COMIC BOOK
REBELS

Also by Stanley Wiater

Night Visions 7 (1989) (editor)
Dark Dreamers: Conversations with the Masters of Horror (1990)
The Official Teenage Mutant Ninja Turtles Treasury (1991)
Dark Visions: Conversations with the Masters of the Horror Film (1992)
After the Darkness (1993) (editor)

Also by Stephen R. Bissette

Taboo, Vol. 1–7 (1988–1992) (editor)
Taboo Especial (1992) (editor)
Aliens: Tribes (1992)
We Are Going to Eat You: Cannibalism in the Cinema (1993)

As Artist:

Saga of the Swamp Thing (1987) (with Alan Moore and John Totleben)
Swamp Thing: Love & Death (1990) (with Alan Moore and John Totleben)

COMIC BOOK REBELS

Conversations with the Creators of the New Comics

STANLEY WIATER AND
STEPHEN R. BISSETTE

DONALD I. FINE, INC.
New York

Library of Congress Cataloging-in-Publication Data

Comic book rebels : conversations with the creators of the new comics
   / [reported] by Stanley Wiater and Stephen R. Bissette.
       p.   cm.
     ISBN 1-55611-355-2 (cloth).—ISBN 1-55611-354-4 (pbk.)
     1. Cartoonists—United States—Interviews.   2. Comic books,
strips, etc.—United States—History and criticism.   I. Wiater,
Stan.   II. Bissette, Stephen.
PN6725.C64   1992
741.5′092′273—dc20   92-54461
                                                        CIP

Manufactured in the United States of America

10   9   8   7   6   5   4   3   2   1

Designed by Irving Perkins Associates

DEDICATIONS

To James Aaron Cooke (formerly Jimmy Cook) and Donald Black; in memory of those hazy, long ago summers when we took off with *Turok, Son of Stone, Gorgo, Tales Calculated to Drive You Bats, MAD, Batman, Journey into Mystery, G.I. Combat, Star-Spangled War Stories, Tarzan of the Apes, Strange Tales, The Twilight Zone, X-Men, The Fantastic Four* (to name only a few of our escape vehicles) . . . usually for no more than twelve cents a trip.

S.W.

To the late, great Harvey Kurtzman and William Gaines, the founders of *MAD*, who tore the blinders off generations of American youth—and to my mentors: Mitch Casey, with whom I drew my first comics; William Cathey, who loaned me *Zap #0* in high school and changed my life forever; and Joe Kubert, who opened the door to a lifelong dream.

S.B.

ACKNOWLEDGMENTS

Beyond the respective artists, writers, and creators who so graciously donated their time and art to make this dream project a reality, we would like to thank the following:

Adam Levison and Andrew Hoffer, Donald I. Fine, Inc.; Joshua Bilmes, Scott Meredith Literary Agency, Inc.; Iris D. Wiater, Shado-Wind, Inc.; Marlene O'Conner, SpiderBaby Grafix and Publications, Diana Schutz, Dark Horse Comics; Jean-Marc & Randy Lofficier, Starwatcher Graphics; Mike Friedrich, Star*Reach, Donna Corben, Fantagor Press; Marie Lisewski, Tundra Publishing, Inc; DC Comics; Fred Greenberg, Great Eastern Conventions & Buffalo Books; Gary Colabuono, Moondog Comics; Terry Fitz, Todd McFarlane Productions.

CONTENTS

FOREWORD

Welcome to the front lines of the war.

Make no mistake about it. There *is* a war going on today throughout the comic book industry. And the personalities interviewed for *Comic Book Rebels* are among those who have shot the most telling blows against the empire.

The business environment in the comic book industry changes more rapidly—and unexpectedly—than perhaps any other form of publishing today. Although these new and exclusive interviews were conducted within a six-month period, we are well aware that there may already be substantial changes between the time this foreword is composed and you take the very first copy out of the bookstores or comic shop.

As is fully documented in the narratives that follow, the first great Comics Revolution occurred when the underground comix burst upon the scene from the mid-Sixties into the Seventies.

In the mid-Seventies and into the early Eighties, the second great Comics Revolution erupted when independent writers and artists decided to use the new marketplace of the direct sales market to bypass the traditional mainstream publishers and self-publish their own comic books.

Now, in the Nineties, a third great Comics Revolution is underway. Perhaps the skirmishes and the sorties are not as blatantly evident to the fans, for it is not necessarily the aesthetics of the medium which are undergoing upheaval again. It is not even the never-ending fight against censorship which is the focus of so much splattered ink and torn paper.

Rather, it's a more or less covert battle currently being ruthlessly fought "in the backroom of the store." The once inviolate corporate fortress where the major mainstream publishers—the dinosaurs of the industry—are finally being forced to come to grips with all the odd little mammals as they grow increasingly underfoot.

Strangely independent, amazingly creative creatures who have finally learned not only to master their craft as artists and writers, but also to be the masters of their professional careers and financial fortunes. This is a side of the comic book industry that the major mainstream publishers would rather not have their "innocent young fans" be aware of, no doubt for fear of overexposure via too much informed enlightenment.

Some critics may charge that almost everyone who agreed to participate in this project has an axe to grind. If that is the case, it's perhaps only because they feel it's time for the hero in the fairy tale "Jack, the Giant Killer" to finally slay the amoral corporate "bottom-line" publishing monster once and for all—even if it takes the combined efforts of the two dozen giant slayers interviewed here, their comrades in arms, and the many more who are sure to follow in their ever greater and wider footsteps.

For without exception, all of them are proud to bear the brand of "comic book rebels."

We are equally honored to bring you this series of uncensored reports, fresh from the front lines of the newest and greatest revolution.

—March 3, 1993
Stanley Wiater
Deerfield, Massachusetts
Stephen R. Bissette
Marlboro, Vermont

Introduction

Comic Book Rebels is, at best, a beginning.

What you are about to read concerns comic *books*, not comic strips. It is not an oral history, though much historical ground is covered in a roughly chronological manner. Nor are we particularly concerned with comic book characters like *Superman, Batman, Spiderman, Cerebus, Teenage Mutant Ninja Turtles* or *Spawn*, though they do play important roles in the stories related here.

Rather, this is a forum for the people who write and draw the adventures of those imaginary beings, among others—the men and women who make comics. These are *their* stories, told by the creative individuals who, through their personal experiences, represent different stages in the evolution of the medium and the industry since the late Sixties.

Since the birth of the American comic book in 1933, the medium has been fettered by the commercial parameters of the industry. These restraints ranged from the publishers' unquestioned ownership of the creative concepts, characters, stories, and the original art they published (a legal propriety later defined by "work-for-hire" laws), to the formation of the Comics Code Authority in October 1954, in order to monitor and enforce the industry-wide self-censorship of the medium. Everything changed in the late Sixties, as the underground "comix" (an adaptive monicker adopted by the movement to differentiate their comic books from the mainstream industry product) revolutionized the medium by understanding the vitality and accessibility of the art form.

Reflecting the youth counterculture they grew out of, comix creators shared an urgent belief that the existing systems of power, whether social, political, religious, or interpersonal, had to be deconstructed in order to build a better world. Student activist Mario Savio stated it eloquently during the University of California demonstrations in

Berkeley on December 2, 1964: "There's a time when the operation of the machine becomes so odious, makes you so sick at heart, that you can't take part—you can't even passively take part—and you've got to put your bodies upon the gears and upon the wheels, upon the levers, upon all the apparatus and you've got to make it *stop* and you've got to indicate to the people who run it and the people who own it that unless you're *free*, the machine will be prevented from working at all!"

Savio and his activist peers were calling for sweeping societal changes. This radical agenda had its converts, its heroes, its traitors, its casualties, and its survivors. Comix chose to simply *ignore* the "machine" that had straight-jacketed the medium for over three decades, establishing their own means of publishing and distribution. Within the relatively narrow focus of this book, we began by seeking out the survivors of the comix era who shared the experiences of the Sixties and found ways to continue their own comix in the wake of the counter-cultural revolution.

We then sought out the creators of more recent generations who grew up with a greater understanding of "the machine"—creators who had a desire to shift its gears and wheels and levers to their own goals rather than martyrize themselves in an industry filled with martyrs. We also sought out the new breeds of creators who have actively been building alternative creative environments or, knowingly, their own "machines."

Of course, a more expansive overview of this nature would certainly benefit from interviews with veterans like Joe Kubert and Jack Kirby, both of whom labored for decades within the confines of the mainstream comic book industry only to emerge in the Eighties as progressive patriarchs for new generations of comic book creators. Jack Kirby had practically invented the vocabulary of the American comic book, and in doing so laid the foundations for the mighty Marvel Comics empire— only to find himself in a protracted legal battle to reclaim his original art from Marvel years later, accentuating his decisive step *away* from traditional work-for-hire practices as the first prominent mainstream creator to work with the new "independent" publishers of the direct-sales market. Also, Joe Kubert's founding of the Joe Kubert School of Cartoon and Graphic Art in the mid-Seventies provided a new doorway for cartoonists eager to enter the industry. And there are many more: Mike Friedrich (publisher and agent, Star*Reach Enterprises), Gary Groth (publisher, Fantagraphic Books Inc.), Cat Yronwode (editor/publisher, Eclipse Comics Inc.), Jim Shooter (editor/publisher, Defiant) and Mike

Richardson (publisher, Dark Horse Comics) could be considered, in many ways, "rebels." Any of these personalities could bring vital perspectives to our project, as would interviews with progressive retailers like Gary Colabuono, Brian Hibbs, and others. Sadly, they all fell outside of the parameters of this project as we sought creators who could experientially discuss the relevant issues.

Choosing the twenty or so individuals who would be represented in this book was not an easy task, and our ultimate decisions to interview creators who *remain* vital in the field were not made lightly. Only Denis Kitchen, Kevin Eastman and Peter Laird were selected for reasons that outweighed their relative paucity of creative output since their respective decisions to *publish* rather than just self-publish—reasons that will hopefully be self-evident in the context of this book.

There are other key creators who should be here, obviously. A few of those on our original "wish list" proved inaccessible for a variety of reasons. Clearly, seminal creators like Robert Crumb, Gilbert and Jaime Hernandez, and Art Spiegelman *belong* in the present company, and we regret their exclusion. It was also unfortunate that our efforts were completed prior to the recent debut of Milestone Media (packaged by founding creator Denys Cowan in conjunction with DC Comics) and the formation of the independent publishers organization ANIA, presently composed of Africa Rising Comics, U.P. Comics, Afrocentric Comics, Dark Zulu Lies Inc., and Omega 7. These seem to herald an ethnic comics movement we will call, for want of a better term, African-American comics—a somewhat misleading monicker in that Milestone also embraces the work of Hispanic and Asian-American artists. Many non-white artists have worked in the industry since the Seventies (including Grass Green, Billy Graham, Trevor Von Eedon, Alex Nino, Milton Knight, Alfredo Alcala, and Denys Cowan), but as with the women and gay comics creators, their respective cultural perspectives had always been sublimated by the dominate industry powers, which remain predominantly white, male, and heterosexual—and intent on crafting entertainments that perpetuate those values. Arguably building upon the example of the Hernandez brothers' seminal *Love and Rockets* (1982-present), which energetically reflects the Spanish-American barrio and punk roots of the creators, Milestone and the ANIA publishers have galvanized multi-cultural creators who found themselves apart from the predominately Caucasian industry norm. It is currently impossible to guess if or how this new movement will change comics, but we look forward to the adventure.

The reader should keep in mind the mercurial nature of the issues discussed herein. Between the time this book's manuscript was completed and this introduction was revised and polished, factors within the industry have changed—some in very fundamental ways—and they undoubtably will change further before this book reaches your hands. For instance, just at the time this book was going to press, we were notified that Denis Kitchen's veteran comix company Kitchen Sink Press had merged with Kevin Eastman's three-year-old Tundra Publishing Ltd. This occurred soon after their respective interviews had been completed, yet long before either could even begin to meaningfully discuss the merger in a forum such as this. The union (and friction) of art and commerce is a constantly transformative proposition, particularly within a multi-million dollar marketplace so dramatically distorted by malleable and even illusory elements (i.e., cynically crafted and orchestrated "collectibles" like 1992's *Death of Superman* comic from DC Comics at a time when *Superman* co-creator Joe Schuster was barely cold in his grave).

Just as *Cerebus, Metal Hurlant, Raw*, Art Spiegelman's *Maus*, Harvey Pekar's *American Splendor* and Joyce Brabner's overtly political comics are potent ideological "blows against the empire," so too have Will Eisner's *The Spirit, Teenage Mutant Ninja Turtles* and Image Comics exacted telling commercial "blows" to a status quo that traditionally demands the subjugation, exploitability and expendability of the creator. Though their importance as an artistic movement within the scope of the Sixties counterculture should not be minimized, the undergrounds were, in part, an attack upon the restrictions of the comic book industry as it existed up to the Sixties. However, comix did not commercially challenge mainstream comics within a relevant arena—just as the comix creators ignored the New York publishers, they in turn could afford to dismiss the comix. It was not until the evolving direct-sales comic book market spawned the "independent" publishers of the early Eighties that the alternative publishing methods had a direct impact upon mainstream comics publishers in their own backyard.

Though the comic book rebels presented in this book are often aesthetically and ideologically at odds with each other, their fierce dedication and devotion to their own creations and themselves unite them. Because of their diversity, the cumulative impact the Comic Book Rebels have had has profoundly changed the industry and the medium.

One of the most fascinating aspects of the contemporary American comic book marketplace is its ability to nurture *self*-publishing as a vital alternative or complement to working within traditional comic book publishing structures. The permutations can be confusing, and demand constant scrutiny. For instance, it is argued by some of the individuals you are about to meet that self-publishing is *the* ideal path for a contemporary comic book creator: a savvy, self-motivated creative individual and businessperson can retain complete autonomy and control over what he or she creates and publishes. There is a demonstrable potential for reaching a readership large enough to fully *support* the creator—financially, emotionally, creatively. This is an option precious few media can offer in late 20th century America.

Inspired by the example of the America underground comix movement and eager to explore the potential of the medium, a group of French and Belgian cartoonists rallied their considerable powers in the mid-Seventies to form a coalition and self-publish their own work. One of the key creators in the movement which founded *Metal Hurlant* was Jean "Moebius" Giraud. Though *Metal Hurlant* gave Giraud the outlet he required for his artistic growth, he ultimately felt the responsibilities of publishing were detrimental to his artistic life. His concerns, and the relevant issues, are echoed and argued in many of the interviews that follow.

By choosing in the mid-Seventies to self-publish his unique character *Cerebus* with a predetermined *thirty-year* life span, Canadian cartoonist Dave Sim and his creative partner Gerhard have successfully built an unprecedented base of autonomy and integrity. Sim has resisted the temptation to profitably license or merchandise *Cerebus*, yet by doing so has persevered and thrived. On the other hand, self-publishing permitted Kevin Eastman and Peter Laird to steer their destinies and those of their creations—the phenomenal *Teenage Mutant Ninja Turtles*—far beyond what would have been possible had they sold their creations to a mainstream publisher. Eastman and Laird chose a path divergent from Sim's to build an empire upon what is one of the great American licensing and merchandising success stories—but at what cost to themselves?

More recently, a collective of mainstream superhero artists who have earned "superstar" status with their work for Marvel Comics chose to break away and form their own publishing imprint, Image Comics. There, they now publish their own work and that of creators they've invited to join them. Marvel Comics management publicly dismissed the departure of these artists as being of little consequence. Yet in the subsequent months, Marvel's status as *the* best-selling publisher of comic books in America for almost twenty years has eroded under the shift of reader interest towards Image Comics. As of this writing, Marvel has lost significant market share due in part to the growth of Image Comics, while the Image creators thrive beyond what would have been possible for them at Marvel.

Note further that what often might *appear* to be self-publishing is not, and vice-versa. The meaningful differences between truly progressive modes of publishing and traditional exploitative methodology are often blurred by the growth or decline of a publishing entity. This is particularly true when an initially idealistic creator-publisher chooses to publish more than *just* his or her own work. The selfish goals essential to self-publishing can become distorted when applied to a partnership or studio division of artistic labor. Just as successful self-publishing can empower the creator, it can also empower that creator to repeat the grievous mistakes made by others.

Consider, a progressive underground publisher like Denis Kitchen, who found himself having to rethink his selfless countercultural agenda if he were to survive as a business—and *again* when he became involved with the packaging and publishing of licensed properties (i.e., *Grateful Dead Comix*). No doubt Kitchen reassessed his position still further with the new publishing entity which emerged from the recent merger with Kevin Eastman's Tundra Publishing. Tundra was itself a noble experiment which had been struggling to maintain its publicized alignment with creators' rights while working to remain commercially viable in a highly competitive and unforgiving marketplace. Dave Sim experimented twice with expanding his base of operations to embrace publishing other creators' work, only to abandon both ventures on ethical grounds, choosing to be responsible *only* to himself rather than an entourage of other creators. The responsibilities of publishing or self-publishing are not to be taken lightly. As Jean Giraud says in his interview, "Publishers are something alive, and therefore they can die. It makes the artist more responsible."

The responsibilities of the artists are vital to the creator/publisher relationships that drive the industry. Too often, relations between publishers and creators become adversarial. The complex dynamics of these relationships are only compounded by the illusory "family" dynamics that have consciously and unconsciously dominated industry practices for years. These family dynamics are nurtured and reinforced by the fact that, at some point in their existence, many firms were (or are) essentially family-run operations, such as National Periodicals/DC Comics, EC Comics, Harvey Comics, Marvel Comics, Archie Comics, Tundra Publishing, etc. This dynamic permits (or forces) the publisher to become a surrogate parent while the creator is relegated to the status of a child, to be rewarded, punished, elevated or disposed of upon the whim of the corporate "parent." These volatile issues are perhaps most pronounced when creators embrace work-for-hire terms to manage and maintain their properties while other creators are busy writing and drawing new material for them.

The roots of this dynamic can be found in the studio system of the Thirties and Forties, when studios were a common fixture of this relatively new industry. Will Eisner's *The Spirit* (1940−52) is justly celebrated as a high water mark in the evolution of comics, and Eisner's ability to retain legal ownership of his creative property was a revolutionary step forward in an era when publishers typically owned creative properties lock, stock and barrel. It is important, however, to remember that *The Spirit* was produced by a studio of talented artists (including Wally Wood, Lou Fine, and Jules Feiffer) working under Eisner's guidance. The studio system provided a modest living for the participating artists while *The Spirit* continued to exist and evolve.

Years later, the fact that Eisner could repackage *The Spirit* for an eager new generation of readers laid the groundwork for his subsequent graphic novels which were conceived and completed by Eisner *alone*. His importance to the medium cannot be overstated, and yet, he owes that stature and his current artistic and commercial freedom to the studio system that perpetuated *The Spirit*. In the context of his interview with us, Will Eisner states, "Jules Feiffer always teases me about the fact that I paid such a low salary. But I didn't feel I was an exploiter, as I recall. The word 'exploitation' is like the word 'sweatshop.' It needs a very careful definition. The reason for the studio system that I set up was to give me total editorial and creative control." Patterned after the motion picture animation studios of the time, Eisner's studio existed primarily to guarantee the creative control he desired while maintaining high quality within tight deadlines.

To this day, similar concerns are the prime motive in the formation of many studios or, on a more intimate level, the hiring of assistants. Studios can yield collaborative efforts that transcend the efforts of any individual member of the unit. Such creative chemistries can nurture healthy mentor and apprenticeship relations, which can and do grow into symbiotic partnerships (i.e., Dave Sim and Gerhard's *Cerebus*) or amicable separation to explore diverging paths. The studio dynamic can, of course, also degenerate into exploitative or parasitic relationships. It all depends upon the integrity, goals, and personalities of the parties involved.

Studios evolve into more problematic organisms when the proprietors of the creative property being produced are also the *publishers* of that material. *Elfquest* and *Teenage Mutant Ninja Turtles* began as self-published creations, though both creator-publisher teams have since formalized work-for-hire publishing practices to maintain their propriety over their original concepts and characters *and* those created by others who write and draw derivative new material. Image Comics was formed as an alternative to the editorial restrictions and work-for-hire practices of Marvel Comics, but a few of the Image creators have, in turn, founded studios which allow them to own and control creative material produced by others. However lucrative the initial profit-sharing from the comic book sales themselves may be, the legal terms necessary to such proprietary relationships are almost identical to those used by Marvel Comics.

It should be evident by now that the traditional attitudes creator and publisher share about themselves and each other must now be irrevocably changed. Neither can afford to perceive the other as being "good," "bad," or a "necessary evil," depending on the circumstances of the relationship. Now that many creators *are* publishers, they are, indeed, more responsible. They will reap the benefits or confront the consequences of their actions in an arena no longer accommodating the simplistic moral standards that united prior generations who too often found themselves at odds with the publishers. The stakes have become higher for publishers, too, who can no longer afford to underestimate the potential that lies within each creator.

Eisner reminds us in his interview that "there isn't a major superhero that has survived through today that is still being done by its originator." Within the ranks of the creators represented in this book, at least one of them—Frank Miller—admits to the important role company-owned characters like *Daredevil* and *Batman* played in his own career. If *Elfquest* and the *Turtles* are to join the rarified ranks of modern mythic heroes like Superman, Batman, or Spiderman, perhaps the process we are witnessing here is a necessary or even inevitable one.

One can also say it is, in part, a corruptive and dehumanizing process, vital to the amoral existence of corporations and pop mythology but destructive to the individual—particularly the individuals who create and/or perpetuate the characters that are the coin of the realm. It is a double-edged sword, in which the rewards can be considerable, but participation in the process can have painful lifelong consequences.

Hopefully, we can all learn from their experiences, just as we can learn a great deal from the example of those who see no reason a fictional creation should perpetuate itself beyond the capabilities or lifespan of the creator. For others, these issues seem irrelevant, as their artistic ventures have little to do with self-perpetuating characters or invented worlds which exist outside the boundaries of a single story or work. For many of these creators, the medium itself *is* the message. Comics harbor possibilities enough for any creator to explore in a lifetime—knowing he or she will only, at best, scratch the surface of the art form's potential.

Undeniably, there are many more questions raised than answers given in the interviews that follow. The questions involve art high and low, aesthetics and politics, society and the individual, sexism and racism, creator rights and the demands of big business . . . all within the arena of that most unusual of mediums, the comic book. Questions which have only intensified as each creator, creative team, or publishing event exposes and explores the possible answers . . .

This volume is only a beginning.

I

BASICS

What are the New Comics?

THE WORLD OF COMICS IS A *HUGE* AND *VARIED* ONE. OUR DEFINITION MUST ENCOMPASS ALL THESE TYPES--

--WHILE NOT BEING *SO* BROAD AS TO INCLUDE ANYTHING WHICH IS CLEARLY *NOT* COMICS.

"COMICS" IS THE WORD WORTH DEFINING, AS IT REFERS TO THE MEDIUM *ITSELF,* NOT A SPECIFIC *OBJECT* AS "COMIC BOOK" OR "COMIC STRIP" DO.

WE CAN ALL VISUALIZE *A* COMIC.

BUT WHAT--

--IS--

--COMICS?

1

SCOTT MCCLOUD
Understanding Comics

Scott McCloud rightfully prides himself as a cartoonist *and* an inventor. Prominent among his inventions
is "A Bill of Rights for Comics Creators," a document
referred to throughout this book. In 1988, *Cerebus*
creator Dave Sim launched a trio of "Creator Summits," gatherings of self-publishing cartoonists and
aspiring self-publishers struggling to define their inherent rights in an industry long dominated by work-
for-hire practices. The concluding summit in No-

vember 1988 (sponsored by Peter Laird and Kevin Eastman, creators of the
Teenage Mutant Ninja Turtles) was galvanized from its outset by McCloud's
proposed Bill of Rights. By the end of the two-day summit, extensive analysis
and debate had only slightly revised McCloud's concise twelve-point document which defined comics creators' implicit rights to their creations. Rights
which may seem glaringly self-evident, but which precious few comic book
creators (with the notable exception of the underground comix creators)
had ever fully understood or retained. (See Appendix I.)

Over the years, Scott has also invented "Five Card Nancy" (a marvelous, almost Dadaist associative card game using panels from Ernie Bushmiller's *Nancy* strip), *The Frying Pan* (a comic art creators' private APA

publication, exchanging business, critical, historical, and creative information), and "The 24-Hour Comic," (without premeditation or preparation, the execution of a coherent twenty-four-page comic narrative within a single twenty-four-hour period). His own comic book creations include *Zot!* (1984–91), *Destroy!!* (1986, special 3–D reprint, 1987), and a clutch of self-published minicomics, such as *Birth of A Nation* and *Fun with Phonics*. (Both 1990). Impressive and engaging as this body of work remains, none of it quite compares with his most recent accomplishment, *Understanding Comics: The Invisible Art* (1993).

Understanding Comics is a remarkable successor to Will Eisner's *Comics & Sequential Art* (1985), its singular worthwhile predecessor. It is most significant that McCloud doesn't study comics via another medium (the written word accompanied by relevent illustrations, as in Eisner's book, or the volume you are now reading). Rather, *Understanding Comics* is a 215-page comic book—an expansive and ever-inventive application of the medium to, in turn, exhaustively study the medium. Like the Bill of Rights for Comic Creators, the inherent concept and application seems, in hindsight, startingly self-evident, but the simple fact remains: no one had ever done it before. McCloud manages the rare feat of rigorously dissecting his chosen subject without butchering it, welding his considerable skills and instincts as a cartoonist to simultaneously demonstrate and preserve the vitality of his chosen subject.

Understanding Comics transcends any previous study of the art form itself. Scott McCloud understands the language and vocabulary of this medium and he communicates that knowledge with passion and clarity.

COMIC BOOK REBELS: You made your initial mark in the industry at a young age, by pulling a proposal for DC Comics to publish *Zot!* when you learned you could not retain ownership of your creation. What made *Zot!* so important to you at the time?

SCOTT MCCLOUD: Actually, the catalyst for that was something that happened in my personal life. When my dad died, I had to contemplate my plans for the rest of my life a little quicker than I thought I would have to at the age of twenty-three. I had actually planned to go the usual route in comics at the time, which was to work my way up gradually. Perhaps learning how to letter, then getting enough lettering work so I would become entrenched enough to maybe get a job inking backgrounds, and eventually pencilling, and maybe I could work my way up to scripting some regular title.

But when my mortality came crashing down on me and I really had to think a little more clearly about my future, I decided to live my life as if it wasn't going to be necessarily all that long. And I wanted to make a statement. So I decided to get to work using my little sketchbook and turn my sketches into a series, and do the work I would be most proud of *now*, rather than wait ten years.

CBR: And *Zot!* truly was unlike most comics of the time, no doubt very consciously so.

McCloud: I wanted to go against the current. Comics were trying to delineate the moral ambiguity and dark shadings that we in comics at the time associated with "real" literature and "real" movies and "real" mainstream fiction. I was trying to find the power locked within very simple and iconic forms instead, something that I had seen the Japanese do in their comics. Even though I had never read any—I'd only "read" the pictures essentially—it seemed to me you could tell very complex stories and generate very complex ideas using very simple elements. The way that an Impressionist uses very few colors in his palate to generate a lot of subtleties of color; I felt the same thing could be done with characters.

CBR: Your *Zot!* isn't really a superhero book: it uses some of the trappings, but it's more of a science-fantasy. Yet the one comic book you've done that clearly appears to be your statement on the superhero genre which still dominates American comics is *Destroy!!* What was your motivation for creating this book?

McCloud: It was a very simple motive. It wasn't so much a parody or satirical piece as it was an expulsion—an exorcism of a spirit that inhabited my body, that I needed to get out as fast as possible. Because I knew that inside of me was that same adolescent fan-boy that was inside *all* artists. And I felt that almost all the artists in mainstream comics at that time were still playing "king of the hill" with Jack Kirby. And they never would win! Because they were devoting their whole careers, unconsciously, to getting that one big punch, and that one massive explosion, and that one way-cool, dynamite, knock 'em out, double-page spread that would blow old daddy Kirby out of the way! It was this huge collective Oedipus complex that everybody had, and I realized that I had it, too!

The only way I would ever fully deal with that was to face it head-on. In one single comic. And I put every single ounce of power I had into trying to blow away Jack. I don't think I did it; I don't think I was quite up to Jack's strength. But what I do know is that I gave it absolutely my best shot. And having done that, I felt that I could then move on to other things while a lot of my colleagues were still playing the game.

A lot of them still are.

CBR: How were you inspired to undertake such a massive project as *Understanding Comics*?

MCCLOUD: These are ideas that have actually been brewing since college. I had a class with a professor named Larry Bakke at Syracuse University, who was a post-McLuhanite, voodoo witch doctor of a professor. He taught us, most of all, that it was up to *us* to learn. That there was no sage out there; nobody who was going to hand us all our knowledge on a silver platter. How we had to exercise a certain amount of reasoning on our own. And, most of all, look for *connections* in places where nobody had ever looked for them before. I took this to heart, and began to commit a lifelong investigation in what I was interested in at the time—which for the most part has been comics.

I've stopped taking my reactions to comics for granted. Whenever I notice in myself that a particular writer or artist or story or character strikes a chord with me, I ask myself, "Why?" I try to investigate my ownn reactions, and try to deduce what could be at the heart of those reactions. And from that, extrapolate how I could duplicate that effect, or enhance it, or increase it in my own work. And try to find those patterns that nobody had ever found before. This process of direct observation allowed me to begin to essentially invent a science of my own, which was pretty much built upon these observations and on very little else. *Understanding Comics* is about ninety percent direct observation. Ideas which I had to develop on my own, and only about ten percent drawn from the observations of others. People from art history, and those few people who have written about comics, primarily Will Eisner.

CBR: To ask the obvious: why have so few studies been written about comics purely as a medium?

McCLOUD: Well, in order for anybody to investigate or write about a science, the first step is to recognize that it *is* a science. Or in the case of an art form, to recognize that it *is* an art form. I see comics as both. But my point is, I had to take that first step: I had to recognize it as a field of study, something which had been done by very few people up to this point.

Most critics see comics as a cultural artifact. They see comics as a product of our culture and our civilization—which it is—but that's all they see it as. They see comics as evidence of *something else*. Pop culture studies of comics have centered around comics as pieces of evidence to give us clues about the culture that created them. But that sets up an unconscious hierarchy: that the culture itself is more important than the products of that culture! This is something we do not do, for example, with music or with painting. We see that the circumstances of the culture that created a Mozart or a Bach as being almost secondary to the products of that culture itself. Yet comics has forever been relegated to that "pop culture artifact" status. And very few people, both in and outside the comic book industry, have seen comics, in and of themselves, as a field worthy of study. Since there is that vacuum, I feel that I do not have to so much as investigate this science, as *invent* one.

That's why I can be a little bit reckless: I can make wild, unsubstantiated claims since most of these claims *have* to be unsubstantiated! [*Chuckles*] I leave it for others to agree, disagree, or offer alternatives. I want to start a debate—not finish it. I don't want to have the last word on comics. I want the first word.

CBR: What is that "first word" then? Using your scientific terms, precisely what *is* comics?

McCLOUD: I see comics as sequential art. Pictures in sequence. I've chosen a very simple definition, and to some eyes, a very soulless definition, one without much poetry. But I believe the soul and the poetry is brought to it by the artist. Comics are just an empty vessel until the artists come and bring their life experiences, their desires, and their passions to it. The longer definition, just to cover my ass, is "juxtaposed pictorial and other icons in deliberate sequence," but it's a little hard to say that in casual conversation! But that helps me distinguish it from film and other arts which might stumble into that simpler definition if we're not specific enough.

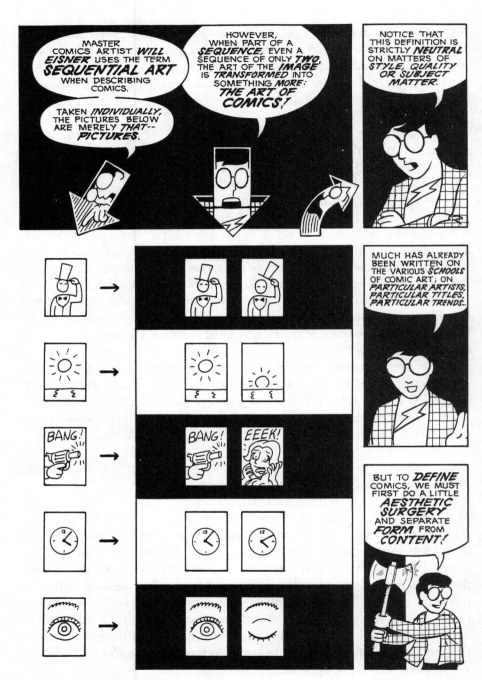

THE ARTFORM -- THE *MEDIUM* -- KNOWN AS COMICS IS A *VESSEL* WHICH CAN HOLD ANY *NUMBER* OF *IDEAS* AND *IMAGES*.

THE *"CONTENT"* OF THOSE IMAGES AND IDEAS IS, OF COURSE, UP TO *CREATORS*, AND WE ALL HAVE DIFFERENT *TASTES*.

=GLUG=
=GLUG=

PTUI!!!

=GAAK=
=WHEEEEZ=
=KAF! KAF!=
GLUGH-GGH...

=ahem=
THE *TRICK* IS TO NEVER MISTAKE THE *MESSAGE* --

-- FOR THE *MESSENGER.*

AT ONE TIME OR ANOTHER VIRTUALLY *ALL* THE GREAT MEDIA HAVE RECEIVED *CRITICAL EXAMINATION,* IN AND OF *THEMSELVES.*

BUT FOR *COMICS,* THIS ATTENTION HAS BEEN *RARE.* *

LET'S SEE IF WE CAN HELP *RECTIFY* THE SITUATION.

*EISNER'S OWN *COMICS AND SEQUENTIAL ART* BEING A HAPPY EXCEPTION.

But by using that definition as a tool, I can ask some simple questions about comics. Such as: how old is the medium? Can we trace comics back any further than 1896, which is what conventional wisdom holds to be the very beginnings of comics, when in fact I hold it to be about thirty-three centuries before that, at least. Are there any comics of our time that have been neglected because they fall outside the status quo definition of comics, while falling inside my definition? And there are a lot of neglected masters.

CBR: Could you give us some current examples?

MCCLOUD: Sure! Maurice Sendak has tremendous respect in the popular culture as an excellent children's book author and illustrator. And yet a book like *In the Night Kitchen* also happens to be comics. The only thing which distinguishes it from what we traditionally think of as a comic book is the format, the format of printing. Which to me is completely irrelevant if we see comics as an art form. Surely the physical format of it—the fact that it has a spine or has hardcovers—should make *no* difference at all! And yet we exclude Sendak from comics because he's slightly different. And perhaps because he's just a little bit "too good." Because he defies our preconception of comics.

Probably the best example of this attitude is the notorious review of Art Spiegelman's *Maus* in the *New York Times Review of Books*, which I believe began with the cheerful proclamation that "*Maus* is not a comic book." And the clear subtext of that was, "Of course! It's too good to be comics!" The moment that comics become too adventurous, or too innovative, they cease to be "comics." And when somebody makes the statement that comics are inherently trivial or incapable of great works, it becomes a self-supporting statement. Because that attitude *is* self-perpetuating; it protects itself from any evidence that might disprove it. If we were to list the honor roll, there would be a lot of names on it: Raymond Briggs, Edward Gorey . . . I heard an interview with Edward Gorey, and the word "comics" never even came up—even though the man has done virtually nothing that *isn't* comics! It's insane.

CBR: Critics often make the mistake of thinking of comics as somehow a lesser genre to transcend, forgetting entirely that it is in fact a totally realized medium.

MCCLOUD: Which makes it even more tragic. It's very frustrating. One of our very first tasks is to convince the public that comics is not a genre, it is a medium. Because comics has been traditionally seen as a subset of two very different art forms—of writing and the graphic arts—and not as an art form in itself.

If other art forms were treated the way comics are treated, we'd get absurd statements like: "So you're reading a book? Have you figured out whodunit yet?" The confusion is of the genre with the medium: just because it's a book, doesn't necessarily mean it's going to be a mystery. Just because it's a play, doesn't mean someone has to die at the end. And just because it's a comic doesn't mean it's going to have to be in four colors, with superheroes punching each other in the mouth, or with funny animals pushing each other off cliffs. There's *nothing* in the essential definition that determines what sort of subject matter it's going to have. And yet this is a misconception that exists outside of comics and, more significantly, inside the industry.

CBR: Is America the chief culprit in terms of this monstrous lack of vision regarding the still untapped potential of comics as a medium?

McCLOUD: America is definitely unique among the three primary producers of comics that I'm familiar with, which would be the Japanese market, the European market, and the American market. In Japan and Europe, comics have penetrated into every level of society. They're read by adults, by women, they cover any number of genres and subjects; they aspire to the higher concerns of literature and fine art—especially in Europe—and they are a tremendously mature business, especially in Japan.

America has been pathetically behind these other two comics cultures. I believe there's a lot we can learn from them, and ultimately a lot that we can teach them, since our take on comics will be very different, and we'll discover quite a few things on our own that perhaps our cousins overseas don't know about comics. We have made some progress in the last ten years, and I don't think we should minimize that. In the past decade, we've increased the number of adventurous and interesting titles a hundredfold.

CBR: Who do you feel is on the cutting edge in the medium?

McCLOUD: *Love & Rockets. Eight Ball. Cages.* Jim Woodring's work. Autobiographical comics like Harvey Pekar's *American Splendor.*

Chester Brown's *Yummy Fur*. More women are making comics, like Mary Fleener and Roberta Gregory. There are comics that are pushing the envelope as far as what's acceptable, like *Taboo*, and again with *Yummy Fur*. We've been seeing an infiltration of comics from Europe and Japan, finally in translation, into the American market. People are taking a harder look at children's comics and seeing that perhaps we don't have to be quite so unimaginative about the sort of comics that come into children's hands.

The revolution is happening on many different fronts, essentially. And while the battle is by no means going well in all cases, it is at least being waged. Something that was not necessarily true only ten years ago.

CBR: What do you hope to accomplish with the publication of *Understanding Comics*?

McCLOUD: I hope that *Understanding Comics* will give reference points to an undiscovered continent. I liken current comics to the shape the American continent had for the settlers in the first few years of discovery when this continent was a very small place—to their perceptions. They had no idea how big it was; they had no idea that there was anything else to discover. And I've tried to send out probes, as far as I possibly can, into the many undiscovered regions of comics. Simply to let people know that they're *there*, so that others can begin to set out and discover what might lie in store in those regions. Eventually to settle and to work the land, as it were, until perhaps we have a clearer idea of the *shape* of comics' potential.

We haven't even begun to explore what comics are capable of, and I want that fact on an emotional level to be received by my readers. That the task of learning how much more there is still to learn is an enormous task, simply to discover how little we know. Because we do have a tendency to assume that the world as we see it . . . is pretty much the only world there is. And as a culture, we're not "seeing" comics at all. It's the invisible art.

CBR: To that end, can you give us a working vocabulary that will aid us to better "see" comics?

McCLOUD: The vocabulary of comics is any element in the great universe of visual iconography: that includes pictures, words, symbols.

Any of the icons that have been invented for comics, such as the panel border and the word balloon. And any icon that could be reinvented to communicate a world of experience. Anything that can be represented by ink on paper, or paint on canvas, or even a stone relief carving. Anything that fits that definition of sequential art—that's our vocabulary. The grammar of comics, to me, is the arrangement of those elements in sequence. It's what we do with those elements, and what happens between the panels—between those images—that we call "closure."

That's the key word when discussing comics. Closure is our ability to complete an action or an idea between the panels. That's the heart of comics, and I think it's a much neglected area. Critics tend to see only what's in the panels—not what's between them. And what's between the panels is the *only* element of comics that is not duplicated in any other medium. Therefore I think it's the most important. Because it's unique.

CBR: Along the way, you also have acquired a reputation as an inventor. What have you invented that is unique to comics?

McCLOUD: I guess I do think of myself as an inventor, maybe because my father was. And though I kind of took the long way around of doing what my father did, I seem to have done just that. When I created *Zot!*, I found the part I enjoyed most was the inventing of characters. I almost wanted to just invent characters, and not have to do anything with them, because I found that the most interesting aspect. So far, my career in comics has been very much geared towards inventions. *Destroy!!* was, in some respects, an invention.

Since *Zot!* and *Destroy!!* I've invented an amateur press alliance in which comics artists can critique each other called "The Frying Pan."

I've invented a neo-Dadaist performance card game called "Five-Card Nancy," in which panels from Ernie Bushmiller's *Nancy* are taken out of context and played like playing cards by players trying to make a coherent—or incoherent—narrative, depending on what mood they're in.

More recently, I've done the twenty-four-hour comic, which was an invention of mine to help jump-start those of us who tend to get behind on deadlines and perhaps think a little *too* much about our work. The twenty-four-hour comic is a challenge, a *dare* to comics creators in which they must draw twenty-four complete pages of comics—a complete story—in under twenty-four hours. That particular dare has been taken up by more than fourteen other comic book artists since I came up with that one.

So I do enjoy that role of inventor. I like the idea of bringing things into the world that did not exist. Especially things which, once they are in existence, seem like they *had* to be invented. Even though nobody was expecting them; nobody was anticipating them, and then they came full-blown from the head of Zeus or whatever! I really enjoy that idea: how something did not exist, and then it did because of me. That gives me a real rush! [*Laughs*]

CBR: Perhaps your greatest invention so far is the Creator's Bill of Rights. How did that come about?

McCLOUD: It was sort of an invention—that was my attempt to put in one place a coherent list of what I felt were the crucial rights of comic book creators that needed to be protected in a corporate environment. The original impetus for the Bill of Rights was as a reaction to a somewhat similar attempt called the "Creative Manifesto," which had been drafted at the first creators' summit in Toronto, Ontario, in the late Eighties. The Creative Manifesto was drafted as an attempt to put into words how the comic industry should work. It was a noble attempt, but I felt that things were a bit simpler than the way the manifesto painted them.

I saw creator's rights as an issue which could be decided unilaterally by the creator simply with a statement of intent. That, for our own survival and self-respect, we would henceforth conduct our business in a particular manner. And that we would no longer sacrifice certain rights. Amongst those being the right to full ownership of what we fully created, the right of creative control over that property, and all the rights that essentially stem from those two. And I found that a simple list was all that was really needed. Simply putting them on paper, for me, focused the debate and allowed us to get down to brass tacks. Which was, "How are we going to implement this in our own lives, never mind what anyone else did?"

I think in the long run that's the way creator's rights have been advanced. Especially in recent years when individual artists take their fate into their own hands and realize *they* are the creative origin of comics. That comics are not created by editors. They're not created by printing presses. They're not created by color separators. They're not created by publishers, by people in board rooms, by demographic charts. They're created by writers and artists. And it's those writers and artists who control their destiny in every respect, except historically. And that control comes with ownership. There is no need to sign away that ownership; ownership is ours by right until we put our name on the dotted line. I felt it was simply time we said, "No thank you." To say, "I will keep this. I would rather this not be published than to sign it away forever to a corporation who does not have the same attachment to it that I do as a creator."

I can't say how many people who've made that decision for themselves were influenced by the Bill of Rights, but I'm just glad it's happening, whether or not that particular piece of paper is what did it. I'm just really glad it's the direction that comics history seems to be taking now: that artists are finally standing up for themselves and realizing that 100% of the power of comics is in their hands.

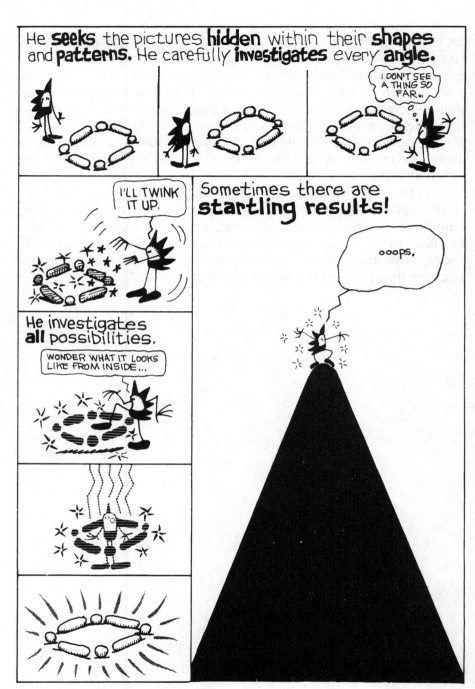

2

LARRY MARDER
Building Bridges

In America and the United Kingdom, many of the most celebrated creators working in the comics medium have been (and often choose to be) perceived as working in something other than this medium. Surely the celebrated likes of Jules Feiffer, Raymond Briggs, and Edward Gorey create *books*, not *comic books*. As already noted by Scott McCloud, this is primarily because the most prevalent *format* for the medium—the physical comic book—has been wrongly perceived as *being* the medium itself, rather than as just one of many possible commercial vehicles.

Having established a workable definition for the comics medium itself, it's only logical at this point to define the parameters of the contemporary American comic book industry. (Bear in mind that events may have transpired which have already altered that marketplace. Dramatic, even profound, events can—and do—happen quite quickly in this most peculiar industry.)

To elucidate some of the basics, it was also logical to turn to Larry Marder. A native of Chicago, Marder's considerable knowledge of the art world was certified with a BFA degree earned at Hartford Art School in 1973. Four years later, he was earning his living as an art director in the high-pressure world of advertising. His experience and expertise in that demanding profession was balanced by a remarkable interior landscape of the imagination that coalesced into the vivid ecology of *Beanworld*.

Beanworld was launched as an essentially self-published comic (though distributed through Eclipse Comics) in 1984. What began as a collection of character sketches and concepts—Mr. Spook, Professor Garbanzo, the mysterious center of the Beanworld universe, Gran'Ma'Pa—soon evolved into what Marder terms "a weird fantasy dimension that operates under its own rules and laws." It is also a reading experience that obeys only its own rules and laws, creating a delightfully accessible, resonant, and almost alchemical bond with readers of all ages.

"*Beanworld* is about the affinity of life," Marder states in the first collected volume. "All the Beanworld characters, whether they are friends or adversaries, understand that ultimately they depend on each other for survival."

As such, *Beanworld* is an ideal metaphor for the comic book industry, though sadly the real-life "characters" who work therein rarely understand their mutual dependency on each other. Working in the marketplace as a creator, self-publisher, and promotional manager for selected publishers (including the Moondog's chain of Chicago-based retail stores), Larry Marder is in a unique position to awaken the members of the comic book community to that often ignored, usually misperceived, yet extremely vital interdependence.

COMIC BOOK REBELS: As an "insider" who is both a creator and a marketing director within the industry, what do you consider the most important changes in the marketplace over the past decade?

LARRY MARDER: Obviously the most important and most significant aspect is that comics are now purchased in comic book stores. They are marketed directly to comic book stores and to the consumers who shop at these stores rather than newsstands. As such, we have a much narrower audience than we had twenty years ago.

CBR: You see it as a narrowing market rather than a growing one?

MARDER: In terms of the last ten years, yes, I would say it has narrowed considerably. On the other hand, I would say it has probably narrowed as much as it is going to. Now, there are concerned people in the business who are trying to expand it beyond the superhero adolescent ghetto which most comic book stores cater to.

CBR: What was the genesis of this direct sales market?

MARDER: A fellow named Phil Seuling went to DC Comics in the mid-Seventies and asked them to sell comic books directly to him on a nonreturnable basis. This was unprecedented because all comics were sold at that time on newsstands on a consignment basis. Therefore, a publisher never really knew how well a comic book sold until the designated period of time had passed when they could accept and calculate the returns.

The comic book stores grew out of the former "head shops" that were first selling underground comix, and then started dealing in back issues of old superhero comics, along with people who were dealing back issues of old comics through flea markets. Basically, they all started opening up stores using their own collections as stock. At some point, Seuling realized, "Gee, we should put new comics in the stores."

The only way they could get every new comic in their stores was to go around the newsstand distributors—the IDs—and make a direct appeal to DC. Sol Harrison, who as the president of DC Comics at the time, decided to take a huge risk and sell their comics directly to the stores. This was a courageous act because Harrison could have alienated the ID distributors and seriously disrupted their ability to distribute comics to the newsstand outlets. When Seuling started buying direct from DC, he became the first direct sales comic book distributor. Within a very short period of time, the new direct sales market started to develop, where publishers sold directly to distributors, who in turn sold through the comic book stores.

CBR: Looking back, what were the most identifiable landmarks in the growth of the direct sales market?

MARDER: First, I would say the emergence of three books between 1976 and 1978: Jack Katz's *The First Kingdom*, Dave Sim's *Cerebus*, and Wendy Pini's *Elfquest*. These were books that were produced for the direct sales market with no attempt to make them available to newsstands. These were the first comics that were specifically made for the customers of these new comic book stores. Even though these new comics had low print runs and were printed in black and white, they were extraordinary in the sense that their creators recognized that artists could make a living feeding the hunger of this new market, and not have to worry about advertising or dealing with the newsstands.

For a lot of people working in the industry today, particularly the alternatives, those three books were very important.

If you want to go a bit further, Eclipse Comics published *Sabre* in 1978, which was significant because it was the first graphic album made available in the United States using the European format—a more expensive product using better paper than anyone had seen previously in the States. It was also significant because the two creators, Don McGregor and Paul Gulacy, were already popular from working in mainstream comics. This was the first example of known talent from the mainstream making an attempt to market their talents to the direct sales market. Again, not worrying about being available through news-stands.

Probably the next landmark would be Pacific Comics, a publishing company formed by the Schanes Brothers in San Diego. They signed Jack Kirby—"The King of Comics"—to a contract to produce *Captain Victory* for them in 1981. It was a color comic book that was indistinguishable from a mainstream DC or Marvel comic—though it was available only through the direct sales market. So in a very short period of time, within five years or so, this new market went from an idea by Phil Seuling to having material produced for it that was indistinguishable from mainstream product. It's really quite extraordinary that it happened that quickly.

I think those three levels of the marketplace established everything we have now. You could point to my book, *Beanworld*, and say that it grew out of the creation of *Cerebus* and *Elfquest*. You could look at *The Dark Knight* or *Taboo*, and say they to a certain degree grew out of the decision to publish *Sabre*. And you could point to the Image Comics line and accurately say that's an outgrowth of *Captain Victory* and Pacific Comics.

CBR: Would Kevin Eastman's and Peter Laird's *Teenage Mutant Ninja Turtles* have any noteworthy place in this chronology?

MARDER: They're important in the history of comic book licensing, but they started out trying to imitate Dave Sim's publishing methods. Eastman's and Laird's success was really the logical and successful extension of what Wendy and Richard Pini were hoping to do with *Elfquest*— aspiring to expand beyond the comics medium into animation, feature films, and merchandising. What's important about the *Turtles* is that they became incredibly popular through the toy line and licensing

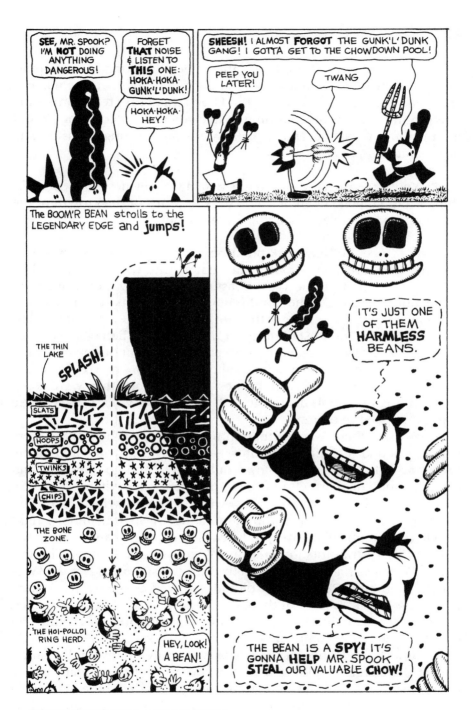

deals. You could say, "Yes, here's this offbeat black and white comic that, in essence, through television and through toys became a mainstream Archie children's comic." But I don't think they really broke any new ground in terms of publishing. When you really take a long view of the medium, what the *Turtles* really are is an amazing licensing and merchandising phenomenon.

CBR: You've defined the landmarks which were evident to the readership; what happened behind the scenes in terms of the growth of the direct sales marketplace then going nationwide?

MARDER: Once the New York publishers started selling comics to Phil Seuling, I believe they almost immediately afterwards began selling them to Bud Plant on the West Coast, so you had two distributors in competition with each other for this new direct sales market. In the case of a book like *Cerebus*, I believe that out of an initial run of 2,000 copies, Dave Sim sold 1,000 to Seuling and 1,000 to Plant. Then what you had were many, many local distributors springing up out of nowhere, and in many cases there were people who worked for the IDs—packing comics or working in the warehouses—who decided they were going to go into comic book distribution, finding new ways to have these comics supplied to them.

So you see, there was a situation ten years ago where there were many local and regional distributors—so many that you could barely keep track of their names. They would merge and go bankrupt and combine and fall apart. Out of these, the main ones when I started in the business in the mid-Eighties were Seagate—which was Phil Seuling—who opened a distribution center in Sparta, Illinois, right next to the printing plant that produced all the mainstream comics. Plus Capital City Distributors in Madison, Wisconsin, and Diamond in Baltimore. You also had American on the East Coast, Sunrise on the West Coast, Alternative Realities in Colorado, as well as Glenwood, Windy City, New Media, Irjax—all these distributors competing against each other for this growing network of comic book stores all around the country. It was *very* competitive.

It's almost impossible for today's fans to really understand what an impact these stores and distributors made on comic book fans ten or fifteen years ago. The most important change was that these new stores were able to rack new comics two to four *weeks* before they appeared on the newsstands. Almost anybody's initial contact with these new establishments was an overwhelming experience: every single comic book on the rack being new, and being able to buy a copy of everything you wanted! At that time, you had to really search the newsstands for the books you wanted, but now it was *all* immediately available.

Then the competition between the distributors intensified as to who could rack the comic books in the stores *first*. If store "A" could rack its new stock before store "B," then all the fans would go to store "A." When you had a situation like you did here in Chicago, where there may have been five or six distributors supplying stores at any given time, it was of utmost importance who racked the new titles first. It used to be measured in days, then in minutes. If a store owner is racking his comics at noon on Thursday, and he finds out that the guy down the street racked his comics at 11:45 A.M., he'd go *nuts*, though it no longer makes any real difference to most consumers.

The system is much more democratic now, in that it has settled down to just a couple of distributors working in any given market. For the most part, everyone gets their new books at the same time.

CBR: What's your view of the current state of the marketplace?

MARDER: Well, to contradict a little bit what I said earlier, I think that things are currently expanding and contracting at the same time. We have a situation where almost all the economic power of the industry seems to be circulating between two distributors—Diamond and Capital—and two publishers, Marvel and DC. And yet, we have up-starts like Image and Valiant coming basically out of nowhere and challenging the consolidation of power in a big way. By saying that, "We're going to open up the marketplace, we're going to come up with new material, and we're going to come up with more innovative ways to merchandise our material." Therefore, it seems like the horizons are expanding again. There are new opportunities for creators to distribute their work, allowing them to survive and hopefully thrive.

Certainly the most interesting situation that I'm involved with is the DLG—Direct Line Group—which is a coalition of fifteen retailers that was put together by Gary Colabuono of Moondog's. It's an opportunity for the large chain retailers to have a forum to discuss their problems and pool their resources to figure out how they can best help them-selves in this new marketplace. Distributors are still focused on opening up new stores; they're not really focused much on helping the estab-lished comic book stores expand. I, as a creator, would much rather that people who already know what they're doing and have a proven track record expand their operations, than constantly have the destiny of my book be in the hands of new people who are making up the rules as they go along. And usually fail at what they're doing. I have a lot of confidence that the DLG is going to promote environments that are going to help alternative comics grow.

CBR: Are we finally at a point where the long-term interests of both the creators committed to the medium and the established retailers selling their creations are beginning to dovetail?

MARDER: We are. Alternative creators, like Dave Sim and myself, are working on long-term projects. We're not just looking for short-term success. The comic book business has been obsessed in short-term profits since day one. But now we need long-term commitment. We need to know that we are going to have places to sell comics today, and places to sell comics ten years from now. Concerned retailers, on the other hand, are looking to expand their horizons beyond just having a constant turnover of adolescent boys: they would like to have customers for life.

One of the examples I use is Levi's. Thirty years ago, Levi's were pants for teenagers. They were cut for teenagers; the only sizes you could find in the clothing stores were for teenagers. Levi's executives didn't say, "As this baby-boomer generation grows up, we're only going to sell our pants to teenagers." Instead they said, "We're going to sell our pants to everyone!" Therefore, they made them bigger, they made them wider—they even have a line now just for people over the age of thirty-five. Levi's recognized they could sell jeans to their customers for life.

This is what DLG is trying to do. We don't wish to sell just to teenagers. We want to get our customers when they're young, yet have the material for them when their tastes change so they'll *still* be customers. Certainly the more progressive retailers have recognized that there is no reason to lose a steady customer just because they grow up and move on to college, or just because they get married and have families of their own.

Customers just don't have a love for the superhero genre; they have a love for the *medium*. Naturally, as they get older, their tastes change. No one is watching the same TV shows that they watched when they were twelve, so why should they only continue to read the same kind of comic books? As long as the material is available, then alert retailers will be able to guide their customers through the transitions. When a customer who has only been reading books about mutants suddenly realizes, "Gee, I've seen this plot used three times before, I guess I don't like comics anymore," the retailer should recognize that this steady customer, this *good* customer, is losing interest in only a certain area, and will get him or her to the next level of books. Books which already *do* exist to further challenge, excite, and entertain every age group and kind of reader.

CBR: Given this mandate, do you believe the recent interest in this medium from established mainstream book publishers is a positive development? Or a blind alley?

MARDER: I'm assuming you're talking about books like Art Spiegelman's *Maus*—it's way too soon to draw a conclusion. It may be a blind alley, but there have been other books that have done well. It seems to me that there were some bad choices made to follow up the success of *Maus*, and the moderate success of the *Watchmen* trade paperback. The book trade either ignored or didn't seem to be able to analyze *why* these particular books were successful in bookstores. The next two or three "successors" that came out—you could see them there, sitting on the bookshelves—and say to yourself, "*Nobody's* ever going to buy these books. Why in the world were they published?"

You have an interesting development with Eclipse. They published graphic adaptations of *The Hobbit* and Anne McCaffrey's *Dragonflight* series, which garnered a tremendous amount of interest on the part of booksellers. They are very eager to sell those graphic novels. But that's because they already know how to sell Tolkien and McCaffrey. They *know* who these people are; they know who their audience is. Yet they don't really know what the audience for *Swamp Thing* or *Sandman* might be. So perhaps what we're going to see for the next couple of years are more successful adaptations of already popular novels. Hopefully the book trade will become more comfortable with selling the comic book/graphic novels. Then maybe we'll all have a better shot at marketing original work to the mainstream bookstores.

CBR: Let's focus on *Beanworld*. How do you sell it to that potential audience? And how do you describe *Beanworld* in order to initially interest an audience?

MARDER: First of all, what is *Beanworld*? *Beanworld* is an ecological romance. *Beanworld* is a self-contained fairy tale about a group of beings who live in the center of their perfect world. They're obsessed with maintaining its food chain. Now, that's a really low concept! [*Chuckles*] The biggest problem with *Beanworld* is that it's harder to describe it than it is to read it. It's also a book that makes the reader work; it's not just a mindless, "sit-back-and-be-entertained" comic book. The reader has to invest a certain amount of mental energy to follow the book. It has maps and a rather long glossary; there're a lot of things the reader has to learn to fully appreciate it.

CBR: And yet, there is no simpler or more iconographic comic book in existence in the world today than your *Beanworld*.

MARDER: Well, that's true when you're talking about artwork. I think *Beanworld* is the exact opposite of most modern comics. The artwork is really simple and the storyline's quite complex. Most comics have complicated artwork supporting very simple storylines. That's not true when you're talking about the alternatives; there are comics that are deeper, more complex than *Beanworld*. It's just that *Beanworld looks* so damned simple that people expect it to read like *Richie Rich*, but they find instead it reads more like *Cerebus*—

CBR: Or Frank Herbert's epic *Dune*.

MARDER: Obviously, *Beanworld* works on two levels. If it didn't, I wouldn't have so many young readers. It works like *Rocky and Bullwinkle* in the sense that there are many levels of complexity the reader can draw from the story, but the surface level is accessible enough for children to enjoy it, which is something that took me completely by surprise.

CBR: Speaking of working on two levels: How do you shift gears between your work at the retail and promotional commitments, and the creative work on *Beanworld*?

MARDER: I just do it. I'm schizo! [*Chuckles*] I don't know—I've always been able to do this, even when I worked in advertising. I'd be struggling with some huge problem, and when I was eating lunch I would be writing *Beanworld*. I can compartmentalize the two mindsets.

CBR: What was the starting point for your book?

MARDER: Twenty years ago, while I was in art school, I was swept up in the conceptual art movement. Everyone else I knew, whether it was painting or sculpture, was saying, "Down with the object. Down with form. Idea is everything." As a cartoonist, I wanted to create comics where idea *was* everything. That immediately meant: "Stop drawing the human figure." So I came up with something that would work in comics: the Bean figures, which were more interesting to me than just stick figures.

That's where it started, with my just goofing around with these figures, doing political cartoons on Watergate and so on, that were published in my college newspapers using these Bean characters. As the years went by, the storyline started coming to me, but bear in mind I came up with the Bean characters in 1972, yet the storyline didn't really come together until 1982. It was a very long, drawn-out process.

CBR: You're essentially a self-publisher. Where do you see the growth of *Beanworld* going, given your knowledge of the realities of the present marketplace?

MARDER: What's the next step? I don't know. Though I still work on it, my book is basically on hiatus while I'm at Moondog's, and I work with other creators trying to figure out what we can do to make this system work better, to prevent these bottlenecks. To find out why we have a situation where retailers *want* the books, and the publishers *have* the books, and somehow they can't get them to more readers. There's no way this business is going to grow until these problems are solved. It seems to me what needs to be done, more than anything, is for these bridges to be built between creators and retailers to figure out better ways to get all of these books on the shelves so the readers who want them can buy them.

Even though *Beanworld* is highly regarded among creative circles and by other cartoonists, and it has a hardcore cult following, it has never been a book that received any critical attention. How can a book grow that is never reviewed, if the press releases about it are never printed? What does one do then?

I decided through the opportunities given me at Moondog's to figure out how this machine works, and in doing so find myself involved in fixing it.

ROOTS

The Undergrounds Ascending

THE POSTWAR YEARS DO NOT BRING AN END TO HOSTILITIES BETWEEN ANGLOS AND MEXICANS — ESPECIALLY IN THE NUECES STRIP. THE WIDE-OPEN BORDER DRAWS LAWLESS MEN OF ALL SHADES AND HUES LIKE A MAGNET.

TH' LAND OF GOLDEN OPPORTUN-ITY, EH ZEKE?

YES, BUT ONLY FOR THEM THAT CARPE DIEM, MY TRUSTED FRIEND.

MANY OF THESE RUFFIANS CLAIM TO BE "MUSTANGERS," LIVING OFF THE HERDS OF WILD HORSES AND ABANDONED CATTLE, BUT THEY ARE MORE ACCURATELY DESCRIBED AS CUT-THROATS AND PRAIRIE PIRATES.

WE'RE RIFF-RAFF AND PROUD OF IT!!

RAIDS ACROSS BOTH SIDES OF THE BORDER ARE FREQUENT AND THE PEACEFUL SETTLERS, ANGLO AND TEJANO, ARE THE ULTIMATE VICTIMS.

LEAVE THESE AROUND AND THEY'LL BLAME IT ON THE INJUNS..

EACH TIME A MEXICAN-BASED BAND ROBS AND PLUNDERS, ANGLO VIGILANTES RETALIATE AGAINST INNOCENT TEJANOS. WHEN "COW BOYS" STRIKE ACROSS THE RIO GRANDE, THE MEXICANS AVENGE THEMSELVES AGAINST ANGLO FAMILIES LIVING IN THE WARZONE.

ZING

WE CAN'T KEEP LIVIN' LIKE THIS, MINERVA...

FROM *LOS TEJANOS.* © 1993 BY JACK JACKSON.

3

JACK JACKSON
The Texas Ranger

The revolutionary underground comix movement of
the Sixties and Seventies forever changed the medium. Exploding from the youth counterculture that
spawned them, the undergrounds reveled in an
uninhibited torrent of concepts, stories, and imagery that flowed from the minds and pens of creators
like Robert Crumb, S. Clay Wilson, Gilbert Shelton,
Vaughn Bode, Greg Irons, Richard Corben, the Air
Pirates, to name just some of the most outrageous.
Resurrecting the bawdy spirit of the sexually explicit "Tijuana Bibles," the
righteous anger and vivid horrors of the EC Comics, and a broad canvas of
artistic influences from the Surrealists and Dadaists to Segar's *Popeye* and
the Fleischer Brothers' *Betty Boop*, the comix creators totally exposed the raw
potential of an art form which had strained for far too long beneath the
constraints of the established (and the Establishment's) comic book industry.

Here all taboos were gleefully broken, explored, exploited, and satirized.
There were no boundaries save those of the cartoonists' imaginations and
the cost of the ink and paper. In the undergrounds, no subject was sacred or
immune from examination.

And Jack Jackson (a.k.a. "Jaxon") was there when the comix movement
began, emerging in part from the college humor magazines of the early

Sixties. Primary among these was *The Texas Ranger*, published at the University of Texas, where Jackson managed editorial duties in the footsteps of previous editors Frank Stack and Gilbert Shelton. It was there that Shelton (creator of the seminal *Wonder Warthog* and *The Fabulous Furry Freak Brothers*) convinced Stack to publish his scathing satire of the New Testament's Christ, yielding what is today considered the very first underground comix, *The Adventures of J* (1962). Jackson's own legendary *God Nose* followed two years later.

When the comix scene finally began to wane, Jackson plunged into an ambitious trilogy of revisionist historical comix: *White Comanche* (1977), *Red Raider* (1977), and *Blood on the Moon* (1978). Revised and presented as the graphic novel *Comanche Moon* (1979), Jackson's rigorously researched and beautifully realized biography of Cynthia Ann Parker and her Comanche warrior son Quanah, set amid the genocide of the Native Americans in the late 1800s, marked a remarkable evolution for both the individual artist and the medium as a whole. This promise of setting the historical record straight on both artistic and moral grounds has been fulfilled by *Los Tejanos* (1982), as well as his more recent adaptations of James Fenimore Cooper's *Last of the Mohicans* (1992) and *Columbus* (1992). Although not a commercial success, his *Secret of San Saba* (1986–1989) masterfully interweaves historical fiction with the Lovecraftian horrors of the artist's early comix work for *Skull* and *Slow Death*.

Whatever the commercial consequences, Jack Jackson remains an accomplished artistic pioneer who remains true to his own rugged paths, tenaciously blazing his own trails.

COMIC BOOK REBELS: Your work goes back to the very beginnings of the underground comix of the early Sixties. Can you relate for us how this revolutionary movement in the medium originated?

JACK JACKSON: I came to Austin, Texas, in 1962. I had just gotten out of college with an accounting degree, so I had a flattop haircut and duck tails, and was working a straight job at the state capital. And I was hanging out with the local weirdos after hours, and trying to make sure that nobody ever learned the truth about what was going on. And in the very early sixties, the collegiate humor magazines were quite the thing. Most of the major schools had humor magazines, like *The Harvard Lampoon*, put out by their communications department. So I fell in with this crowd of weirdos who were involved with a humor magazine called *The Texas Ranger*. That was how I picked up on Frank Stack's *The*

Adventures of Jesus (1962), through people like Gilbert Shelton and various others involved in the college humor scene. It was rather like a little oasis for us, this wonderful little mimeographed thing called *The Adventures of Jesus*.

CBR: The historians now consider *The Adventures of Jesus* to be the very first underground comix. What did it mean to you at the time?

JACKSON: For somebody like me, who had all these religious hangups that I still hadn't shaken—I was going to be a fundamentalist preacher, that was what my road in life was supposed to be—this was just a breath of fresh air. It poked fun at the Scriptures and the sanctity and Godhood of Jesus and all that, and rather made him like a normal guy. Frank Stack, bless his heart, is finally getting some belated recognition on that.

CBR: What inspired your work on *God Nose* (1964), one of the earliest of the undergrounds?

JACKSON: We were doing a lot of peyote in those days. Aldous Huxley had written this book called *The Doors of Perception*, and there was really a lot of academic interest in what happened to your mind under the influence of psychedelics. And we had no idea what could happen, and being quite foolhardy, we thought it would be nice to try some of this stuff. Peyote was quite legal at the time; you could buy it at any cactus shop or cactus farm that sold ornamental cactus for about twenty-five cents a bud. A bud being about the size of your fist. And part of the group we were hanging out with were people studying chemistry, so they quickly devoted themselves to how to render mescaline from peyote, and psilocybin from mushrooms, and just about anything else we could get them.

This was just about before the Beatles broke, I believe. So there would be a group of us sitting around munching on these mushrooms, listening to classical music. There was a *lot* of classical music, which was in keeping of course with the intellectual explorations involved. So we got to taking that mind-altering stuff, and you get up there, and you don't know if you're ever coming back, and you're like a blithering idiot, you know? And, among other things, it makes your nose drip. So under the influence of this stuff, sitting around with some of these

NERVOUSLY HE FUMBLES WITH HIS KEYS AS THE CIRCLE TIGHTENS AROUND HIM.

EVADING THE HORDE OF MERCENARY BANSHEES, YOUNG FRED TODD RIDES THE FREIGHT ELEVATOR UPWARD INTO THE PITCH-BLACK VOID.

IT MIRACULOUSLY LABORS TO A HALT ON THE 3RD FLOOR AND FRED PICKS HIS WAY THROUGH A MINEFIELD OF COUNTERCULTURAL ACTIVITY.

WAY DOWN ON THE END, PAST THE NUDE DANCING TROUPE, THE LIGHTSHOW SETUP, THE IMPROVISED BANDSTAND, AND ASSORTED WORKSHOP/LIVING SPACE, IS A PARTITIONED CORNER.

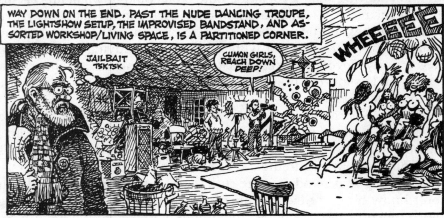

loony guys, we came up with a character called "God Nose." It was strictly drug-induced.

And I'm not apologetic at *all* about those old days. "Just Say No." I don't go for it for a minute! I think that as long as you don't totally abuse drugs, like anything else in life, there's a great deal to be learned from it. Unfortunately, a few of my friends did go whacko; they just took so much they never really got all their marbles back together. But I really felt that it woke up an artistic side of me that had been slumbering. It also allowed me to put my act together in this world, and shake off a lot of this religious crap that I had that had been strangling me. So I think, all together, it was a very exciting period.

Anyway, *God Nose* was an attempt to render some of the ridiculous absurdities that had come through from these peyote sessions. Like I say, it was legal then. All you had to do was to stay out of your car, so you didn't hallucinate the Grand Canyon and crash into a tree. [*Laughs*]

CBR: Then how did the underground comix movement eventually begin on the West Coast, and what part did you play in it?

JACKSON: Well, as you can well imagine, this period of time completely prepared me for the scene in San Francisco. We had already done all the stuff that was being done there, though on a much smaller scale, for the past three or four years. But the humor magazine scene fell apart— people got too crazy and did things that alienated the school censors. We tried a little off-campus humor sheet for a while, but that never really got going. Then people started splitting off.

Meanwhile, people would occasionally stray through from the West Coast and said, "Forget the Village, it's all happening out on the West Coast." So I went out there the summer of '66. There was a small network of Texans out there even then, which steadily grew and grew over time until it was quite a little colony out there. Detroit had a similar colony, as did New York City of course. You see, as a correspondent and editor of *The Ranger*, I exchanged humor magazines with other colleges, and kept in touch with a lot of people who later on you met in the scene. Jay Lynch, and various people from around the country who were in the humor scene, were familiar just from correspondence. But there was always this small group of humor-orientated people that later got together on the West Coast. It was a very strong-willed community of artists and writers doing this same type of thing, some of whom later went on into publishing.

CBR: But how did the idea of doing underground comix come out of that sense of community? Was there a conscious collective goal among these expatriate artists to produce them?

JACKSON: No, the "comix" as such were out of the tail end of the rock poster trip. All the visuals in the Haight-Ashbury scene had been in the underground newspapers and the rock posters. And I had gone to work for one of the old peyote-party people from Austin named Chet Helms. His group was called the "Family Dog." They were Bill Graham's archenemy. Graham was the bad guy, and we were the good guys. He was a crass mercenary, and we were doing it for the love and flowers: "We're just doing the art because it's great to do, man, not to get rich."

That turned into comix because so many people had done work there in posters, once the posters started taking a slide—because there the market was glutted due to overproduction—these people started getting disenchanted. "I don't want to work in this medium anymore. It's all fucked up." People like Peter Max were coming in and taking the charisma of it and turning it into really big bucks. And so when R. Crumb comes along, with his little *Zap* #1 (1968) comix there, hawking it on the street, it was just like, "Oh, wow! Here's something we can do! Why didn't we think of this before?"

So you had all these people who were into psychedelics who had done really dazzling visuals with the rock posters, all of a sudden, they decided to start doing some comix. We couldn't afford to do the interiors in color because of the economics of self-publishing, but at least the covers could be nice and colorful. Everybody tried to get cover gigs, because that was where they could really strut their stuff with colors, as they had done with the posters.

But in a sense it was a natural setup, you see, because the market already existed for the posters in the head shops. We could go around to them and say, "Okay, you're not selling many posters? Well here—try these. Comix." So the rock posters laid the groundwork which enabled us to publish the underground comix. The distribution system and printers were already in place; we didn't have to start from scratch. And since none of the mainstream distributors would touch this outrageous material, it was really essential that we had that "underground" system. If we hadn't had that system of head shops and various alternative outlets like that, the comix movement just wouldn't have gone anywhere. We all would have been sitting around with boxes of unsold comix.

CBR: At what point do you feel the underground comix were reaching a sizable audience, and thereby possibly having some effect upon the popular culture of the time?

JACKSON: We *never* felt like we were reaching a sizable audience. [*Laughs*] The comix were for aficionados and dopers and whatnot from the beginning. We were just entertaining our friends, so to speak. We of course hoped that there would be a tie-in with the hip people out there. This is why the head shop connection was so critical, because any city of any significance had at least one head shop in those days. And the dopers really loved them: comics that had an updated sensibility to them, none of the plastic shit that you would get from the big corporations. These were the home-grown variety. And of course a lot of the comix did deal with dope, you know. *The Fabulous Furry Freak Brothers* (from 1968 to the present). And Dave Sheriden's "Dealer McDope" character. They were just about this incredible humor surrounding the ritual of doing some kind of dope.

CBR: Was there a personal vision that each of you were trying to explore as artists, with the mind-altering drugs just another tool to expand your artistic horizons?

JACKSON: Sort of like that, yeah. That's a pretty grandiose statement, though. Basically we were just trying to have some fun, and avoid having to work a straight job. [*Laughs*]

CBR: What're your best memories of your life as a cartoonist in that period, in the early Seventies?

JACKSON: I enjoyed working on *Slow Death* (1970–1979) a whole lot, much more so than *Skull* (1970–1972). To me, *Slow Death* had some kind of social significance because there really was this awareness of "Hey, if we don't stop this mad rush we're in with our culture, we're going to trash the whole goddamn world, and there'll be nothing left in a hundred years." So, in that sense, it was a "mission" we were on in that we felt, if we could wake people up to some of the issues we were trying to explore there in the name of progress, that maybe we could halt the juggernaut. Or at least slow it down a little. It was not a unique vision, but it was a persistent one. You still have people doing that kind of work with that vision in mind today.

We were not the only ones with this idea. Later on, Warren Publishing had this magazine, *1984* (1978–1981), that kinda followed in the same footsteps. *Slow Death* is where I got turned on to Richard Corben, because his work was just so *powerful* in terms of that ecological vision. Something like Corben's "How Howie Made It in the Real World" in issue #2 (1970)—that just knocked my socks off! Every once in a while somebody does a strip that reaches a plateau, and then you make a jump from there, make another quantum leap. I felt like that was one of those type of stories.

CBR: What was your personal favorite, though, of your own work?

JACKSON: I saw myself as always a second- or third-stringer. I was never on the cutting edge, but I would get inspired by what other people were doing, and try to work in the same vein. One of my one-shot books that I was really excited about was *Up from the Deep* (1971). What I wanted to do with that book was explore other dimensions. Basically I just wanted to get into psychic stuff; what goes on in your dream world. I didn't really follow it up, and one reason why was because that was the first underground to come out with a full color insert. (Richard Corben had a color insert in there, too.) In terms of economics the use of color was a mistake, because in black and white the book might have sold enough to be successful and would have encouraged us to do more.

CBR: Not that *Slow Death* was ever a walk in the park, but some of your wildest and most outrageous work appeared in the bloodsoaked pages of *Skull*.

JACKSON: Well, *Skull*, on the other hand, was just kind of a jerkoff book. [*Chuckles*] Everybody just had fun with that: we got as gory as we wanted to get. Greg Irons and Tom Veitch did one story which typifies the book for me, about a guy who goes to clean up a wreck on the highway—"Cleanup Crew" in #3 (1971). And that's the kind of book that it was, just off the wall, bananas kind of stuff, with utterly *no* socially redeeming value! But with *Slow Death* we were very conscious of what we were doing, and were really trying to strike a blow, as it were, for Mother Earth.

CBR: You were one of the first underground artists to adapt the stories of H.P. Lovecraft and Robert E. Howard. How influential were those pulpmasters from the 1930s to your work?

JACKSON: Oh, they were *very* influential. For some reason, I don't know why, somebody turned me on to that horror specialty press Arkham House. And I believe there was also an entire line of paperbacks by Lovecraft coming out for the first time then, as well as a number of books by other writers who wrote in that vein. Those guys—it was hard to read this stuff without thinking they must have been doing some kind of drugs back in the thirties—they were just *bizarre*. I read every goddamn thing I could find by Lovecraft, then went on to other people who had been originally published in *Weird Tales* and the like. I found a lot of these stories really fun to try and adapt into comic books.

I missed out doing more of them because I had had hand surgery around the period of 1969 to 1971, where there were muscle transplants in my hand. I was in the hospital twice, and so my drawing arm was in a cast for three or four months. Then I had to go through a rehabilitation stage before I could see if I could even draw again. It worked out pretty well in the long run, but during that period of time when the undergrounds were starting to come out full force, I was kind of laid-up, and there was a time when I had to say to people, "Gee, I'd love to be in your book, but my hand's not strong enough yet."

But that period was really exciting, we had a lot of fun with it. As long as we were making enough to pay the bills, we felt like we were making it pretty well.

CBR: Yet in terms of profiting from your creations, none of you ever were truly making much of a living, in spite of your undeniable wealth of artistic freedom.

JACKSON: I think we were working in those days for something like twenty-five dollars a page, advance against royalties. And even though we worked so hard for this idea that the creator would share in the royalties of the book, it was so disappointing because there never seemed to be any profit, you know? There just never seemed to be any more money than the advance. So basically you were working for starvation wages, that's what you were doing. And on payday, even though we were careful that the artist would have the advantage of owning his own work, it just never seemed to pan out.

CBR: Do you remember when you felt that "the Movement" had finally run its course?

JACKSON: Oh, yeah, no doubt about it. I think it was around 1973, when Stanley Mouse—who was one of the great poster artists of the time—went to Detroit to visit his friends and family. He was one of the prototype hippies—and he came back with short hair! And Rick Griffin, who had sworn he would never cut his hair, was there when Stanley comes back from the airport, and when we saw him it was just total *shock*. We knew that the end had come when one of the hardcore, cutting-edge artists suddenly goes straight on us, appearancewise.

But the scene itself started getting real ugly and nasty at that point in the mid-Seventies. Everybody pretty well acknowledged to themselves that something had gone wrong, you know? The things that were supposed to work, and the changes in society that were supposed to have come down, just didn't come. People were just doing bad stuff. You had people like the Hell's Angels taking the same kind of drugs we were, except they were bashing people's brains in when *they* got high. Instead of doing groovy things, like being soul brothers, you know? I went to the concert at Altamont, and that was just another nail in the coffin. You tell from the vibes of that place that somewhere somebody—if not all of us—had taken a wrong turn.

So about this time I was doing "White Man's Burden" for *Slow Death* #6 (1974), and a couple of other depressing comic strips which talked about the circularity of it all: What goes around comes around. Where first you're the oppressed, and then all of a sudden you become an oppressor just as bad as whoever was first oppressing you. Just remember that comix were just a reflection of the larger scene; so it's hard to talk about the undergrounds without talking about the social turmoil that was going on simultaneously.

CBR: One of the key transitional stories for you at this time appeared in *Slow Death* #7 (1975) called "Nits Make Lice." This was clearly a precursor to the *Comanche Moon* trilogy (1977–1978) the first of your historical comic series. Why the changeover to history from fantasy?

JACKSON: That was my first venture into real history. That is, what we're told about history as opposed to what *really* happened. For some reason, I just began getting interested in history. I remember going down to the San Francisco Library and checking out history books. The one that got me was *Bury My Heart at Wounded Knee*, in terms of my interest in the Indians, and the way their history had been written. So reading that book was an inspiration for my doing "Nits Make Lice."

I had also, as a youngster, been given in school a book of the history of Texas that had been done entirely in comic book form, *Texas History Movies* (1926–1956). It was first published in serial form in the late twenties by a newspaper artist named Jack Patton and author John Rosenfield, Jr., and later collected into a book. It always stuck in my mind; I've still got my copy that I had gotten in the sixth grade, with "Jacky Jackson" signed on it. I knew that since I had gotten it in the public school system, it must be legit, you know? So when I got tired of doing the dope and sex comix, the idea of doing history just kind of came to the forefront.

CBR: But how can the idea of doing historically accurate fiction about real people and events be as challenging as doing horror and fantasy stories, where you have the complete freedom to make it up as you go along?

JACKSON: Oh, no! One is easily just as free as the other! Because when you can do this—by virtue of being able to tell the truth—you *can* show the massacres with all the gory details. You are *more* free than any of these other people who ever tried to do history in a comic strip! You don't have to abide any more by the old, standard presentations. You can show someone who's been scalped by Indians and the atrocities that were committed against them by us . . . you can do *anything*. Nobody dared do this before. You can now fully address the political issues of the way we had treated the Indians, and every other important issue.

Before you had just had that "Tonto" bullshit.

I simply took the freedom I had been accustomed to in the undergrounds and applied it to not telling the standard, or sanitized version of history, but going to great pains to research what actually happened. To fit the pieces together.

CBR: Between the three-issue underground comix series and the revised book edition of *Comanche Moon* (1979), you went back and redrew some panels. Basically self-censoring yourself after the fact, yes?

JACKSON: Oh, yes. The reason why I did that is because you become aware as you go that you're not going to get your book into a lot of places—like libraries—you're not going to reach a lot of the young minds you're hoping to reach. So you realize you have to cut some panels out, or you have to cover these beautiful little titties up—or else. This is why, when you attempt to do a "legitimate biography," even though you're trying to tell it from a revisionist point of view, historically speaking, you have to pay more attention to what you're doing in certain areas, like sex or nudity. Otherwise you're not going to reach an audience that is interested solely in history. Also, some granny-lady is going to come in and make them take your book out of the school library.

CBR: Considering the vast amount of artistic freedom you had as an underground cartoonist, how do you keep your sanity if you have to rein in certain aspects of your imagination to gain acceptance in a mainstream marketplace?

JACKSON: Well, what I have done to solve that dilemma, and it *is* a creative dilemma, what I have done is to compartmentalize my work. In other words, if I just want to get my rocks off and do some wild, sexy, perverto thing, I'll just do it in a strip for that means. But I also have a parallel life. I do this kind of straight-ahead biographical material. But I know when I do the biographical work, I already know not to get too wild and crazy. So I just compartmentalize it. What a cartoonist should do in that situation is, depending on what you feel like doing at that time, you just do that type of a strip, and then try and feed it to the right particular type of a market. You tailor different kinds of work to different kinds of projects.

CBR: If the underground comix were once considered truly revolutionary in every artistic, sociological and political sense, do you think there will ever be another revolution?

JACKSON: Well, these things come in cycles. There won't be another until the situation gets as stagnant as it was when the first undergrounds had their little revolution. And the scene with the undergrounds was part of a larger social revolution, so you have to keep that in mind as well. Maybe it's time for a swing of the pendulum back the other way. But I don't see it happening any time soon.

It's kind of like the undergrounds broke enough creative ground, and opened up enough possibilities for us to explore for quite a while. On

many different fronts, and in many different directions. It's like anything else; young artists are saying, "Gee, these guys went so far, what
can we do now?" So you have these "punk comix" coming out, trying
to do us one better, as it were. Trying to go farther. So I don't see any
problem with worrying about the next revolution. I think we now as
artists have the latitude and the freedom to do pretty much whatever
we damn well please.

SO ENDS THE SAGA OF THE *LAST CHIEF OF THE COMANCHES*, WHO PERHAPS DID MORE TO RECONCILE THE RED AND WHITE RACES THAN ANY OTHER MAN. BUT HIS SPIRIT LIVES ON! EACH YEAR THE DESCENDANTS OF QUANAH AND THEIR PARKER RELATIVES GATHER TO HONOR THE MEMORY OF CYNTHIA ANN AND HER REMARKABLE SON.

END

FROM *RIP IN TIME*. © 1993 BY RICHARD CORBEN AND BRUCE JONES.

4

RICHARD CORBEN
Up from the Deep

A soft-spoken, reclusive Midwesterner who shuns the spotlight of celebrity, Richard Corben is a rather mysterious figure to even his most devoted readers and fans. However aloof the artist himself may remain, his stories and art burn into the international comic book arena with an aggressive clarity and seductive skill. However wildly impossible the adventures and anatomies of his oversexed heroes, heroines, and monsters may seem, they will forever pulse with an almost tactile sense of elemental life.

While his early artwork for the science-fiction and horror fanzines of the late Sixties showed obvious promise and steady growth, Corben's affinity for the comics medium blossomed with the fanzine publication of *Rowlf* in *The Voice of Comicdom* #16 and #17 (1970–71). *Rowlf* boldly demonstrated his remarkable grasp of chiaroscuro, drama, and movement to tell the compelling tale of a humanoid canine battling mutants to defend the woman to whom he is devoted. A giddy adventure by turns touching and bracingly violent, *Rowlf* established the post-Apocalyptic landscape peculiar to much of Corben's finest work. This includes his ongoing saga of his adventurer *Den* to his collaborations with acclaimed writers like Jan Strnad (*Mutant World*, 1978–79) and Harlan Ellison (*Vic and Blood*, 1987–89).

After the collapse of his first self-published fanzine *Fantagor* (1970), and while still unaware of the underground comix movement, Corben was contacted by San Francisco comic-shop owner Gary Arlington who had just published *Skull Comics* #1 (1970). Excited by the possibilities, Corben responded with the story "Lame Lem's Love," which Arlington promptly published in *Skull Comics* #2. Neither Corben or comix were ever the same again. He all but erupted into the undergrounds with an astonishing torrent of memorable stories. Though Corben was occasionally attacked by other comix creators who considered his sensibilities at odds with the established countercultural agenda (so to speak), his culminative output from this period in his career rates with the very best of the undergrounds.

Corben's dazzling experiments with color comix stories began with "Ci-Dopey" (*Up from the Deep*, 1971), "Going Home" (*Funny World* #14, 1972), the comix incarnation of *Fantagor* #2 and #4 (1972), and the first chapter of *Den* in the full-color *Grimwit* #2 (1973). Along with the concurrently published color stories in James Warren's newstand horror magazines *Creepy*, *Eerie*, and *Vampirella*, these tales were unprecedented achievements in contemporary American comic art.

His extraordinary color narratives opened new horizons via reprints in *Metal Hurlant*, and subsequent wider exposure to a domestic readership when the French magazine spawned America's first "Adult Illustrated Fantasy" periodical *Heavy Metal* (from 1977 to the present). Freshly inspired by the success of the *Teenage Mutant Ninja Turtles* comics of Kevin Eastman and Peter Laird, Corben returned once more to self-publishing in the mid-Eighties. Still based in Kansas City, Richard Corben continues to produce his unique stories and art, satisfying an appreciative international audience as he quietly works to please only himself.

COMIC BOOK REBELS: Growing up in the Fifties, how much of a creative impact did the now legendary EC Comics make upon you? Did they influence you primarily as a developing storyteller?

RICHARD CORBEN: I think it's something a little more fundamental than that. They were great stories, sure. But they also hit upon a fundamental need or expression that kids a certain age need to explore, which they need to work out for themselves: Exploring the meaning of death, and everything that goes around with it.

CBR: Regarding your influences as a cartoonist, we've always had the sense that you were a fan of Dell Comics' *Tarzan* artist Jessie Marsh,

FROM *DEN SAGA* #2 © 1993 RICHARD CORBEN.

primarily because of the way you draw your animals. Are you familiar with his work?

CORBEN: If I collected anybody, it was Jessie Marsh's *Tarzan* books (1948—65). I collected those for years, and he was one of my stars. Most people can't see the connection at all, and it may in fact be a little tenuous.

CBR: Was Russ Manning an influence in any way? We're thinking in terms of the semiparody of Manning's *Magnus Robot Fighter* (1963—68) you did in *Slow Death* #4 (1972).

CORBEN: Yeah, but probably to a lesser extent. In some ways he was much more finished as an artist than Jessie Marsh, but by the time he took over, I was getting too old for comics. I went away from them for a time.

CBR: So what brought you back to comics as a reader?

CORBEN: Well, I don't know if I ever really came back to them as a reader. I came back to comics because of something I felt a need to do for myself: I wanted to be a cartoonist.

CBR: We know that you've used sculpture as a means of better visualizing your characters. Has that always been an organic part of the creative process for you as an artist?

CORBEN: Well, that goes back to some of my earliest efforts. I did character heads because drawing the same character over and over again, from different angles, the sculpture became an aid in doing that more effectively. But it was sort of limiting in that my drawings were only as good as my sculptures. I mean, they had the character, but they weren't always that lifelike.

CBR: One of the aspects of your art that instantly hits people upon seeing it for the first time is your amazing use of dramatic lighting. Where did that develop?

CORBEN: Now, I think that is definitely from the EC Comics. Most noticeably of all, probably, from Wally Wood. If I learned lighting from anybody, it was from him. And Will Eisner.

CBR: Any influences from your life-long interest in the cinema?

CORBEN: Some influences are unconscious, and you don't realize them until they come out later, often in an odd sort of way. It may have been an influence, but in terms of making a connection by watching a film and saying, "That's a neat lighting effect. I should use it in a comic," well, I really don't remember ever coming to a decision like that in my work.

CBR: You've done some short films of your own, primarily in clay animation. In some ways, pursuing filmmaking and animation has been as important to you as cartooning, hasn't it?

CORBEN: There were some decisions that were made very early on in my career. When I was going to high school, I said, "Well—I either want to be a comic-book artist or I want to be an animator. Whatever the fortunes bring to me, that's the way I'll go." I went one way for a while, and then went another way, and then went back—it's a mix in the early part of my career before I settled, almost exclusively, on the comics. But for the first ten years after college I was working for an industrial movie company in Kansas City, and so I was—sort of—working in the movies.

I think if I had been a little more independent, at a very young age, I think I might have taken off for Hollywood, and things would have been different. But being the person I am, I didn't, so I just stayed at home. I've had a few opportunities since then to possibly do some work in feature films, yet I can see that these people don't have all the freedom that I thought they might have.

CBR: You developed a most distinctive style for your work very early on in your career. In a certain sense, your style seems purposely "overdone," especially in the incredibly voluptuous manner both your male and female characters are rendered.

CORBEN: My style is kind of like watching television with the intensity of the colors turned up a little bit. It's also taking the idea of classic heroes and heroines and turning up or exaggerating the archetypes a little bit, too. But it's all done with a straight face. And in the early part of my career, the development of style was not a conscious thing, it just sort of happened. Normally I don't question my motives of doing things. I just do them.

CBR: One of your early works was *Tales from the Plague*, which was first published as *The Plague Years* (1969). Was that initially conceived as a single "novel"-length tale?

CORBEN: Well, it was conceived and done as a two-part "novel," and it was published that way. Actually, it was published together in two sixteen-page sections—two versions of the same story. That was me getting my feet wet, too, in terms of doing comic art for publication. It may have been a bit overdone.

CBR: How did *Rowlf* (1970–71) come about, which was entirely your own concept and story? The post-Apocalyptic theme of his world has been one you've returned to repeatedly in your work.

CORBEN: He was partially based on the dog we had as a kid. When I was growing up we had a dog, and I think there's a bunch of him in *Rowlf*. My concept of Rowlf's world was that this would be a clash of fantasy and science fiction. We have fantasy elements like the castles and medieval costumes and sorcerers, and then they clash with these mutants with their sort of "Panzer" tanks.

CBR: Of the many comic book writers you've worked with over the years, one of the first was Jan Strnad. How did you connect with Strnad?

CORBEN: I met him at the World Science Fiction Convention in St. Louis, in '68 or '69. He had published a fanzine called *Anomaly*, and I bought one there, and we took up a correspondence, and then later we took up work together. We've worked together on and off through the years. My favorite work with him is probably the one he found the most difficult because he had to pick up on something I had started and then didn't know what to do with—that would be *Mutant World* (1978–79). At the time I had only done the first chapter, and I had some vague ideas of what I was going to do with it next, and then I realized my ideas were no good! [*Laughs*] We later went back and did a sequel to that series, *Son of Mutant World* (1990–91).

CBR: Were your experiences with Strnad in the fanzines what made you decide to start your own company, Fantagor Press, so as to have a vehicle to best showcase your own material?

CORBEN: Partially. I can't remember where I saw my first fanzine, but I remember writing to the editor and sending him some of my drawings. He decided he was going to use them, and then decided I could do a story, too. But then, after seeing such a great variety in quality and points of view in other fanzines, I thought, "Heck, I can do this!" So I did a fanzine or two, and when the underground comix came out I thought, "This is basically simple: you just write and draw your own comics. And I can do that, too." So I did. There's a little more to it than just that, but basically that's what I've been doing ever since.

CBR: You did a considerable body of work during the height of the popularity of the underground comix in the Seventies. Was that where publisher James Warren first saw your stories?

CORBEN: Yeah, I did a lot of work. I can't say I made a lot of money, but I did a *lot* of work. [*Chuckles*] But I was being published in the undergrounds at about the same time I started doing work for Jim Warren. I had been trying to cultivate working for Warren for several years, and just as I was getting into the underground comix, that was when Warren decided he would give me some strips to do.

CBR: In hindsight, was your involvement with the legendary—some would say infamous—James Warren an enjoyable experience?

CORBEN: Well, Warren was a hard taskmaster. I had to go over several of my stories and change this and that, and fix this and that, just to meet his demands. I could talk about my personal memories of the man, but they may not be suitable for publication! [*Laughs*] There was always a tension between Warren and the people who worked for him. I wanted desperately to do comics, and he was publishing the only kind of comics that I wanted to do, so it was either play his game, or nothing. So I felt like I had to put up with some abuse . . .

I also had to censor my work on a couple of occasions. There was that dinosaur cover I did for *Eerie* #125 (1981) with the woman up in the tree. She had a little more breast exposed than they cared for, as I recall.

CBR: Did you ever feel a sense of community with the other creators working in the underground comix scene?

CORBEN: That was a *very* diverse group of people. I did feel a camaraderie with some of them, but with some others, they were just too, too different for me. A lot of them had a real political agenda, and that has never been overt in my work. But the freedom I had there probably spoiled me.

CBR: To what extent do you still consider yourself an "underground comix" artist?

CORBEN: Well, I'm not sure what that term means. But I am a misfit in terms of mainstream cartoonists in that, though I work hard at what I do, I just can't see working for people who seem to be doing things for the wrong reasons. I mean, I have friends who are in the mainstream comics industry, but I just couldn't hack it myself.

CBR: *Den* is the one character that continues to thread throughout your entire career, going all the way back to your work in the underground comix. What's your continued interest with him as a character?

CORBEN: To me, he represents a universal individual. He's sort of a hero in spite of himself.

CBR: How much does *Den* reflect your inner landscape as an artist?

CORBEN: Probably far more than I care to admit! [*Laughs*]

CBR: Can you tell us how *Den* came to appear in the 1981 animated feature, *Heavy Metal*?

CORBEN: The people who ran *Heavy Metal* wanted to do an animated version of the magazine. And they wanted to include all the characters that they possibly could have from the magazine in the movie. So my input for that was, because *Den* was in the magazine, they wanted my work in the movie. It wasn't anything I actively promoted, really. Oddly enough, *Den* originated in a short animated film of my own called *Neverwhere* back in 1968 before I even did the comics.

The producers offered me the chance of going to the studio and doing some supervisory work of my segment, but I was too tied up in other comics projects at the time. So mainly what I did was some model sheets for my characters and did some approvals of their designs, and that was about it. I didn't choose John Candy for the voice of Den either, but in retrospect I think he did a pretty good job. Looking back, I'm not all that strong on the animation, but I think they came pretty close with the tone of Den's world.

CBR: With the many writers whose classics you've adapted to the comic medium over the years—Poe, Lovecraft, Howard, Bradbury—were those projects you initiated for purely personal reasons, or were they the most commercially viable to do at that point in your career?

CORBEN: Each circumstance was different. In some cases, the opportunity just presented itself, and I jumped at it, as was the case with Robert E. Howard and Ray Bradbury. And Lovecraft, too, come to think of it. On one of my current books, *Den Saga*, the project is something I initiated myself, with three adaptations of Clark Ashton Smith to be used as backup stories. The first adaptation is "The Seed from the Sepulcher," which is a story that takes place in a South American jungle and there's this mutant orchid growing out this guy's head . . . [*Laughs*] The one I've just finished for issue Number Two is "The Vaults of Yoh-Vombis," which is a Martian story. Some readers might see the origins of some situations that were later used in the movie *Alien* there. Actually, when I was negotiating to get the Clark Ashton Smith properties, that was when I was publishing the *Horror in the Dark* (1991–92) and they would have been perfect for that title. But then *Horror in the Dark* didn't quite make it in the marketplace.

CBR: You were responsible for one of the very first graphic novels—published before that term really existed—with your adaptation of Robert E. Howard's *Bloodstar* (1976). Wasn't artist Gil Kane involved in that project as well?

CORBEN: Like I said before, this was an opportunity that was presented to me. It *was* a graphic novel, but I didn't put it out, it was published by a company called Morning Star Press. But it was a great opportunity for me at the time, and I considered it then to be my best work to date. Gil Kane was a partner in the Morning Star Press, which unfortunately broke up very shortly after that book's publication.

CBR: You've done numerous wonderful stories with Bruce Jones, not only in the Warren publications, but your more recent *Rip in Time* (1986–87). How have your collaborations been conducted with him and other writers?

CORBEN: I've had some very good collaborations with other writers. But with one exception, they've all been done long-distance. They've been done by letter, phone, fax, and everything else. Bruce and I loved the stories we did for Warren, but they were done simply on a job by job basis, with no thought of any thematic goals, I must admit. We weren't organized enough to have any long-range goals, but we did love the work, and that's what kept us going.

But each collaboration was different. I worked with Jan one way, worked with Bruce another way, and I worked with Simon Revelstroke yet another way. When I worked with Simon I believe the results had merit, but boy did it come out of conflict! [*Laughs*] I fought with him constantly.

CBR: Is "Simon Revelstroke" a pseudonym? It certainly sounds like one.

CORBEN: Yes, it is. But it's not mine, though. All I can tell you is, he's a local writer who lives here in Kansas City. I guess he was just self-conscious about being in comics.

CBR: Considering the universal appeal much of your work has to fantasy and science-fiction fans, have you had a good experience with other foreign markets over the years?

CORBEN: At first they were just ripping me off—there was this under-ground comix movement over in Europe, too. And they thought it was all right to reprint or publish anything they could get their hands on! Fortunately, at the point when I got an established European publisher who wanted to publish my work, he took it on himself to help me police the reprinting of my work over there. So it's since become, for me, very good. At least, in comparison to the U.S. markets, it's very good.

CBR: In spite of your success with commercial markets both here and overseas, what brought you back to self-publishing in the late Eighties?

CORBEN: Probably the same reason that every other would-be comic book creator and cartoonist jumped in at the same moment: because of the incredible success of Eastman and Laird's *Teenage Mutant Ninja Turtles*. At that time, when we started self-publishing again, every title would sell at *least* 50,000 copies. In fact, at that point in my career I was getting pretty fed up with a lot of things, and said, "Well, we'll give it one more chance . . ." as self-publishers. So I made a deal with Bruce Jones to write *Rip in Time* and fortunately we did very well.

CBR: An obvious question: Why is it so important for you to be in total control over your own projects?

CORBEN: Well, as a cartoonist the work you do is like your children. And you want to give them the best possible chance to be fully realized. That means the best publishing, the best printing, the best—well, distribution may not be the best!—but you try to get them to the people who will really appreciate your efforts. The downside is that it's kind of isolated when you're working for yourself, in that you work really hard on a project for months, and then you throw it out into the marketplace to see what happens. And it sinks or floats—it sells or it doesn't sell. So you may break even, or you may not break even. Most of the time it's very close.

CBR: We've noticed that some of your earlier artwork has been re-worked to tone down the nudity now that you're self-publishing again, primarily for distribution through the direct market. What led to that decision?

CORBEN: I had to give a lot of thought as to whether or not I wanted to do that. But it was either redo the art, or they could not be included in the new collections. There's a new distribution system now with the direct market and the comic shops, and I wanted to get to the widest possible audience that I could. I felt that I was not destroying the original, just making a new version. So that's what I did.

CBR: You're one of the very few self-publishers who, from time to time, continues to publish in full color. Given the enormous time and production costs, how and why do you continue to do it?

CORBEN: We might not do as much color work as we do except our foreign markets demand it. They'll pay a certain amount more for color than they will for black and white, and so it becomes a business decision. To try and keep the costs down, we've printed in Europe, we've printed in Spain, we've printed in Holland, and in the United States, too.

CBR: After basically creating your own unique system to reproduce your color work, you've more recently done this process using computer technology. How is that working out for you?

CORBEN: Yes, I've gone high-tech. I'll either do the color work myself and then scan it into the computer and then the computer does the color separations. As for the type, and the hand-lettering, the computer does it much faster, and I have more control. But I'm still never satisfied with the reproduction. At this point I've been using the color computer for about two years, yet I really don't perceive giving up pencil and paper.

CBR: Any opportunities in the medium that you feel you have yet to obtain or have just not come your way?

CORBEN: As a publisher, we try to make short-range goals, and long-range goals. But we haven't figured out what our long-range goals are right now! [*Chuckles*] The main thing is to make good on our promise to express ourselves truthfully about what we think; to try and produce work which reflects society, not in an obvious way, but in subtle ways. As to how far I've gone in keeping that promise, I sometimes really question my career, here and there. I have no fear that I'm going to starve to death—but I question if I've always made the right decision, here and there, along the way.

CBR: No regrets then as to how your career eventually turned out?

CORBEN: If we're supposed to be masters of our own fate, I don't know how we should measure regrets. Whatever success we've had—it's all ours. We worked for it, and if we didn't get it, it's not because we didn't work as hard as we could for it. I simply don't think I could ever work for another publisher, except on a very temporary basis. I just want to do things my own way too much. Regrets? No—we could have done a lot worse.

CBR: Any practical advice for a young person wishing to follow in your footsteps, then?

CORBEN: Don't do it! [*Laughs*] Seriously, I'm always saying how great freedom is, but there's a price to pay. And that's going through some hard times. It's all right to put yourself into this lifestyle, but if you have to put your family through this same situation, you have to really decide if it's worth it. Especially through the lean times.

Some great artists—and I'm not saying I'm a great artist—but some artists *never* have any recognition, except maybe years after they're dead. And then you've got to ask yourself, "Is that some kind of cosmic joke, or what?"

Why pick a career which may seem glamorous to a kid? Because in this industry it's not usually the cartoonist who gets the money, power, or the glory; it's the publisher. There are only a very few cartoonists whom I would call successful in this business; for most of them it's just a mediocre job that they're lucky to make a living at. Only a few are able to rise above that reality. So I would say be *very* careful in picking your career. You have to be sort of nuts to want to keep going on when faced with that, but I and a lot of people do.

5

LEE MARRS
Burning Down the House

Just like hundreds of other women cartoonists before her, Lee Marrs found the comics profession to
be yet another restrictive "boy's club." Unlike many
of the women who preceded her, Marrs was fortu-
nate enough to drift into the field during the flower-
ing of the underground comix movement. She was
soon able to find a community of like-minded artists
eager to start their own "women's club" to create
and publish their own comix.

Taking its name (and most of its contributors) from California's pioneer
feminist newspaper, *It Ain't Me, Babe* (1970) was the first comix book ever
created exclusively by women *for* women. A necessary and intellectually
volatile statement against the comix patriarchy in particular, and the comics
industry at large, *It Ain't Me, Babe* proved successful enough to galvanize the
growing coalition of female and feminist artists. The maiden voyage of
Wimmen's Comix (1972) followed, and Marrs was of course there. Six issues
soon appeared, along with sister comix like *Tits 'n' Clits* (1972–80), and *Wet
Satin: Women's Erotic Fantasies* (1976–78), among many others.

Along with Marrs, the eye-opening efforts of Trina Robbins (who also
edited many titles), Willy Mendes, Sharon Rudahl, Aline Kominsky, Melinda

Gebbie, and Shary Flenniken offered a healthy opposition and comple-ment to the predominantly male-created fantasies and comix. If the underground patriarchy redefined the parameters of the medium, the underground matriarchy redirected its scope and potential.

One of the few comix artists to have emerged from the comics main-stream (inking backgrounds for *Prince Valiant* and freelancing for DC Comics), Marrs had already begun work on her solo project *Pudge Girl Blimp* even before appearing in *Wimmen's Comix #1*. *The Further Fattening Adventures of Pudge Girl Blimp #1* (1974), and the scatalogical parody *The Compleat Fart and Other Body Emissions* (1976) were to follow, along with many notable contributions to the anthology titles. Marrs's autobiographical narratives soon aligned her with the growing lesbian comix movement. Her work, as well as that of Mary Wings, Roberta Gregory, and Alison Bechdell, moved far beyond the heterosexual orientation of almost all comix up to that time, and was often revelatory in its emotional depth and clarity.

As the underground movement began to falter, Marrs's subsequent issues of *Pudge Girl Blimp* found a home with Mike Friedrich, a former mainstream comic book writer turned publisher. Friedrich founded Star*Reach Produc-tions in 1974 to nurture a new kind of comics for the burgeoning direct sales market, which he dubbed "ground-level" comics. Along with a number of artists seeking alternatives apart from the West Coast comix and the New York mainstream comics scene, Marrs found Star*Reach to be a haven for her transitional work as she juxtaposed assignments as an animator and a computer graphics expert with her intensely personal scripts and art for *Heavy Metal* and publishers like DC Comics and Eclipse.

Having successfully grown beyond the constricting boundaries of "boy's" *and* "girl's" clubs, Lee Marrs continues to effectively tell her own stories in her own exquisite fashion.

COMIC BOOK REBELS: Considering you were involved to some extent in mainstream comics in the late Sixties, how did you get involved in the undergrounds?

LEE MARRS: What I was also doing, with a couple of other people, was running an underground newspaper and college newspaper features service called "Alternative Features Service." We distributed feature articles, artwork, and political cartoons to newspapers all over the world. It was a counterculture service. It was a really exciting time to be out on the West Coast, but it was certainly no way to make any money! [*Laughs*] So the straight comic books really helped out.

And in working on the comic books I had really fallen in love with the comic book as a way of telling stories. It turned out that my natural storytelling pace was not to do a one-panel cartoon, not to do even a comic strip. I'm a blabbermouth in real life, and it turns out I'm a blabbermouth in print, so to me to have four or five or ten pages to tell a story was really the most comfortable. But the constraints on what you could do then in comics was enormous! I mean, name something—and you couldn't do it in comics! Of course, I was living out here on the West Coast where all kinds of exciting things were happening, and at that time, there was nobody telling those stories.

Just as people would write short stories and novels about parts of life that they're experiencing that they're just not seeing in print anywhere, that was what the underground comix were all about! Being able to draw and write the stories you saw happening around you, or which you wished were happening, and then finding a place to at least get them printed and get them out there to the public.

So I got into the undergrounds through Alternative Features, because we were actively looking for cartoonists, and some of the folks that we hired were people like Trina Robbins and Spain Rodriguez. Another person who we first gave national exposure to was Howard Cruse. His *Barefootz* scripts were perfect, because they looked totally clean and Disneylike, and it wasn't until you actually read them that you saw that they were saying all these amazing things! [*Laughs*] So as for myself, I ran around to some of the different publishers, asked them what they were interested in, and then began doing *Pudge Girl Blimp* in 1973.

CBR: How did you get involved in the formation of the Women's Comics Collective, and why was it necessary to even have one?

MARRS: Well, for most of the other women, it was because they had no chance to get in print whatsoever unless they banded together and started their own "club." I mean, it was like *Little Lulu*: the "boy's club," no girls allowed! Well, that had been true in the undergrounds as well. There were a few women, most of whom had been girlfriends of male cartoonists who had managed to get one or two stories in one or two comix. Remember, we're not talking about a ton of books being put out in those days; there was really only a handful of titles.

So the idea of getting together to "do our own thing" was not something that only the Black Panthers had in mind, the same thing was happening in regard to the women's movement. A lot of the women in the collective were just starting out, and that was wonderful because they didn't know *anything* about any of the rules! So they kept coming up with these marvelous stories that were really invigorating. So in the sense that when you're creating *anything* with any group of people, it makes *everything* you're doing better. I think that was what worked with us.

CBR: Looking back with 20/20 hindsight, what did you feel was the most lasting effect the undergrounds had on the medium as a whole?

MARRS: What was most interesting to me about that period, as the years go by, was that we began to learn that that kind of self-confessional, or deeply personal story, sparked a revolution in Europe. The whole women's comix movement out of the West Coast of California was a megahit in Europe in terms of inspiring all kinds of other people to do this kind of storytelling. In Sweden, and in Germany, and Finland—for Heaven's sake!—we're in graphics history books as being the torchbearers for this complete change in the way that comic book storytelling is done.

Of course, none of this registered here in the United States! [*Laughs*]

No matter what kind of books we did, we couldn't get them sold in women's bookstores because they weren't "politically correct." Because the stories were about rape, or we made fun of sacred cows that had to do with feminism—I mean the very freedom of self-expression, the fact that we weren't taking any sort of a party line—that denied us any kind of real distribution in women's stores! And the fact that we showed penises and naked boobs and that kind of thing kept us out of regular comic shops, even though there weren't that many in existence back then. It was just the head shops.

So there was just no way to really get the word out, as far as the United States was concerned—and that wasn't true in Europe. A bookstore is just a bookstore there.

CBR: Then what excited you and your colleagues most about working in the undergrounds, considering the low distribution and even lower financial returns?

MARRS: The fact that we owned all of our own work, and the reprints checks have since become a way of keeping track of just how long-lived some of these stories are! It's astounding to see how long some of them go on, and I'm still getting royalty checks from overseas on some really old stories.

Quite a few of us had various opportunities to move further into the mainstream, but the work conditions—not being allowed to own any of our work, and not even having any say over their use—really made a *lot* of difference. So, for quite a few of us, that was the crux for not continuing down that road.

CBR: Have you seen any of the influence you had on the European scene reflected back at you since the Seventies?

MARRS: Yes—our kind of personal storytelling, the inclusion of mundane, everyday matters even into fantasy storytelling has crept its way into the mainstream. Alan Moore, for instance, has talked about how inspired he was by the work that we've done. So there're a couple of generations of folks—not necessarily just in Europe—who saw the power of that kind of story. Even in things like *Animal Man* (1988 to the present), I can see a lot of the presence of that attitude in comics, even now.

CBR: What led to your participation in the "ground-level" comics, an unwieldly term which unfortunately hasn't weathered time too well?

MARRS: I was visiting New York City at the same time that Mike Friedrich was there, and he was just getting ready to move back to California. So I was introduced to him, and he said he was going to start up his own comic book there. And he had been very impressed with the power of the stories that he had read in the underground comix. So we lived in adjoining towns back in California, and at that time I was doing a lot of science-fiction work with the man who I was living with at the time. Who was a science-fiction writer, Mel Warwick. So Mel and I wrote and drew stories for Mike's title *Star*Reach* (1974–79).

CBR: Getting back to your work in the women's anthologies, do you recall what happened with that censorship incident dealing with *Wet Satin*?

MARRS: It's been a long time, but as I remember it, there was a Midwestern printer who refused to print it. It was not so much a publisher as it was a printer who looked at the material—and this was somebody who had been printing totally raunchy material for males—but the fact that it was obvious that it was women who were doing this completely freaked him out. And so he refused to print it. It got shopped around to various places until somebody was found who would print it. I mean, all the comix that the women's comic collective put out had overt sexual material of one sort or another, but. . . !

I mean, it's always been interesting to me that the anarchistic, totally radical, burn-down-the-town attitude that was in most of the undergrounds never seemed to bother anyone! [*Laughs*] The fact that Spain's *Trashman* character is machinegunning half the known political entities and policemen of the Western World: Oh, well, that's *adventure*! But let's see a naked penis there—immediately everything *stops*. So it does point out what people are afraid of in our society.

CBR: You did an entire book parodying our culture's obsessions with *The Compleat Fart*, published by Kitchen Sink.

MARRS: Denis Kitchen, over the years, has been a really wonderful and ingenious person in the sense of giving folks a chance to create what they love and what they're truly interested in doing. I think he would have been happy to do *The Compleat Fart* #2 and #3 and #4 if there had been any money to do it, but we get back to what we said before about the problems with distribution.

CBR: It seems to us that the "ground-level" comics sought a happy middle ground between the underground and the "above-ground"— i.e., mainstream—markets. Was there ever a specific political agenda or aesthetic direction there?

MARRS: Mike Friedrich—because he had been a comic book writer himself—had spent all this time in all these people's studios where they were drawing the latest boring rerun of the usual stuff that they did. And late at night they would confess to him, "If only I had the freedom to do the stories that I love to do, I would do this, and I would do that. . . !" Neal Adams in particular was in the forefront of this. So Mike's idea was totally focused towards giving mainstream talent a chance to do what they would love to do if they were unleashed. That was the plan. Although Mike was something of a fan of the undergrounds, I don't believe it was ever his idea to mesh the two, or set up a "middle ground" in that sense. It was more of a freeing up of the mainstream people.

And it turned out—in my opinion—that what a lot of the mainstream talent did when they were "unleashed" was to do the same stories they had done before—only the girls didn't have clothes on. Wow—what a breakthrough!

True, Mike did open the door for people like myself and P. Craig Russell, and especially for people who were coming up in the ranks. And folks who had never had a story published—at all. People saw this as an avenue to tackle subjects that had never been done before. For people whose interests did not fit either the undergrounds—at least what most of us think of as "undergrounds"—or mainstream comics, this situation was perfect. By now there were comic shops, and other publishers came along once they saw a pattern had been set and that these subjects *were* selling, and that there *was* a market for them. But for me, the main value I saw in what are now called the ground-levels is that it was the first chance a lot of people had in doing stories on the widest possible subject matter.

CBR: Was there any special freedom because this group was not tied up in either the industry's expectations of either what the underground comic were "supposed" to be, or what the mainstream comics had always been?

MARRS: Yes, because although we haven't talked about it, there was *enormous* pressure among the underground publishers to have sex in everything you did—and the more explicit, the better! If you wanted to do a parody on TV commercials, fine, but they wanted you to get a fuck scene in there somehow. Especially for the women artists! I can remember so many conversations with so many publishers who wanted a raunchier cover, an even more "far-out" cover. So there was pressure from them in just the *opposite* direction than the mainstream.

But I don't remember anybody sticking in "extra juicy stuff" in order to placate a publisher, either. The levels of raunchiness were always naturally healthy ones. [*Chuckles*]

CBR: What led to your more recent work in animation and computer graphics?

Marrs: Storytelling was really the initial interest in animation. And of course making pictures move is *great*. Because when you're doing comics, you're imagining these stories as movies. You're imagining everything you've done in your story as happening in a moving sense, anyway. So to start to actually make pictures *move* was a wonderful experience. Plus the fact that you're paid five times as much money in this industry was also a great appeal—aesthetically speaking! There's also a whole other intellectual part of my life that came alive when I began working in computer graphics. It's like working very elaborate puzzles and games. It's very challenging, and a lot of fun.

It was also fun to be physically working with other people rather than being alone in one's dark little room at two o'clock in the morning, drawing away. The disadvantage of not living in the same town where all this art is published is gone. Let's face it, even on the best comic book projects I worked on, these things go off in boxes and people read them, but unless you go to a lot of comic book conventions, you never even hear what their response may have been. "Did people get this?" You know: "Did they laugh?" It's like your work just goes off a cliff.

So I have gone to conventions, and people have come up to me and said, "Oh, my favorite piece of work of yours was—" And it was something that you did fifteen years before and you don't even know what they're talking about! But when you do animation, it's immediate in that it's on TV, and even your mom can see it! It doesn't even have anything to do with being famous—it's about that *connection*, and since all of us love to communicate, that's why we're doing all this in the first place! There's an immediate feedback, and a feeling of teamwork, of doing good work with other people. That's really warming and rewarding.

CBR: When you do go back to comics, is there anything different or special here that you still treasure above all other mediums?

Marrs: Well, in a weird way, the very advantage of doing work in those other fields—namely, that you're doing it with a lot of other people—still means that *you're doing work with all these other people*. And sometimes all these other people have total control over what you're doing. You're doing these projects for other clients, and a lot of the material is very commercial. You do all these wonderful, artistic things and you sell—a car. "Oh, boy! I'm such a wonderful artist—somebody just bought an Isuzu Trooper." The capitalistic end of it is not all that rewarding, plus the fact that maybe nineteen other people had their fingers in the baking of the pie.

But as we all know, when you do comics you're *everything*. You're the director, the cinematographer, the screenwriter—it's all your creation. And it's also more *direct* storytelling. You really are able to express your personal feelings and the subjects that are really important to you in a way that doesn't get as filtered as it can in those other, larger concerns.

CBR: What impact has the women's cartoonist's movement had on the mainstream industry? Did it change in any fundamental way how the publishers deal with women today?

MARRS: It's a completely new universe! I mean, there are quite a few women who are working in the field now. Not just as creative people, but on the business end; a lot of the companies are employing women in very influential and pivotal areas. I don't know about the maturing of the subject matter, though. The subject matter has gone from once having a range from "A" to "B" to now having a range from "A" to "D." So we haven't yet reached "W" as far as the mainstream is concerned.

6

HOWARD CRUSE
"Dancin' Nekkid with the Angels"

Like many artists who find themselves at the forefront of a movement, Howard Cruse did not ever
intend to become identified with any specific group
or cause. He was only being true to himself and his
art—and in doing so, broke new ground within his
chosen field of endeavor.

By the end of the Seventies, Cruse had established himself as a moderately successful freelancer whose breezy style set his work apart from
that of his "heavier" underground peers, yet still allowed ready acceptance
in numerous mainstream markets. He straddled commercials jobs for Scho-
lastic Magazines and Starlog Press with his comix semiconfessionals in *Dope
Comix* (1978–79), and miscellaneous underground work for *Snarf* (1973–
81), and *Bizarre Sex* (1973–80), among many others. For a time he was
content to allow the suggestive and playfully subversive undercurrents to
quietly simmer beneath the humorous narratives of his *Barefootz* stories and
comic series (1973–79).

But by 1979, Cruse found himself aching to openly express himself on a
deeper and more intimate level through his comix work; to forthrightly
explore his personal life as well as his perceptions of (and from) the
gay subculture. So in 1980, he founded *Gay Comix* to provide a nurturing

anthology for homosexual and lesbian cartoonists. As the women's comix movement gave voice to lesbian sensibilities via the works of artists like Lee Marrs, Roberta Gregory, and Alison Bechdell (whose *Dykes to Watch Out For* is available in a series of collected volumes from Firebrand Books), the gay comix provided a vehicle for male and female creators. However, whereas the predominately male gay comix of the Sixties and Seventies were content to render mostly sexual fantasies, Cruse sought to mobilize the talents of his dedicated peers to explore creative alternatives which would be marketed beyond the usual parameters of the subculture.

Cruse's work in particular has achieved well-deserved recognition and longevity. His character strip *Wendel* was successfully serialized for years in *The Advocate* newspaper, since available in graphic novel format as *Wendel* (1985), *Dancin' Nekkid with the Angels* (1987), and *Wendel on the Rebound.* As embodied in his work, and that of cartoonists such as Tim Barela (*Leonard & Larry*, 1985 to the present) and Ivan Velez, Jr. (*Tales of the Closet*, 1987 to the present), their efforts are expansively reflecting gay sensibilities rather than just sexuality. The subsequent volumes of assured, skillfully told stories, rich in humor, characterization, and resonant depth have considerably enriched the art form and the industry as a whole.

By integrating his personal life with his commercial work, Cruse obviously has taken a highly calculated risk with his career, yet it apparently remains a positive turning point, both personally and professionally for the man. And by doing so, he has, for a time, been a trailblazer for a vital subcultural movement within the comics field.

With his current work in progress for DC Comics, *Stuck Rubber Baby* (1994), Howard Cruse has extended his considerable talents in yet another new direction, fearlessly exploring the possibilities of his love affair with the medium.

COMIC BOOK REBELS: You were in your late twenties when you started publishing regularly in the undergrounds. What led you there?

HOWARD CRUSE: It took me six years to finish college, so I was on a slightly late track. Then I was in graduate school very briefly, and dropped out after one term. And I lived in New York for a year, then moved back to Birmingham, Alabama. Because I had had a playwriting fellowship at Penn State, I was interested in doing something in the theater. But I had always been into cartooning as well. Perhaps it was the fact that it was so much more complicated to get a foothold in the theater world compared to breaking into cartooning. Because in cartooning you can sit down with a piece of paper and start to draw—you don't have to have a production company involved!

But I had seen underground comix as early as '67 or '68, but didn't see the best of what was out there. It was only after I returned to Birmingham that I sent for a package of sample undergrounds that Denis Kitchen was offering. Then I was pleasantly surprised to see that Denis was publishing undergrounds that had a kind of low-key sense of humor, in contrast to the very aggressive *Zap!* comix sense of style. Later on, I became very appreciative of what *Zap!* was trying to do, and became a big R. Crumb fan.

But at the very beginning, I just didn't see myself in that world. I did not feel I was a particularly "hammer it home with sex and violence" kind of artist. But Denis was publishing—I hate to say this about an underground!—a "nicer" sort of comix. I also appreciated the fact that Denis could get into the spirit of *Barefootz*, which was a very personal strip, and was coming out of my own experiences at the time. It was not aggressive, but rather kind of wry—and very cosmic and psychedelic. So Denis kind of eased me into the undergrounds.

CBR: *Barefootz* ran for almost a decade. At what point did you feel it had run its course?

CRUSE: Well, I began to question myself a lot when I began getting heat from members of the underground press, especially the fan press, that bothered to notice my work. People said that *Barefootz* was too "cute." And I began to question whether there was a part of me that was trying too hard to please, that maybe I needed to examine whether I was being cowardly about dealing with the taboo subjects the other underground artists were tackling. So this self-questioning side of me was affecting my work in the mid-Seventies. And you can see it exhibiting itself to some degree in later issues of *Barefootz*.

By the end of the seventies, I was really running into a block in that I was becoming more politically minded. And anxious to talk about some of the really tough issues in the world. And though I tried to do that to some degree within the context of *Barefootz*, I found myself just running up against a wall because the format simply didn't allow me to go as far as I wanted to go. I decided it was holding me back.

It was like trying to make social statements in the superhero mode: you can go so far, but after awhile you start to think, "Gee, if I just didn't have to deal with these costumes, I could get down to business."

I found I couldn't do anything with the characters that really cut to the bone. And I finally actually became totally blocked. It took me years to finally finish the last *Barefootz* comic book because I just didn't have another Barefootz story in me.

CBR: In hindsight, your autobiographical pieces in *Dope Comix* and *Bizarre Sex* provide some sense of that uneasy transition of discussing homosexuality while still trying to strike a sense of camaraderie with the presumably straight readership.

CRUSE: I became really uncomfortable with the sense of complicity that exists throughout the culture that everybody's straight, with participating in that. I felt very dishonest. But it was a gradual process, concluding with my actually "coming out" with the publication of *Gay Comix*. It was a process of seeing if a big hammer would come out and strike me down for doing so. Eventually I just decided that this was really a moral issue; I couldn't go on the way I had been going in my career, and not letting it "all hang out." In other words, I feel I should be able to continue to write and comment about the straight world, but I think I should do it with people knowing that I'm gay. As opposed to the automatic assumption that everyone is straight—unless they tell you otherwise.

CBR: In terms of your work getting out into the mainstream, did the short-lived *Comix Book* further your career in any way?

CRUSE: There were a number of people who first saw my work in *Comix Book*, and who had mentioned that was how they first took note of me. This includes several art directors who gave me commercial work when I moved back to New York. So it was beneficial for me to be in there, and it was extremely exciting to be in a magazine that was sold on newstands across the country. Basically I was doing the same things for *Comix Book* that I was doing for Denis Kitchen's underground comix, except I couldn't have done more sexually explicit work if I had wanted to. But even with the material I was doing for the undergrounds, I hadn't really started to get sexually explicit at that point.

CBR: So what finally caused you, as you state in your introduction to *Dancin' Nekkid with the Angels* to "drop lingering evasions and begin drawing stories about my life as a gay man?"

CRUSE: Well, it was really Denis Kitchen who offered the opportunity. I had made the decision, as early as the early Seventies, that I wanted to be "out" professionally and do openly gay work. But I was protective of my career in that I did not want to rise to prominence on that basis; so that people would see that as a gimmick by which I had built a career. This is not to say that anybody who used that route would be seen as using it as a gimmick, but I had a traditional notion that I wanted to be viable in various arenas, including mainstream arenas. And I wanted people to know my name before they knew I was gay.

I also didn't want to do it in any way that was confessional; I didn't want there to be any sense that I was telling some sort of "deep, dark secret," because I felt very good about being gay at that point in the mid-Seventies. Then Denis suggested we start the *Gay Comix* series, and asked me if I would edit it. And so that became the perfect opportunity to take the step. It was still scary, even though I knew I wanted to do it, and there was no question in my mind that I was going to say yes. But it was still scary because I didn't know how it would affect my career.

CBR: Again using hindsight, have you since been able to judge if it had any adverse effect on your career?

CRUSE: Basically, any negative impact my doing gay work had on my career was not voiced to me. I'll never know what opportunities I might have had, from people saying, "Howard Cruse? Well, wait a minute . . ." You know? "We like your work, but we don't know if we want to deal with this issue." As far as within the gay community, with extremely scattered exceptions, I found nothing but support. At that point, gay people were so starved to see themselves treated with dignity as human beings by the mainstream media, and here they were visible outside of what was strictly the gay media. There had been some earlier gay comic strips in gay periodicals, but none of them were very ambitious by today's standards. But considering that somebody had to break ground, I honor them as my predecessors.

Larry Fuller's *Gay Heartthrob*, the underground comix book had, to some degree, broken new ground. But also the solo comix done by Mary Wings and Roberta Gregory, which were the *real* inspirations to me for getting off my ass and taking a stab. I really felt, "Okay, this is being done, now I want to get in there and do that as well." But *Gay Comix* was kind of magical because you had people like Mary Wings and Roberta Gregory involved, you had a lot of credibility in the gay community, and I felt unshackled. I look at that time as really a beginning of a new voltage level to my personal artwork. To me, it's just the perfect example of why there's nothing like honesty in work to raise the quality level overall.

CBR: Your early stories, particularly "Jerry Mack" and "Billy Goes Out," show a remarkable sense of maturity within the medium, with both stories offering a sense of their whole being greater than the sum of their parts. Were you conscious how vital those works would be in expressing yourself honestly as a gay artist?

CRUSE: I believe you can almost feel the release I had at talking about things that I had deeply experienced, and felt, in contrast to those pieces where I was playing games where it sort of looked like I could still be straight.

I had learned, from reading some of R. Crumb's stream-of-consciousness work, that you *can* make the whole be greater than the parts. If you push people's buttons in a lot of different ways, at the same time, you create an effect that is something more than simply what those individual panels would seem to indicate. You send people off on trips, based on your own experiences, and your own feelings.

For even though I had included very little information about Billy in that story, I've had people tell me that they become very involved, emotionally, with him as a character. I can only attribute that somehow the little information I gave on the page plugged into a large number of internal connections from the experiences of the reader—both straight and gay. Though with gay people it was particularly important because I was dealing with issues that had been essentially treated as something to hide in the past. So it was very much of a relief to readers to see it out there, just as it was a relief for me to *put* it out there.

CBR: Even as casual readers, it struck us that the gay characters you portray in your work seem to have an emotional life that basically is no different from the emotions experienced by those of us in the straight life.

CRUSE: Well, that's interesting. [*Laughs*] That's an amazingly simple insight that a lot of people are amazingly resistant to getting.

CBR: Whether autobiographical or not, your stories seem to be trying to deal with real human emotions at all times, regardless of whether the characters are gay or straight.

CRUSE: Many of the women artists in *Comix Book* really struck me with the emotional realities of their stories. And basically they triggered the desire in me to work as much as possible from an emotional reality— even if I was going to use a satirical or comedic or exaggerated format. Actually, that had been going on for some years in my work. From the time that I began to do undergrounds, I quickly developed the feeling that, if I didn't feel it in my heart, it basically bored me to do it. And I mean that in my comix work, not to confuse that with my commercial projects.

Even with religion—even when I am using a very burlesque style, and seemingly ridiculing religion, I am coming from the fact that my life will always be influenced by my being a person who grew up being the son of a preacher. As well as my experience with psychedelics, this would also fall under my personal views of religion.

CBR: You have a quietly subversive style—one that appears very playful and innocent, yet deals with subjects which, to many, would be considered quite perverse and unpalatable. Is this a conscious decision on your part?

CRUSE: As for style, I am limited by where I am as an artist at any given moment. My style is essentially the *Wendel* style, and it may not be to everyone's taste, but I feel confident that I've demonstrated the ability to deal with some pretty nitty-gritty subjects, including some subjects of great pain, with that style.

And I've moved people with it.

Always, even going back to *Barefootz*, I had a certain strategy in mind of drawing people in to my work with a very "reader-friendly" style. So they accidentally got into my world—perhaps even further than they might have intended to! So that they could deal with some things they might otherwise find too troubling. But ultimately I think I asked more of that style from *Barefootz* than it could provide. Yet a lot of people can read *Wendel* and think, "Oh, this isn't too scary." You know? "I may be scared of gay people on some deep, subterranean level I'm not willing to admit, but this doesn't seem too bad." And they get into it, and then maybe they will have to actually spend some time looking at the world through gay eyes. Seeing how things appear when you're gay.

I think that all art that has any merit has different levels of meaning. And one of the ways that you utilize things that are pleasing to an audience is that you get them to let down their defenses, and relax them into going somewhere where they might not otherwise go. *Then* you deal with issues on an emotional level. It's not in terms of slipping in some secret message, but simply getting people to let down their barriers so they can better experience the artist's world.

CBR: You've parodied this in a couple of your strips—but how concerned are you that some of your readers may feel you have the responsibility of acting as some sort of "spokesperson" for gays in America?

CRUSE: Well, I do not feel I'm under any responsibility to be a spokesperson. I do feel that as an American citizen I do have a responsibility to give thought to what sort of attitudes I'm putting out, so that I don't unnecessarily add to the pain people experience in this world. But I think it has to do with a level of sensitivity that shouldn't hamstring you any more than learning not to use the word "nigger." As long as it's not done in any stupid or unnecessary way, I also feel I have the absolute right—and the responsibility—to feel free to defend my views, when the point of the art is to make people uncomfortable and make them reconsider their attitudes. But I just do this as an individual artist—I'm all too aware that there is no unanimity of opinion in the gay world.

CBR: What kind of battles have you had on the censorship front as a cartoonist?

CRUSE: Almost none, personally, other than the kind of censorship which comes with binders refusing to bind your books. Printers refusing to print them. I think it's a horrible, unethical thing for binders and printers to serve as censors. But there are plenty of other comic publishers who can tell you their own sad stories about that situation. But basically, I've been real lucky. With my work under Denis Kitchen's sponsorship—he never asked me to change a thing. And my contract with *The Advocate* was that I had total freedom, with the understanding that I wouldn't do anything that would make it impossible to get the publication across the Canadian border. And on the graphic novel I'm working on now, I'm getting total cooperation from DC Comics. I've had no interference with *anything* from them, which is quite a nice experience, considering it was with great trepidation that I got anywhere near the mainstream publishing world.

CBR: Could you tell us a bit more about your current project, which we understand just may be your magnum opus?

CRUSE: The book is called *Stuck Rubber Baby*, and I expect it will be out in 1994, unless it's further delayed by problems with raising money to have the time to draw it. It uses no characters which previously existed in my work. If it can be compared with anything that I've done in the past, it would be "Jerry Mack." The story is set in the South, in the early sixties, and deals with homophobia, and racism, and the gay subculture of that period. This is six years before the Stonewall riots, which were named for the Stonewall Inn, a gay bar that was raided by the police in 1969, and this incident precipitated a series of riots, like none the New York police had seen before. It's basically considered the symbolic beginning of the gay rights movement as we know it today: one that's built on street activism, one that did not ask for tolerance, but demanded rights. So it predates the contemporary gay rights movement.

CBR: What are the parameters of this project? We understand you've already put two years of work into it.

CRUSE: Yes, this is going to take me something like three and a half years to write and draw. It's over half done now, so it *is* possible to do it. It's going to be put out under the Piranha imprint from DC Comics, as the situation stands now. *Stuck Rubber Baby* is going to be a work unto itself. For better or worse, I don't think there's going to be another book anywhere like it.

CBR: How do you deal with the idea that you're writing a graphic novel, while the industry—and most of the public—perceives the comic medium as basically telling tales in a periodical, short-story format? What changes do you see necessary for a comic creator to take on a project this ambitious, and still be financially able to work on it full time, as most successful prose novelists are able to do?

CRUSE: Well, that's certainly the sixty-four million dollar question, isn't it? I wish I had an answer for that. [*Pauses*] To put this in perspective, all of the best work that I've ever done has been done at a loss.

Maybe *Wendel* breaks even; doing it for *The Advocate*, I was making a reasonable living. But all the underground comix were done at a loss, and they had to be subsidized by my doing commercial work. The thing that is unusual about this project is the *degree* of shortfall, due to the extreme length of time that is required to complete it. Now DC has been *very* generous with their advance—they were not stingy. We originally thought this would be a two year project, but it turned into a three and half year project. So this is what makes it a challenge to finish.

But the fact of the matter is, if somebody had made a Howard Cruse movie from my work, if someone was selling Howard Cruse T-shirts . . . If there were any number of things in my career that could have become cash-cows, then they would have made doing a project like this much easier. It so happens that nothing of mine has been picked up in that way. Consequently, I don't have anything else to fall back on for a subsidy.

CBR: Finally, any lasting misperception that you wish you could change about how the straight world interprets your work?

CRUSE: I'm not sure that I'm different from most artists in that, for all of those people who think they've got me pegged, I wish they would first just read my work and then reconsider! [*Chuckles*] Basically, I think my work is undervalued. Yet I think most artists feel that way—even after they've won the Nobel Prize.

But I do think a lot of straight readers have an absolute terror of spending time with something that might, you know, take them into the world of gay people. I regret that, because I'm trying to do sincere work about human beings—and considering all the time I spend in the straight world, I don't think it would hurt them to spend some time in the gay world.

III

MAVERICKS & MOGULS

Publish or Perish

Script: **DAVE SCHREINER**   Art: **DENIS KITCHEN**

7

Denis Kitchen
America's Most Wholesome Comix

Denis Kitchen's career as an underground artist and publisher was launched in Racine's Horlick High School in Caledonia, Wisconsin. In 1960, the first hand-drawn issue of *Cleptomaniac* circulated his eighth-grade classroom, promptly causing trouble for the young cartoonist. Under the new monicker *Klepto*, Kitchen's maiden comix voyage graduated to mimeographed status, and ran twenty-five issues to the end of his senior year.

During his formative University of Wisconsin years, Kitchen worked on a new college-humor zine, *Snide* (1967), which collapsed just on the verge of becoming an all-comics publication. Still unaware of the volatile West Coast underground comix movement, Kitchen purchased a copy of Jay Lynch's Chicago-based *Bijou Funnies* #1 (1968) and decided to create his own comix title between freelance art assignments. *Mom's Homemade Comics* (1969) ushered in his love affair with the medium to its first sizable audience under the apt "Kitchen Sink" masthead.

After a brief relationship with San Francisco's Print Mint (distributing a second printing of *Mom's Homemade Comics* #1 and publishing issue #2), Kitchen decided to return to self-publishing. He soon became a publisher when he took on subsequent issues of Jay Lynch and Skip Williamson's *Bijou Funnies*, and Robert Crumb's classic *Home Grown Funnies* (1971).

Kitchen Sink was originally based in Wisconsin (which provided a relatively central warehousing and shipping location for all of North America), where it built its own distribution network amongst head shops, independent record stores and early comic book shops. The company has since adapted to the best and worst of times: surviving the 1973 implosion of the comix market (and subsequent outlawing of the drug paraphernalia that was the backbone of the head shops) to rebuild with the steadily growing direct sales marketplace. Kitchen Sink has since broadened its publishing base to reprint venerable treasures like Al Capp's *L'il Abner*, Ernie Bushmiller's *Nancy*, and the *Batman* comic strips, while still embracing new work from Will Eisner, Charles Burns, Mark Schultz (*Xenozoic Tales*, 1987-present), Kate and Reed Waller (*Omaha, the Cat Dancer*, 1984-present), and many others. In April of 1993, Kitchen Sink merged with Tundra Publishing and moved operations to Northampton, Massachusetts, for what promises to be a new chapter in the company's history.

Kitchen himself has little time for his own cartooning these days, though he remains a vital figure and force in the current comic book industry. In 1988, he formed the Comic Book Legal Defense Fund, establishing an important organization which continues to offer legal and financial aid to retailers on the front lines of the never-ending battle against censorship—even while more powerful and considerably richer publishers (including Marvel and DC) and distributors ignore the issue.

Fortunately, Denis Kitchen's lifelong love for the medium has forged an approach to publishing comics that transcends the "business as usual" role many of his competitors choose to play.

COMIC BOOK REBELS: What led to your working in the underground newspaper and comics movement of the Sixties?

DENIS KITCHEN: I began drawing cartoons as far back as I can remember. Probably what was different is that I was actually making money from drawing comics; at the age of thirteen I self-published an illustrated newsletter in grade school that I continued to publish through high school. So I had the experience, very early on, of being both an artist and a publisher. Like so many others of my generation, I was very politically active during the Sixties, and naturally the underground comics and newspapers made me very curious to try them as markets for my work. Also, like some other young Turks, I was becoming increasingly aware of the dark side of comics—the creative restrictions of the Comic Code Authority, and the economic reality: of how great writers and artists were being shut out from sharing with the major publishers in the wealth that their creations brought about.

In 1968 I graduated from college with a journalism degree, because at that time there were no academic programs for cartooning in the art department. So I opted at the time to use my writing skills and my journalism degree. It was only a year or so after graduation I formally cofounded both "Kitchen Sink Press" and an underground newspaper. I started them both in the same month. At the same time I was also running for a government office. So it was a crazy time. [*Laughs*] But it was also an exciting time, because a lot of us thought the Revolution was around the corner.

CBR: What prompted the birth of "Kitchen Sink Press" as a publishing entity for the comics medium?

KITCHEN: Well, I think it was partially because, early on, I had had this entrepreneurial experience. And the very first comic I did, called *Mom's Homemade Comics* #1 (1969), I self-published, and it did very well. I could only afford to print 4,000 of them, which was a fairly arbitrary number, but I was able to sell 3,000 of those right in Milwaukee, which I think at the time was pretty remarkable. Then an underground publisher on the West Coast had asked to reprint it, but this was at a time when Rip Off Press was just getting off the ground, and this was a couple of years before Last Gasp appeared. So otherwise there was no other place to go to get my work out there. Yet at that point I decided to self-publish again instead. There was only regional distribution at that point, but who knows—I may have evolved to be an earlier version of Dave Sim!

But then I received a call from Jay Lynch which dramatically changed my life. He had learned that I was self-publishing and self-distributing again, and he asked if I would publish some issues of his work, since he was having problems with his publisher. And he really caught me off guard, but I recall thinking about it for a whole two seconds before giving my reply, because I really thought it was no big deal then. Which at first it wasn't. But from that moment on, whether I realized it or not, I had become a real publisher. And I now had obligations to other people than myself. Seriously, I still don't know if I should kiss Jay or punch him. But in any case, before I knew it, I had a full-time career as a publisher—schlepping cartons, paying royalties, hiring employees, working with other artists—even though I never completely stopped drawing. It was just that drawing was no longer how I was making my living.

CBR: Even as an "underground" artist, you didn't seem to embrace the harsh, violent edge that so many of the cartoonists of the time, like R. Crumb and S. Clay Wilson, were championing.

KITCHEN: Right. At that point in time, there was more of a playfulness in my work, with even a kind of self-deprecating attitude about it. I remember the blurb on the second issue of *Mom's Homemade Comics*: "America's Most Wholesome Underground Comic!" [*Laughs*]

I don't know whether to attribute this attitude to being happier or more "well-adjusted" than my counterparts or what. But I do know that relative to a lot of my counterparts back then I did not ever do drugs, and I did not uproot myself from my surroundings. A lot of the underground cartoonists had migrated out to the West Coast, and were caught up a lot more in the counterculture. While for me, I was still living in the city where I'd been raised, and I was just having *fun* not having any rules in my life. I was just having fun doing whatever I wanted to do. I had no particular place or direction to go, although I certainly appreciated what the others were trying to do.

CBR: Given the fact that you were a creative peer with many of those in the underground movement, how did it affect your relationship with the other creators when you made that major transition into publishing?

KITCHEN: In general, being known as an artist helped me as a publisher because I could better relate to their needs. Sometimes with newer artists, I could offer technical advice and that sort of thing. But generally I was a kindred spirit—and that went a long way. By definition, artists are not publishers or businessmen. But as a kindred spirit, I was able to make things happen a lot easier. On the down side, by being an artist myself it almost made me extend the Golden Rule too far: I had established royalties to these artists that were so generous I couldn't make a profit! After a year or so of this, without my drawing a salary for myself, I then hired a business manager, and he helped me steer a course between the generous and the stupid in terms of my business practices.

CBR: What was the shape of the marketplace for "comix" at that time? This was back in the early Seventies.

KITCHEN: Well, this was *way* before comic shops were commonplace. There were literally only a handful of comic shops at that time. For me, this would go back to 1969, when I self-published *Mom's Homemade Comics* and literally went around to every place I could to try and have them stock it. This obviously included head shops, record stores, corner drug stores, campus bookstores, gift shops—any place I thought I could get a foot in the door. Partly because I was a local artist, a lot of these places gave me a break. And I was able to get myself into a remarkably diverse group of outlets at that point.

But as I went around and collected on consignments, it became clear that head shops were the strongest outlets there were for these kinds of comics. I think it was also probably because as underground cartoonists we were cultural outlaws, and our "comix" were too outrageous of course for regular newsstands—that was out of the question. And our primary audience was, basically, the counterculture. They were the ones most frequenting these head shops. Let's face it—most of our customers were known then as "hippies," although, as I recall, we liked to call ourselves "freaks." And these freaks would go into a head shop, buy pipes or rolling papers and wrappers—and comix. On the other hand, the young soldiers on military bases around the country were also steady customers back then.

But gradually the pioneer comic shops came into their own. That partially came about because of a Supreme Court ruling on obscenity, which put a real scare into a lot of the previous outlets, and also there came in 1973 the first real glut on the market. We refer to it as the "Crash of '73." A lot of people came into the comix market simply to try and make a quick buck off what was popular at the time. And so the junk began to come in, and a lot of the shop owners couldn't distinguish between a Robert Crumb and a Robert Crumb imitator. Fortunately the customers could, and left the junk on the racks. And the next thing we knew, there was a nonreturn system. Shop owners were calling up and complaining that they had had a lot of product on the shelves that wouldn't sell. Of course we knew that things had come to a critical juncture in the industry—the retailers knew what would sell and what wouldn't, but back in '73, that sorting out process had to first take place throughout the entire marketplace.

CBR: It was around this time you developed *Comix Book* (1974–1976), which was first published by Marvel Comics, and then later by Kitchen Sink Press. It was a pretty bold experiment at the time, wasn't it, to bring the underground comix into the mainstream of newsstand retailers?

KITCHEN: When I first did *Mom*, I sent copies out to anyone I thought might be interested—especially fellow cartoonists, people that I respected. And I happened to send a copy to Stan Lee at Marvel. As a college student, I was a big fan of his. To my surprise, I got a very nice, chatty letter back from him. We began to regularly correspond. He was rather fascinated with what was going on in the counterculture, but mainly he was interested in getting me to come to Marvel. But I wasn't at all interested in working for Marvel; I enjoyed working for myself. But a couple of times he called and said point-blank, "Come and work for me." And I'd say "No, I have my own company." And he'd say, "Well, we'll buy the company!"

Well, when the Crash of '73 occurred, Stan Lee wasn't aware of how bad things were with the counterculture movement; it was in pretty terrible shape. So at that point I told Stan I would consider working for Marvel, but it would have to be on something that I was pretty comfortable with. So I went to New York and after some internal debate at Marvel, we worked out a deal where I could work out of Wisconsin, and so they trusted me to produce *Comix Book*. That's how it began. It originally was called *Comix International*. Jim Warren had made a similar offer to me to work for his Warren Publications, but mainly because of his personal reputation, I decided to go with Marvel.

True to form, Warren rushed his own *Comix International* (1974–1977) into production, so I came up with the title *Comix Book*, which I didn't think was as good. I always felt the title was a bit awkward, but we went with it. The premise of course was to try and come up with this hybrid which was to take the underground comix and put them into a newsstand publication. Stan was actually quite nervous about this; because on the one hand, he thought it would be very innovative and he would get a lot of slaps on the back for it. On the other hand, he was afraid the underground cartoonists might do something too outrageous and he would get into big trouble because he had a reputation as a family-orientated comics creator.

So he couldn't quite bring himself to put his name on the masthead as publisher. And at the same time, he wanted to make sure he received credit for it if it was successful! So he finally came up with the title "instigator." And his reasoning was, if the publication got him in trouble, he could say, "Hey, I *just* instigated it." But if it was successful, then he could say, "Hey—*I* instigated it!" [*Laughs*] And if you look at the masthead, that's what he really did. And to further play it safe, Marvel's name as a company was also not on the front cover.

But from the start, of course, *Comix Book* was a marriage that was destined to fail. For a lot of reasons. Yet I was able to get a lot of major talents, mainly because the page rates at that point were exceptionally good. Marvel was willing to pay a hundred dollars a page at a time when the undergrounds were paying only close to twenty-five dollars a page. And I was able to work out a compromise where the contributors were able to put their own trademark and copyright on their material after the first issue. We were able to bang out so many compromises between the artists and Marvel that that ultimately caused the problem. Artists at Marvel who were work-for-hire started saying, "Whoa—why are these guys getting breaks we aren't?" So the magazine became a political hot potato. Marvel ended up publishing the first three issues of this experiment, and we did the last two.

CBR: But why did the experiment fail if Marvel had the capability of printing something like 200,000 copies per issue, with newsstand distribution nationwide?

KITCHEN: First of all, there was nothing like *Comix Book* out there! They simply didn't know where to put it. Newsstands that I checked—if I could find it at all—I would put it next to *Mad* magazine. At least it would reach an audience there that was in high school. But we certainly didn't think we were going after the same market that read *Mad*. I think if we had our choices, we'd have placed it next to *Playboy* or *Ramparts* or *Rolling Stone*—anything that would have appealed to a more sophisticated audience. But we got absolutely *lost* on the racks. Now, in retrospect, it seems like a pretty inefficient way to distribute anything. I'm sure the majority of the issues just got pulped up.

CBR: So it was simply coincidental that, after the demise of *Comix Book* in the mid-Seventies, comic book shops came into their own?

KITCHEN: Well, the growth of comic shops at about the same time the head shops were being shut down was fortuitous, certainly. But in many respects, we were still selling to the same kind of customer at that point. To my recollection, many of the owners of the original comic shops were these long-haired, bearded guys who were still into undergrounds. And so they captured many of the same readers who used to frequent the head shops. You have to remember that at this point Marvel Comics had nowhere *near* the market domination it has now.

There were also people like Phil Seuling and Bud Plant at that time, who were just beginning to develop the early distributor and retail mechanisms. They were kindred spirits, too, for recognizing the importance of comics. The people who first started comic shops in those days all seemed to *love* comics, and supported everybody, and that's a critical distinction from today, where there's much more of a ''bottom line,'' speculative, cutthroat business.

CBR: You carry a lot of underground comix in your catalog, and Kitchen Sink Press is still publishing comix. Is there a valid market for them today, or are they now seen more as nostalgic or curiosity pieces?

KITCHEN: Well, we stock a lot of undergrounds because we think there still is a demand for them, and it's a demand that's served very poorly by most comic retailers. And also because they represent my roots. I can't deny that some of the people who are collecting them today probably did so years ago, and are collecting them again out of nostalgia. But there are still a lot of undergrounds being done today—''alternative comics'' or whatever you want to call them—which function as a safety valve for today's new generation of artists.

In a weird way, there're actually more ''undergrounds'' today than there were before because there're not enough diverse outlets now to support them. It always astonishes people when we tell them that we sold far more undergrounds through that rickety old ''head-shop'' system than through today's direct market, with theoretically thousands of outlets. When there was a vast counterculture in the sixties, there was also an easily identifiable audience, and a way to reach them.

CBR: •Has that audience intellectually matured since the Sixties, or does the stereotype of the adolescent fan-boy the critics describe as the typical reader of comics still apply?

KITCHEN: That's a good question. I can't offer any real quantitative information there because we've never done a formal survey. But we have found a goodly number of customers have stayed with us over the years. From our mail-order service we have seen that a number of doctors, lawyers, professional technicians of all kinds are ordering from us. It's certainly not just because they can afford to buy the books—but I think it's also because we try to publish books that serve them on an intellectual basis. The average superhero comic just doesn't hold that same kind of appeal to them.

CBR: Lately you've expanded your territory into licensed properties such as *Batman* and *Nancy*. How much of this is a balance between what the marketplace demands and what you, Denis Kitchen, wish to carry in your catalog?

KITCHEN: I certainly wouldn't last long carrying just what I personally like, yet generally I've successfully avoided the traps of the superhero speculators. But as you correctly point out, we did copublish some *Batman* books: *Batman: The Dailies 1943–46* and *Batman: The Sunday Classics 1943–46*. And that was certainly partially driven by market forces, as I'm sure you're aware. But my rationale for doing that was that we chose a historical period to reprint, it was material that had never been collected before, and we frankly felt someone needed to do it.

Something like *Nancy* may seem like a completely commercial undertaking, whereas actually it's less commercial than some critics would suspect. I will come out of the closet and say I consider Ernie Bushmiller a surrealist, while others feel he's the dumbest cartoonist who ever lived! And they're both right! [*Laughs*] But there's a general audience they appeal to, as well as a cult audience.

But as far as licensing goes, the only item we've really licensed is the *Grateful Dead Comix* (from 1991 to the present). Nowadays you have to become *very* successful to make a licensed product work on a modern scale. There are so many people cutting out pieces of the pie, there're generally very few slices left for you at the end. So I don't see that as a trend for Kitchen Sink, and I'll do the copublishing ventures on a case by case basis.

CBR: While daydreaming, do you ever imagine you'll return to your previous career as a cartoonist? Or is publishing enough to assure your voice is heard out there in the industry?

KITCHEN: Well, that is a question I ask myself very, very often. It's a cliché, but with Kitchen Sink I've created a monster, and the monster controls me. And sometimes I feel like I'm holding on to its tail and it's dragging me along behind it. But in many ways, being a publisher *is* creative, it's just on a different level. It's more like being the producer of a movie, rather than being the star or the writer or the director. It's a step removed, but you know the Big Picture, and you certainly have an influence over how that movie finally comes out. And by choosing specific areas, and certain creators to work with, you do have an impact on the rest of the industry.

At the same time, it *is* frustrating because being back at the drawing board is something I enjoy. But partly there is the reality of having a family, and if I just did art for a living, I might not make enough to support my family. Now that my family is no longer a day-to-day consideration, my company has grown even more, and it's become an even bigger monster than before.

So I still fantasize about being an artist, but I don't see it becoming a reality in the foreseeable future.

FROM *MONDO SNARFO* #1, 1978 © 1992 DENIS KITCHEN.

8

DAVE SIM
One Man Army

Dave Sim is the most infuriatingly independent and ethical man working in the comics medium in North America. His anchor and sole, driven creative focus is *Cerebus* (from 1977 to the present), which he and his creative and business partner Gerhard self-publish on a monthly schedule.

Cerebus began as a periodic homage to artist Barry Windsor-Smith's seminal contribution to *Conan the Barbarian* (#1–24, Marvel Comics, 1970–1972). "Cerebus the Aardvark" was the absurdist barbarian hero, and Sim's title quickly matured into a remarkable vehicle for barbed (and often hilarious) perspectives on life, love, politics, power, religion, and reality. The expression and projection is uncanny: Dave Sim *is* Cerebus.

With precious few peers, Sim and Gerhard are producing volumes that truly fulfill the term "graphic novel." Of the six collected volumes to date, *High Society* (1986), *Church and State* (1987), and *Jaka's Story* (1990) are most remarkable for the breadth and depth of characterization which fuels the Machiavellian stories—each over 500 pages in length. These are, in every sense of the word, true novels, with an acute eye for nuance, action, and detail, and an ear for dialogue that is second to none. *Jaka's Story* is arguably their most accomplished work to date: compelling, moving and audacious; though *Melmoth* (1991), a haunting meditation on human frailty and mortality, is perhaps a more deeply felt and evocative work.

Equally impressive is Sim's long-term commitment to *Cerebus* as a self-contained 300-issue novel.

When Sim announced his ambitious, unprecedented plan in 1979, the comics industry simply shrugged. Sixteen years later—and well past the half-way point in his thirty-year plan—Sim's unswerving commitment to the art form, his creation, and chosen marketplace, demands far more than the industry's acknowledgment or applause. Yet Sim pauses for neither; he is too busy working on the next chapter of *Cerebus*. So far he has paused only to better the creative and business environment of comics, particularly for those creators who also choose the even more difficult path of self-publishing.

The current novel, *Mothers & Daughters* (serialized in *Cerebus* #151–200), returns Cerebus to the foreground of the action, erupting with a breathlessly orchestrated series of battles which in turn launch an expansive reevaluation of the entire Cerebus canon. With over a decade (at least three more novels to go), Dave Sim's and Gerhard's unique accomplishments are clearly to be celebrated and savored. Beyond our applause, their efforts to enlighten both the creative and business interests of the North American comics community deserve careful scrutiny and assessment.

COMIC BOOK REBELS: What you've done with *Cerebus* is unprecedented in comics history. We can't find a record anywhere in the world of someone writing, drawing, and publishing 150 issues of their own work. Do you know of anyone?

DAVE SIM: No, no.

CBR: Why do you think the industry seems so afraid of this achievement?

SIM: I think it's got a lot of the same quality as the twenty-four-hour-comic. It was a great experience, but as soon as someone asks me if I'm ever going to do another one it's, like, probably not. Doing a long story like *Cerebus* is a lot like that: it has so much to recommend it, but at the same time it's not difficult to see why someone would avoid doing it. Obviously you can only do one of them, for one thing; I can't really start another when I'm done.

I was out for dinner at a convention one time and talking to someone who was asking me, first of all, why on earth would I do 300 issues, and

second of all, now that I am doing it, why don't I stop and start doing something else? Coincidentally, Marv Wolfman happened to be sitting across the table and I was sort of looking to him for help. I said, "You did *Tomb of Dracula* for seventy issues with the same creative team, Gene Colan and Tom Palmer. Can you not back me up on this: that there is a quality to doing an extended story in terms of getting to know the characters, the story sort of writing itself and amazing things coming out that you are really convinced have nothing to do with you? You didn't come up with that, it just sort of appeared there?"

And of course he's nodding vigorously and is saying, yes, there's no question about it, that in his experience of writing nothing has approached *Tomb of Dracula* for what it did to him, how it felt; but at the same time he's not at all keen to do another seventy issues of something. It's an attraction/repulsion thing. As much as you're attracted to it—that's why I compare it to the twenty-four-hour-comic—the sheer amount of energy and large bits of yourself that are required to do it make it completely understandable why someone would *not* want to do it.

CBR: Have there been any disadvantages in doing *Cerebus* on a monthly basis, producing roughly a page a day?

SIM: No, I can't say that has ever bothered me or ever caused any kind of real problem. I did the first fourteen issues bimonthly, and I found there was a psychological strain of *stopping* doing it for the month in between to do advertising or whatever it was that I was doing in the month in between to make revenues. The psychological wrench of getting out of this world I created and doing something to please somebody else where the check was on the line and then psychologically getting back into it was wrenching. I think even at this point, where I could do the book bimonthly and probably do nothing the other month, would be too psychologically wrenching to keep pulling myself out of it and putting myself back into it.

I found it interesting with John Byrne saying that he was leaving the trenches, he wasn't going to be doing a monthly book anymore, and then just found it was in his blood. I hope to hell that I don't find that out in the year 2004, that inside of six months I'm back doing a monthly title again because I'm just too badly hooked to do anything else. It wouldn't surprise me!

It's such a unique skill to be able to produce a whole comic book in a month. There are so few people who can do it. There're very few people who can produce a comic book every four months. If you take an average illustrator out of commercial art, and tell him you've got to produce thirty pages, and you've got to be able to draw this character from any angle, keep it interesting, you've got to draw it fast, and you've got to be better than you were last month, and you've got to keep everybody's attention engaged and you have to do it for probably a tenth of what you made drawing that toaster, they would look at you like you were nuts!

Our whole field is full of guys who could probably do the average commercial artist's year's worth of production in four or five afternoons and then take the rest of the year off. But we don't do that because the only reason to do comic books is because you love them.

CBR: Maintaining the pace of writing, drawing, and publishing a monthly comic book is no day at the beach. It has to take a lot out of you, doesn't it?

SIM: Yes, but at the same time, *everything* does. It is still the line of least resistance in my life. I've always been a big advocate of at least *trying* it. If self-publishing is not for you, you'll know pretty quickly that it's not. You're a guy who, for good or ill, should be working for other people or should have somebody handling all the business side. I tend to think it really hasn't taken a toll. I remember seeing an interview with Dennis Hopper where they were asking him about his crazy life style—all the women and all the drugs. That's the stuff that takes a toll on you. The work doesn't take a toll on you; *Cerebus* has never cost me anything emotionally.

Everything that has to do with having a real life, marriage and girlfriends especially, I've always found *that* to be what has taken a toll on me. At the same time, I still feel that I am about sixteen years old. I don't do anything different on a day-to-day basis that I didn't do during my summer vacation between high school years. I just sink right up to my neck in comic books and I exist there, but now it's 365 days a year. I used to take weekends off until I realized that I had more fun on the weekend drawing without the pressure. If I get a page done, that's fine. If I only get a panel done, that's fine, too. If I do something that is never going to get seen by anybody but I got the joy out of drawing . . . there's where the back cover of Issue 150 came from, "The First Half," with Cerebus as the football player.

I had no idea that I was going to use that, but I was in on the weekend and I thought, "Yeah, that would be pretty cool." I've always wanted to be a football player, and to draw Cerebus as a football player, and then ultimately it became a back cover, and now it's going to be a poster and a T-shirt, and the response to it has been phenomenal. *Everybody* commented on it—which is what usually happens when you do something just because you wanted to do it. If you really, really wanted to do it, and it just dropped out of your pen, that's what people are going to respond to.

CBR: When you reached Issue 150, you didn't even get so much as a shrug of notice from the industry trades. Does that pain you or doesn't it matter to you anymore?

SIM: Not really, no. There was enough of a time period when there was *so* much attention paid to *everything* that I said, and *everything* that was going on in the book, that I know what that's like, and consequently I don't miss it. You get to a point where you realize that what you're doing is doing the thing for yourself. It's a really good job. It's a lot of work, but it is something that I enjoy doing. And I get fan mail. How many people do their job all their lives and will get maybe one or two pats on the back from the boss? And on a day-in and day-out basis I'm getting letters from people who are saying I'm a god, or whatever . . . That's a very unique kind of job to have.

CBR: In terms of influences, what was there in the comic community when you started *Cerebus* that prompted you to have such a grandiose dream, to pursue thirty years of doing one story? Was there something other than just the love for the medium that you obviously have?

SIM: Well, that would be it. I think you have to remember that I first said that I am going to do *Cerebus* for 300 issues in 1979 and it was, easily, five years before anybody took it even half seriously. It was just *completely* unheard of. At the time I started doing Cerebus, comics was not something that you did as a life's work. Comic books were something that you did to attract the attention of somebody so you could do something *else*. Like *The Studio* guys (Bernie Wrightson, Barry Windsor-Smith, Jeff Jones, Mike Kaluta) when they started doing their pictures: "I have learned from comics and now I want to move into a more mature form."

CBR: As a publisher, Dark Horse might be a perfect example of that, given their recent move into feature film production.

SIM: Yeah—or the guys who move into storyboarding. Paul Chadwick walked away from *Concrete* for a specific length of time because somebody offered him a movie.

CBR: Bear in mind that Paul Chadwick came out of storyboarding, too.

SIM: But that doesn't tempt *me*. If somebody came and offered me a really interesting, artsy thing to do that I had never done before, I would not feel a wrenching choice between *Cerebus* and that. Or even in comics. If someone came to me and said, "We want you to do a 'Rolling Stones' comic book, we want you to do it basically as Issue #86, but do it without *Cerebus*," that would still not be a temptation. I would love to do it; it would be fun, as opposed to taking over, say, *Batman*, which I would treat as a joke. Compared to developing and continuing the Cerebus story as I have done for fourteen years, I mean, there is *no* comparison.

CBR: Let's talk about some of the temptations that have been put in your path. You're one of the few people in the industry who has resisted licensing. Why?

SIM: As Henry David Thoreau said, "Simplify, simplify." If it's simple already, examine it and see what it is that is good, *maintain* that, and then see what is bad, and if it's bad, just pass it by.

By that I mean, I was never much tempted by merchandising and whatnot, because you are then dealing with those guys in the three-piece suits. I love the story of your once talking to Peter Laird about merchandising, and you met one of the "Turtle Suits" for the first time. You took an instant disliking to the guy. One of those people you would not allow to pet your dog, let alone invite him to dinner. And Pete looked at you with that very blank look that Pete does so well, and said, "Well, they're *all* like that!" There's not an amount of money in the world that would compel me to sit in the same room with somebody like that. I passionately disagree with them; I am at the opposite end of the spectrum and dealing with them would diminish what it is I enjoy about *Cerebus*: the autonomy, and *not* having to talk to people like that. If I don't have to talk to an editor, I certainly don't want to talk to somebody who is a licensing cop or a senior agent, or whoever it is.

What makes me feel good about *Cerebus* is working on the book. Working on the actual story. After the first three or four years of doing it, once I had established a kind of "name" in the field, I got invited to conventions. Somebody was willing to pay my plane fare and my hotel room, and take me out for dinner and agree with everything I said, so that seemed to me like the reason to do it. I got to travel, I got to go to these conventions, I made a lot of money doing sketches and all that . . . but obviously the novelty went away. Then I realized "Well, son of a gun, that's *not* why I do it" because I didn't want to be away from the board any more. Realizing I never *had* to do another comic shop signing, and I never *had* to do another convention for the rest of my life, that I can just sit and draw my comic book—I leapt at that chance. *That's* what I wanted.

Once you realize the creating of the book is everything, then there are very few temptations.

Anything that I agree to, or anything that I go after that I accede to is something that takes me away from the drawing board. Consequently, it has to go on the back burner . . . But if you start doing licensing, merchandising, translating, and all of those sorts of things, they all have to be accommodated into your day. Then you have to start allocating specific amounts of time . . . But that's part and parcel of *Cerebus* being the central thing in my life; the thing I derive the most happiness from; the thing I am best at, and the thing that I get the best results out of the effort I put in.

CBR: But what led to the decision of compiling all the published issues of *Cerebus* into graphic novels, or as they have since affectionately been termed, into "phone books?"

Sim: It was a problem of keeping the issues in print. If you're only reprinting four back issues at a time, what do you do when you get up to *Cerebus* #40? I forget which issue was out at the time, but I could just picture this situation as an ongoing nightmare: How do you keep fifteen four-issue volumes in print, simultaneously? And it was also necessary to keep them in print to build up the readership. It may not have been possible to read the whole story at once—*Cerebus* has always been a treasure hunt, but you can't make it *too* much of a treasure hunt, or people are going to be very resistant to the idea of ever starting it.

CBR: You began issuing these huge collections before the mainstream publishers, such as DC Comics, began their first experiments with the higher priced "prestige editions."

SIM: Yes, it was definitely a breakthrough in terms of *Cerebus* being a twenty-five dollar comic book! [*Chuckles*] To a great extent, DC was— and still is—experimenting with how much you can make people pay for a comic book: How few pages can you get away with, at how high a price? The issue is still not adequately settled, because it does really depend on what it is that you're selling.

CBR: Yet on sheer aesthetic grounds, you clearly asserted the initial parameters under which a graphic novel could—and perhaps should— be technically defined.

SIM: Well, *I* thought I did. [*Chuckles*] But there weren't a lot of people who agreed that I had, and that was the beginning for me of a very isolated time period, from 1986 on, which continues to this day. People are still calling my reprint volumes "phone books," whereas anything that's published that's a hundred pages in length is called a "graphic novel." With a lot of that definition being because there's just nothing else out there that's 500 pages in length. I think there eventually will be, as it becomes obvious with the volume of material going through the stores that there is enough in terms of issues for other creators to collect.

CBR: There was a time when you were publishing the works of other cartoonists, for example, Stephen Murphy's and Michael Zulli's *Puma Blues*. What stopped you from pursuing Aardvark-Vanaheim as a publishing house?

SIM: Essentially I found myself caught in the trap that you see everywhere with publishers in the direct market. That the people in the office—the bureaucrats and the functionaries—are paid a salary, while the creative people are only being paid a percentage of the revenues that are coming in on their books, once the book is done. And theoretically the money comes in to them thirty days later. You end up with a situation where, if you totaled up what the creator made through the course of a year, and matched that against what my office workers were making, it was probably a two-to-one ratio in terms of salary over royalties.

This is a straightforward business, but it is the creator's obligation to make his own book work, to stay in touch with everybody, and to do his own promotion. We would also get a certain amount of flak from the creators that not enough promotion was being done. But when you're barely making enough to pay these two office salaries, there's not a lot of money left over for advertising. And if you're going to do advertising for all these different individuals' books, you're ultimately forced into a situation of doing "company" ads. I never liked that sort of centralization. And of course, at that point, *I* just became one of the artists working for Aardvark-Vanaheim.

Although *Cerebus* was doing quite well at the time, the other books were always just marginal by comparison. There was just an awareness that a lot of the money that was coming in because of *Cerebus* was going towards paying the salaries of my two office workers, as well as paying for advertising, and the usual office overhead. What finally ended it was our trying to insure the entire company to replace me if I left, which ultimately proved untenable.

CBR: You played an important role in the series of Creator Summits in the late Eighties. What led you to gather a group of primarily self-published comic book creators together?

SIM: At the time, business people were always in the superior position. Basically, I was making five times as much money doing things my way as by doing things their way, in terms of dealing with the distributors and the retailers. It just seemed natural to get together a group of people who were reasonably close to the present business situation, and who understood how the market functioned, and to make up a set of rules by which to work. At the time, there were no rules. I wanted to get some input from people whose opinions I respected, to find out just what was the right thing to do here. Ultimately that led to the summit being held in Northampton, Massachusetts, and that led to Scott Mc-Cloud coming in with his Creator Bill of Rights.

One of the things I was looking to find an answer for, "Does a creator have the right to chose how he sells his work, and who he sells it to?" Whenever that issue came up with people who *weren't* creators, there was always this "Yes, that's a foregone conclusion—you should sell to whoever you want to in whatever way you want to." But the flip side of their argument was always, "But that's not fair!" There was still a very large degree of animosity between some in attendance saying that "your way was the wrong way," and my saying "my way *is* the right way," and it seemed really unresolvable at the time. But that was largely because I had retreated from the whole idea of personal appearances as well.

But once I did establish through the summits that I was on pretty strong ground for saying that "I have the right to sell my work the way that I want to sell my work," it no longer seemed necessary to go out and interact with the marketplace. By the beginning of 1989, there was a definite sense that I really didn't have a place here; I was being heralded as the problem, and everything else in the industry apart from what I was doing was fine. So essentially I thought, "We'll just sit back for a couple of years, and since everybody else knows what's best for the direct market, and I'm the one causing trouble, we'll just see how it goes."

CBR: Yet in 1992, you did return to making personal appearances, and in fact devoted a good part of your career to purposely interacting with the marketplace. Why did you return?

SIM: I essentially came back in once I started seeing that, left to its own devices, the industry was pursuing exactly the *wrong* course of action. When you consider all the controversy that was raised when *Watchmen* and *The Dark Knight* were first coming out, by the time I came back in in 1992 to do essentially a year-long fact-finding mission, all of the promise of *Watchmen* and *The Dark Knight* had been frittered away on gimmick covers, the editor as superstar, and massive crossover, year-long storylines that ultimately went nowhere. I found there was a far more receptive audience among the retailers who had felt, if not consciously, at least unconsciously, that things had gone seriously wrong in this business.

But the biggest thing I noticed in the first couple of months of my tour, which kept getting reenforced from that time forward, is that there's a 90–10 split in the direct market. And that's among creators, distributors, retailers, fans, collectors, and investors. Ninety percent of the people are very happy with the way things are going, or at least are very much adjusted to the fact that this is how things are today. And they don't want to rock the boat, and they're not very interested in new ideas.

Then there is this newly vocal ten percent who are interested in change, who are no longer content to sit back and say that "Quality material doesn't sell. Only crap sells." And I think we have the *Comics*

Journal to thank a great deal for that being such a widely held view, both among people who want change, and people who don't want change, because it seemed to reinforce both viewpoints.

Among that ten percent, the biggest development for change has been Larry Marder's very enlightened view of the direct link between retailers and creators. The creator who really wants to change things, who wants to see better material sell, who wants to produce better material. Who is *not* looking to do another line of superheroes; is not looking to do another revisionist take of *Green Lantern*. Working in tandem with the store owners who would be tickled to death if the next *Punisher* title just dies on the vine, and the circulation of *Love & Rockets* triples.

Direct communication is needed between those two forces, not at the expense of the distribution network, but as a way of developing that end of the market. By finding ways of making the better material sell: by actually getting out and pushing the books on the retailer's part, and on the creator's part to produce better material, rather than just capitulating to the market forces by saying, "All they want is crap, so that's all I'm going to write and draw."

We have to get over the notion that everybody is the same in this business. Not all retailers are the same, not all creators, and not all the people working in the distribution system are the same. There are good people at every level, and the more we can stay in communication—to talk to the people who already have it as an article of faith that change *is* necessary, that's where all the potential lies.

THE ORIGINAL CEREBUS FROM *CEREBUS* #4 (1978) © 1978, 1992
DAVE SIM.

9

KEVIN EASTMAN &
PETER LAIRD
Beyond the Turtles Empire

"Mutation" is the key word when discussing the careers of Kevin Eastman and Peter Laird: the mutation from struggling, unknown, underemployed
artists to their current worldwide popularity as the
cocreators of the phenomenally successful "Teenage Mutant Ninja Turtles." And phenomenomen is
also a key word, as the Turtles phenomenon has
produced no less than a best-selling action-figure
toy line, a weekly cartoon series, a Saturday morn-
ing cartoon series, an official fan magazine, and (so far) three hit motion
pictures . . . not to mention a few thousand products bearing the name or
likeness of the four reptilian characters.

By the beginning of 1993, the simple fact is that the four silly words
"Teenage" "Mutant" "Ninja" "Turtles" have mutated themselves into a two
billion dollar global industry. Almost as incredible to comprehend, it all
started at the end of 1983, when Eastman was working in a restaurant and
seeking underground publishers for his comix stories, and Laird was getting

the princely sum of ten dollars an illustration from a local newspaper in Northampton, Massachusetts.

Indeed, of all the creators interviewed for *Comic Book Rebels*, Eastman & Laird are undeniably the most well-known to the general public. (It's been reported that ninety percent of American boys between the ages of three and eight own at least one Turtles action figure.) Their ever growing universe of mutated characters is widely considered to be among the most widely merchandised and promoted in the history of the licensing industry.

What must not be overlooked is that the Turtles first appeared within the pages of an oddly oversized, black & white, self-published *comic book*. A comic book which had an initial print run of 3,000 copies, and was financed mostly out of their own usually empty pockets for $1,200. A comic book which is still being published by Eastman and Laird to this day, out of the offices of their own Mirage Studios. (More information on the creation of Mirage Studios and the Turtles can be found in Stanley Wiater's *The Official Teenage Mutant Ninja Turtles Treasury*, Villard Books, 1991.)

Like all creators who have the relative good fortune to see their creations become wildly successful in the marketplace, Eastman and Laird have still had their shares of heartaches and mixed blessings. Most crucially, however, they were wise enough from the outset to properly copyright and trademark their creations, and were never tempted to ever give over control to anyone but themselves.

Not content to rest on their shells, both Peter Laird and Kevin Eastman have initiated a number of behind-the-scenes contributions to the industry. While still co-managing Mirage Studios, Eastman has moved further into the publishing arena. Here, too, "mutation" is the key word: Eastman's three-year old Tundra Publishing company recently merged with Kitchen Sink Press (a dramatic change our interview just pre-dates), while Laird is only beginning to unveil his own unique publishing alternatives.

Together, both artists do their best to carry on a daily routine to keep their creative offspring under control. Seperately, and at their own pace, they explore the paths that lie ahead of them. Even in the face of their whirlwind success, "slow and steady wins the race."

COMIC BOOK REBELS: Kevin, considering the massive success of Mirage Studios, what prompted you to create another entire business, Tundra Publishing?

KEVIN EASTMAN: One of the reasons was because of our having so much success with the Turtles. Having created it, having kept ownership of copyright and trademark, being able to control what was done with it and what was *not* to be done with it—the business was going along so well we didn't even realize we were being spoiled as much as we were spoiled. When Pete and I started talking to creators who were working for other companies in the industry, we learned about a lot of the hardships and sacrifices they had to undergo to control their own work. They all had stories to tell, whether they were creating and doing their own characters, and not having the freedom to do with them as they wanted because of company restrictions, or they were writers over-writing so editors would delete stuff they wished deleted anyway so they could end up with the story they wanted, or with artists dealing basically with the same frustrations.

So here we are—with all these rights that we take for granted as creators—and there are all these people that we respect and admire, and you see all the hardships that they are going through. It all hits you kind of hard.

I felt it was time to do something about it. So with the control we had, and the success, and the connections we had with the various movie companies and toy companies and everything else that might offer possibilities for these other creators, my first thought was to expand the publishing arm of Mirage. But the more sane of the two partners said, "What are you, nuts?" [*Laughs*] We were working pretty much full time just on the Turtles. Pete told me, and I agreed, that he didn't want to have anything else on his brain in terms of publishing at the time. So with his blessing, I started Tundra Publishing.

As Dave Sim would say, "Somebody needs to carry the ball." Being part of the group that got together to form the Creator Bill of Rights, someone needed to carry it beyond the document, and I sort of took that to heart and tried to expand upon it in forming Tundra.

CBR: So you felt that with Tundra Publishing you could realize the comics projects that you couldn't do at Mirage Studios, as well as your own personal projects. Any surprises along the way?

EASTMAN: Working at Mirage, I thought I had a pretty good grasp of what a publisher should be, and what a publisher needs to do—boy, was I *wrong!* Tundra was *not* like publishing the Turtles.

When you're working on such a successful animal that it kind of runs itself, you only have to nudge it here and nudge it there to keep it moving along. You drive lawyers and consultants nuts trying to learn everything about the ongoing situation. But when you try and force *new* things that you personally believe in into a similar situation, it simply doesn't work that way when you find yourself building from the ground up. It was a lot more work than I'd ever thought it'd be. The company grew very fast, and grew too big, too quick. Three years later, I think we've finally reached the point where we're slowed up enough, and gotten enough experience under our belts as a company, to be giving individual projects the time and attention they require.

CBR: You've also stated to us that you wanted to reach more mature readers with these Tundra projects. Do you feel that most fans simply grow up and out of their interest in comics, or do they simply become more difficult to reach?

EASTMAN: Besides my desire to do my own projects, that was one of the reasons it was inappropriate at Mirage to do adult books. Pete and I had discussions on this early on, that Mirage really seemed to be geared towards this whole "Turtles children's program." (Even though the black and white book remained ours, and was rougher and more adult in its content.) It did seem inappropriate to try and place more adult-oriented material there.

So I wanted to focus on that older readership with Tundra. But that was another early problem—it was like being too rock 'n' roll for country, and too country for rock 'n' roll, in the sense that our publications were too booklike for comic book stores, and too comic-booklike for bookstores! We were trying to build an older audience based on those who had grown up and grown out of the comics books intended for a younger audience. I thought that the audience was a lot larger than it actually was. I figured naturally people would grow up through *X-Men* and discover *The Sandman* and then *Dark Knight* and *Watchmen* and beyond.

But every time you add another year to a comic reader's life, in terms of that age group, you automatically lose a certain percentage of that audience. It's *not* that the potential audience isn't there, it's mainly that it's not easy to reach. You don't have to have been insane about comics all your life to know that when you show people what is going on in comics nowadays, they are truly blown away. It's like, "Oh, I read them when I was younger, but I didn't know they had advanced to this stage."

But if they don't see it in a bookstore, they won't feel it's easily accessible. Ninety percent of them will not go into a comic book store. For those of us who have been in comic book stores, what you unfortunately see ninety percent of the time are these horrible little places where neighborhood kids hang out. And that's too bad. It's past time for the industry to try and reach a new audience.

CBR: Peter, what led you to create the Xeric Foundation?

PETER LAIRD: The word "xeric" means dry or desertlike, and it has absolutely no direct connection with the foundation; it's just a word I like. It actually originated out of a Scrabble game with my brother Don.

The Xeric Foundation is actually two foundations in one. One half of it is for charitable organizations, and the other half is for creators who want to self-publish their comics. That procedure involves the usual application, financial statement, an explanation of how much money you want, what you want it for, when do you need it, and so forth. And there's a process that we've set up to keep track of what was done with the money. There also is an advisory committee made up of three members, and they are people working in the industry, whose names I probably shouldn't divulge.

I'd been thinking about doing this for a while. It seemed like an appropriate way to give back something extra to the comics world. And given my past experience with the Turtles and self-publishing, and going through that whole learning process myself, I felt that it would be very valuable to other people to go through that, too. Which is not to say every self-publishing project will generate the kind of licensing and merchandising empire that the Turtles have generated, but the experience is worthwhile in teaching creators about themselves, about life, about the hard reality of business. Even if the published comic doesn't sell, and they end up sitting on big boxes of unsold comics, it's still going to be a worthwhile experience for them. I also think a lot of people have a very naive outlook on what it means to completely produce and publish something that someone else really wants.

CBR: Rather than a foundation, why not form another publishing company like Kevin did with Tundra?

LAIRD: Well, quite frankly because it was like Kevin said—I had far too much to do as it is with Mirage. I didn't want to start up another huge business and end up running around, losing my mind, because there's just so much you have to take care of. I knew that if I said to Kevin, "Well, I've got some money here, let's put it to good use in terms of getting people's work out to the public." If I had gone that route—even if I never *did* anything—it would have required setting it up, overseeing it, making sure the right people were working there, worrying about it, you know? [*Laughs*] I've got enough business worries as it is! So I preferred to do something where it was more of a transfer of capital, and all the worries are on *other* people's shoulders. It just made no sense to me personally to set up a whole other publishing company.

CBR: How much of the Xeric Foundation came about from the experiences you had at the Creator Bill of Rights summits?

LAIRD: I think my decision to start the foundation was informed to some degree by all that happened at those summits. But in terms of the charitable end of it, I was getting so many requests for money that I needed a way to deal with it in an organized fashion. In this way, people know where to send their material, and I don't even have to look at it in the sense that it's first evaluated by a team, I look at the team's recommendations, and then I make the final decision. But it really came out of a desire to use some of my good fortune, in the financial sense, to help people out both as creators and those involved in charitable organizations.

In my own experience, it was Kevin's uncle Quentin who loaned us a thousand dollars to print *Turtles* #1, and we paid him back right away. But if we hadn't gotten that loan from him at that point in our lives, it might have taken us a couple more months to raise that money from other sources, and who *knows* what might have happened differently as a result of that delay? It just seems to me there must be so many times where a self-publishing venture can sink or float on the strength of a thousand dollars or five hundred dollars or whatever. And if that's all it takes to have somebody put out something that they're passionate about, it seems worth it to me to help.

Hopefully, knock on wood, God willing, and the creek don't rise, if we go on for another couple of decades, and I'm able to put more money into the basic funding of the Xeric Foundation, then the amount of money that can be given out can really be raised significantly. Then we'll be able to give out hundreds of thousands of dollars instead of just thousands of dollars, and then we can support some pretty impressive projects, along with a lot of small ones.

CBR: Kevin, you publicized your support of the Creator Bill of Rights at Tundra. Is it possible for the Bill of Rights to work in reality as a publisher, and not just in theory?

EASTMAN: Absolutely! My impression of the Bill of Rights' main purpose is to know your rights, and to know what as a creator you should decide to give up or not to give up to see your work realized in the way that is most faithful to your original vision. Whether you go to a publisher like Marvel or a publisher like Dark Horse or a publisher like Tundra, there are going to be different levels of what you're going to have to give up in order to see your work finally realized. I haven't worked with other publishers, so I don't know what their feelings are towards creator rights.

All I know is, what I'm offering is, in my opinion, the most rights for the creator to retain. It's like the cliché "The customer's always right." Here the creator's always right. Now that has its good sides and bad sides, but we've had to offer that to the creator because I wouldn't be comfortable any other way; I wouldn't have Tundra if I couldn't preserve those sensibilities. I want the creator to be involved in all the important decision making. *Everything* that is needed to make a book successful is put into the form of a budget, and is put in front of the creator, and they are told, "This is what it's going to have to be to make it work. This is what we need. Is this what you need? Is this what you're comfortable with?" It has to be agreed upon then, and if it is, then we can go ahead and start production on the book.

As a creator, I believe in the Bill of Rights, because I had all those rights, and I could decide what I wanted to do with them. I try to offer all those rights to creators who bring their projects to Tundra.

But as much as there are rights for creators, there are also rights for publishers. And a publisher needs to have its rights and interests protected so it can protect a creator's rights. You have to work together; it has to be a mutually satisfying situation. So we're still pushing ahead. We're trying to create a balance between the financial realities and the artistic goals without compromising. But dealing with reality . . . it's a bitch!

CBR: Was it your ongoing search for more mature readers and that untapped adult audience which led you to purchase *Heavy Metal* (1977 to the present)? We know you've been a lifelong fan of the magazine.

EASTMAN: I would imagine that it was the same reaction for most of the other people in this book; I don't want to sound corny, but it was the skies parting and the heavens shining down when *Heavy Metal* presented all this art from Europe that had never made it over here before! Beyond Jack Kirby's influence on me early on, *Heavy Metal* was where I discovered the second greatest influence on me, an artist named Richard Corben—not to mention a whole group of strange and weird creators that just blew me away. It was kind of like the same feeling when you first discover underground comix—that there's a whole other place to show your work. A whole other audience out there, somewhere. The magazine seemed to offer a lot of creative possibilities and yet it wasn't as harsh or extreme as some of the underground comix—but it was *definitely* intended for an older readership.

So when I learned that *Heavy Metal* was for sale, it brought back all these memories. "Oh, wow! *Heavy Metal*! That's pretty wild." It made a big difference on me when I was younger, so I decided to look into it. The price was very reasonable, and the more I looked into it, the more lightbulbs went off over my head. So, yes, with the intents and hopes of Tundra reaching an older audience, the magazine really became the final piece of the puzzle that just fit into what I hoped for Tundra in terms of reaching that audience. In my life, too many things have happened in a weird, sort of shit-luck sort of fashion for my liking. [*Laughs*] And *Heavy Metal* seemed to be one of them, and we purchased it in January of 1992.

CBR: How do you plan to use your new vision of *Heavy Metal* to influence its readers, many of whom may have no awareness of the rest of the comics industry, including even Tundra?

EASTMAN: The audiences *have* for a long time been separate. Most of the audience who read *Heavy Metal* buy it off the newsstands; they're not going into comic book stores. They don't even know what the direct market is! So we're trying to expose that readership to what is going on now in the rest of the industry with numerous crossovers from the cutting edge of comics creators. I'd like to do that as often as I can, and it doesn't have to be just comics, but anything from the visual media that can cross over and explore these other possibilities.

I've also had a dream for a long time, being a fan of the European comics and visiting the comic book stores in Europe, and having seen what they call a "comic book" compared to what we call a "comic book." Ours are typically thirty-two pages, and you can use it to swat flies with when you're done or throw it away. But theirs are typically forty-eight pages, deluxe, full-color books that a writer and an artist would come out with once a year; a laminated hardcover, on beautiful paper—it'd be a *book*. It's something you'd be proud to leave on a coffee table or have on a bookshelf. Whereas with our comic books, for the most part, it'd be something you'd shove *under* the couch!

So I've started to bring in the European hardcover books for sale here. We've met with a fairly cool response so far. The books aren't cheap, but they're worth it to someone that they're worth it to. We came up with a program where we can expose the material by running an album section in *Heavy Metal*, and then later bind it in a laminated hardcover for a better price, then pass that better price on to the average direct market consumer, which is still a very small part of the *Heavy Metal* readership. For me it's a way to get the best of both worlds: I want comics to be looked at as *art* and as *books*, and not so much as disposable entertainment.

CBR: Peter, on a more personal note, how did you get through your artist's block of a few years ago, and how did it come about?

LAIRD: It was pretty scary. It was a combination of a number of things, primarily a lot of burnout from the intensity of the Turtles experience. Burnout from having been overwhelmed by the incredible growth and complexity of the business; concerns I'd never ever even *considered* I'd be involved in, let alone be swamped with. I suddenly discovered to my horror that I no longer enjoyed drawing. It was a real shock, because if I ever had anything that I could rely on, at the very basic limits of my existence, it was that I loved to draw. And having to admit to myself that I got no enjoyment out of drawing anymore was . . . it really freaked me out.

I'm not exactly sure how I came out of that block, but I did after about a year of feeling, "What the hell *am* I doing?" I think getting involved in learning about computer-generated art helped a lot, because it was so different from what I had been doing, and allowed me to set aside the pencils and brushes and go off in a different direction. Gradually, my desire to draw came back. Which is not to say it won't ever happen again. But even after coming back, drawing does feel different to me now. It's not exactly how it used to be—I think I take it less seriously, which may be a bit of an overreaction to the sort of desperate anxiety I felt when I thought I had lost it forever.

But the experience *has* taught me that I can't count on drawing as that big a part of my life, and to do so is really dangerous. I'm trying to do new projects that I simply *enjoy*. Maybe at some point later on I'll take it more seriously, but . . .

CBR: Besides possibly triggering that block, any other regrets on how the Turtles have apparently taken over your life, creatively speaking?

LAIRD: You know when Kevin and I started the Turtles it was a goof; it was not anything we envisioned directing our lives in any way, shape, or form. It was like, "Hey, this looks like fun! Let's self-publish it! Let's see what happens!" What we really wanted to do was some comics here, paint some book covers there, do an album jacket, do some posters, do magazine illustrations. Suddenly, and just completely out of the blue, this Turtles phenomenon emerged. And really—from day one—just took over. It was a rapidly accelerating process which culminated in essentially taking over our lives. Completely. Ask me how many other comic books I've drawn?

CBR: Okay, how many other comic books have you drawn?

LAIRD: Zero!

CBR: All right, how many book covers and album jackets have you done?

LAIRD: Zero! Zero! It's all been the Turtles! I always feel kind of odd talking about this, because it's kind of like "Yeah—complain about all this fucking success!" But I feel like I have a right to, because it *did* happen to me, and it has taken over my life. Any kind of successful thing that you start and that is your baby, is like a tar baby in a way. You can't really get away from it: it's like abandoning a child. Unless you're a real shithead, you can't abandon your child! And yet you have to wait for that child to grow up before it can finally leave the nest on its own. And Kevin and I had these four children together—the Teenage Mutant Ninja Turtles—and until they're ready to leave the nest, I don't really feel I can *do* much else.

I think I might finally be getting to that point now, where enough has been learned about the business so that Kevin and I can both turn over a lot of responsibilities that we used to have to worry about and handle ourselves to other people. And then get on with other creative ventures. It's not an easy thing to do, especially when it's something you've created. Something that's the fruit of your mental loins, so to speak.

CBR: Kevin, any regrets with the way the Teenage Mutant Ninja Turtles phenomenon has affected you as an artist-writer?

EASTMAN: It's so *weird* every time I think back on it. But what was the main reason Pete and I started Mirage? The number one reason was that we loved comics, and wanted to tell our *own* stories. And that was like a dream come true at the time.

I remember when we solicited for issue #2 of the *Turtles*, and we had advance orders—and it seemed to us like a million copies—of 15,000 copies, which basically ended up with us clearing a profit of two thousand dollars apiece. Which allowed us to write and draw stories full time: it was enough to pay the rent, pay the bills, and buy enough macaroni and cheese and pencils to live on.

We were absolutely 100% convinced that we were living a dream, that nothing could possibly top that.

But as time went on, with the decisions we made and the roads we decided to take, suddenly it was fifty percent of the time we were drawing rather than ninety percent of the time. And then it became totally crazy, and we were spending ninety percent of the time doing business, and ten percent of the time drawing! Although I don't regret a moment of what we learned on the business end of things, it was critical to these two wet-behind-the-ears dreamers, and it was all part of the Big Picture. Finally it got to the point at Mirage where we were just starting to get some of our creative time back.

And that was when I made the decision to start Tundra. [*Laughs*]

Eight years ago, when we did *Turtles* #1, I had a stack of stories that I wanted to tell, and we did the first Turtles issue *never* expecting to ever do another one. I thought that we would go on to something else, and I'd get through this backlog of crazy ideas that I wanted to do. But it'll happen! *Melting Pot* is finally going to come out in 1993—I hope—and the original layouts and story notes were done in 1988. But the main goal for all these other stories that I want to do is the same sensibility that we had when we created the Turtles: Good, bad, or ugly, I'm going to write something that I enjoy, misspellings and all! [*Laughs*] Something that's totally self-satisfying, and *that's* the only way I think any artist or writer should ever approach his or her work.

CBR: Any advice for young self-publishers hoping to follow in the footsteps of Eastman & Laird?

LAIRD: It's an old Chinese proverb that goes, "Be careful what you wish for, you might get it." And there's a lot of truth in that statement.

I mean, you have to play with the hand you're dealt, and Kevin and I were dealt a surprise hand. But we played it. Anyone who gets into self-publishing shouldn't expect anything except to work really hard if they expect anything to happen. I can impart sparkling gems of wisdom such as: watch your ass, do everything by the book, make sure you're covered in all legal ways—those are all lessons we've learned through hard experience.

CBR: Do either of you feel you've done any harm to Western Civilization by creating the Turtles? Not everyone in the world is a fan of their exploits, especially the way they're portrayed on the animated cartoon series.

LAIRD: No, not really. I have to confess to a feeling sometimes that the licensed forms of the Turtles, specifically in animation, have not really done much to advance the shining path of Western Civilization—or Eastern Civilization for that matter. Certainly the Turtles comic books that Kevin and I did—or any of the books that we have published—are never going to be regarded as Fine Art. Of course, no comics are Fine Art. But I think the point of the Turtles is not to be "Fine Art," but to be enjoyed. If there's anything I can take pride in, it's the fact that most people who encounter the Turtles find them to be enjoyable.

CBR: So you believe that the power to entertain on a purely popular level has a value equal to some level of art?

LAIRD: Oh, yeah! I think entertainment art *is* perhaps the most important art. It should be done well, but entertainment art can also inspire serious thoughts and careful ruminations.

I was just reading this book about highbrow, middlebrow, and lowbrow culture, and I think the Turtles fall in the middlebrow area, which is really where most entertainment art exists, and it's the level that means the most to most people. But it will always be derided by the intelligentsia, the "cultural elite," who think we all should just be . . . strung up and butchered!! [*Laughs*]

CBR: Kevin, you've also launched the Words & Pictures Museum, in part to enlighten the public regarding comics as a legitimate art form. What was the genesis for its creation?

EASTMAN: This specifically goes back to the very first piece of original art that I ever bought, which was at the first convention Pete and I attended, which was in Atlanta in 1984. Pete and I were invited guests—which was a total shock: somebody was going to invite us to a show and actually going to *pay* our way! [*Laughs*] I was able to meet a lot of artists and writers who had original art for sale, and I bought a couple of pages that were penciled by Michael Golden and inked by Bob McCloud for Marvel Comics' *Howard the Duck*.

It's one thing to see the material in its printed form, but it's not until you see original art—especially with somebody who was as eager to learn as I was in terms of, how did Corben do *this* and how did Frazetta do *that?*—you can't see that until you have the original. And then you can get the art an inch away from your face and go "OH!!! Yeah—that's how they did that!" So that's where I started collecting art.

It's been quite an addiction for a long period of time. And as the years went on, I collected more and more art, for the sheer beauty of it, but also for what I was learning. But always first the beauty. So then friends of mine would come over to my house and say, "Let's see all your original art!" and I'd be pulling out these portfolios for hours. And I got to thinking more and more that it was a shame that the only time these beautiful drawings and paintings got seen were when people visited the house.

The thought also goes back to when I applied to Arts college—or should I say "Fine Arts" college—and bringing in my "best" work. Which was my best Jack Kirby homage or whomever I was really into at the time. And having the portfolio reviewer look at me like I'm literally a walking waste of time! [*Angrily*] Like, ''What are you doing here? This stuff is shit! It's horrible!'' That's always bothered me. I can go into any museum in the country and look at a lot of different things that people interpret as art that don't even come *close* to what I would interpret as art! And yet those kinds of critics who were calling that material ''Art'' always pass judgment on what I call ''Art.''

Again, it's from being exposed to Europe and what they think of their artists. For example, Moebius is heralded as one of the major talents in France and throughout Europe—and he does *comic books*! The French government has a state sponsored museum dedicated to comic book art, and we've got nothing like that here. The appreciation just isn't there yet, for a great many reasons. It's been a dream for a long time to open a museum that would be dedicated to a little bit of what brought us here, a lot of what's going on today, and also a look to the future of comics.

CBR: Does it ever seem a daunting task to look at your own future in comics as individual creators, when you're already world-famous for creating the Teenage Mutant Ninja Turtles?

LAIRD: You carry it in the back of your mind. It's always there—that no matter what Kevin and I do in the future—it's a virtual certainty that it won't have the same impact or same level of success as the Turtles. And that's an odd feeling. It's kind of like, ''Why bother doing *anything*?'' So now it's an internal psychic barometer of how I feel. This may have been part of the burnout I experienced a few years ago: ''Why bother doing anything else? Why bother continuing as an artist?'' And the only conclusion I ended up coming to is like Kevin's: the only reason to continue, the only reason to draw any more is for my own pleasure. And if it benefits anybody else, great.

But I should *first* do it for myself.

THE FIRST TURTLES ART BY EASTMAN & LAIRD—FROM *TEENAGE MUTANT NINJA TURTLES #1*, 1984, © 1984, 1993 MIRAGE STUDIOS.

PLUS I SIGNED A CONTRACT WITH A PUBLISHER, FOUR WALLS EIGHT WINDOWS, TO WRITE A "GRAPHIC" NON-NOVEL WITH MY WIFE ABOUT THE HOUSE BUYING AND THE CANCER AND HOW IT WAS FOR HER TO TAKE CARE OF ME WHEN SHE HAD OTHER PRESSING RESPONSIBILITIES.

C'MON, HARVEY, EAT. YOU'VE GOT TO KEEP YOUR WEIGHT UP.

UHHH, I CAN'T EAT ANYMORE.

OUR NON-NOVEL'S SCRIPT'S DONE, BUT IT'S GOING TO TAKE AN AWFUL LOT OF WORK BY US AND THE ARTIST TO ILLUSTRATE IT. GETTING PHOTO REFERENCES IN ITSELF IS A MAJOR EFFORT IN A BIG PROJECT LIKE THIS, WITH A DEADLINE.

THERE'S AN AWFUL LOT RIDING ON THIS FOUR WALLS PROJECT. IT ENRAGES ME THAT THERE IS. I'VE ALREADY DONE ENOUGH T' PROVE MYSELF, BUT THE FACT THAT I WRITE ABOUT EVERYDAY LIFE IN MY COMICS RATHER THAN, SAY, WAR, THE FACT THAT I'M ISOLATED IN CLEVELAND AND NOT IN A POSITION TO GET THE NATIONAL MEDIA BEHIND ME, IS A DRAG. SO NOW MY WIFE AND I ARE WRITING ABOUT CANCER. MAYBE THAT'LL AROUSE SOME INTEREST IN MY WORK, MAYBE THAT'LL BE A CROWD PLEASING SUBJECT.

EVERY DAY I WAKE UP THINKING ABOUT HOW TO HUSTLE WRITING GIGS, HOW TO GET PAID THE MONEY I'M OWED, HOW I'M GONNA GET MY NEXT COMIC AND THE GRAPHIC NON-NOVEL OUT, I WORRY ABOUT GETTING CANCER AGAIN, ABOUT HOW MY HIP'S HOLDIN' UP. SOMETIMES I JUST... I DUNNO.

OH MY GOD, MY GOD, HOW'M' I GONNA GET THROUGH ALL THESE THINGS? ONE TASK COMES UP AFTER ANOTHER, 4' RUN AROUND LIKE CRAZY TRYING TO DO THEM, THEN 4' DIE.

BUT I KNOW I WANNA LIVE, NOT DIE, THESE DAYS, SO FUCK IT, I KNOW WHAT I GOTTA DO TO ACCOMPLISH WHAT I WANNA ACCOMPLISH. I'M GONNA TRY TO DO IT, WORK AT IT EVERY DAY THROUGH THE PAIN AND HOPE THINGS FALL INTO PLACE, THAT MAYBE SOMETIME IN THE FUTURE I'LL START TO FEEL BETTER AGAIN. THAT'S EASIER SAID THAN DONE, BUT SO FAR I'VE BEEN ABLE TO KEEP GOIN'.

END

10

HARVEY PEKAR & JOYCE BRABNER

By the People, For the People

There is a certain prophetic resonance in the fact that Harvey Pekar's first comic book effort appeared in *People's Comics* (1972), drawn by his friend Robert Crumb for the back cover of Crumb's underground comix classic. Both Pekar's and Joyce Brabner's comics, from Harvey's autobiographical *American Splendor* to the broad political scope of Joyce's *Real War Stories* (1987–91) and *Brought to Light* (1989), are in every sense of the term "for the  people, by the people." Pekar's stories are primarily by himself and about himself, while Brabner uses her own experiences to frame broader investigative narratives about America, and the impact our social, political, and military institutions have upon not only ourselves, but the world.

As journalists, authors, packagers, publishers, *provocateurs* (and husband and wife), Harvey and Joyce have tenaciously pursued a path dedicated to the truths of the human condition, contrary to the lurid escapist fantasies that fuel the main engines of the comic book industry. Mobilizing a wide variety of cartoonists (from R. Crumb and Jim Woodring to Tom Yeates and Bill Sienkiewicz) to illustrate their projects, Harvey and Joyce have worked hard to approach the medium solely on their own pragmatic terms. They continue to approach their intended audience with the same ruthless honesty and unflinching introspective integrity they demand of themselves.

Within the parameters of the countercultural comix movement, Pekar's early efforts seemed out of place. Despite their kinship to the occasionally autobiographical comix created by Crumb and others, Pekar's earnest, unembellished "slice-of-life" clarity stood in stark blue-collar contrast to the hallucinogenic excess of the material which surrounded him. Pekar decided to present his autobiographical stories as a self-contained comix, self-publishing his first issue of *American Splendor* in 1976. Maintaining his day job at a Cleveland veteran's hospital, he has continued (with Joyce's assistance) *American Splendor* to this day. Though his own print runs remain modest, Doubleday has collected two volumes for the mainstream book market, which in turn has landed Pekar on the David Letterman late night talk show.

American Splendor clearly played a vital role in Joyce's decision to build upon her work in prisons and schools, to apply the medium to controversial investigative ventures like *Real War Stories* and *Brought to Light*. She also cites the historical role of comics in social and political arenas. For example, when in February 1960, four black college freshmen sat down at a segregated luncheon counter in Greensboro, North Carolina, they initiated a nonviolent sit-in demonstration. That demonstration lasted for weeks and subsequently prompted similar nonviolent sit-ins in over 100 cities across the country within the year. When asked by the press what prompted their decision to protest, one of the four students cited a comic book, *Martin Luther King and the Montgomery Story* (produced by Al Capp Studios), for the inspiration and instructional guidance it had provided them.

Harvey Pekar and Joyce Brabner, in their own way, are to be commended for their continuing inspiration and instructional guidance.

COMIC BOOK REBELS: Harvey, some of your earliest scripts were published in titles such as *Bizarre Sex* #4 (1975) and *Snarf* #6 (1976). What originally brought you into writing for the undergrounds?

HARVEY PEKAR: What happened was that I was personal friends with Robert Crumb. Crumb used to live in my neighborhood in Cleveland. When he left the area, I kind of followed his career. I also was starting to theorize about comics. I found that, although the underground comic book artists were writing about a lot of different topics, they were concentrating on their lives as part of the counterculture of that time. I thought, "You know, comics can be about *anything*. Alternative comics don't just have to be about the counterculture."

I thought more and more about that, and while Crumb was staying with me in 1972, I showed him some scripts that I wrote that were about my life. You know—about a guy who's working a forty-hour-a-week job as a file clerk at a Veteran's Administration hospital. Crumb liked them. So he was with a guy named Robert Armstrong, and they illustrated some of these stories, and they got published, and that's how I got started.

CBR: How did this lead to your self-publishing *American Splendor*?

PEKAR: At that time, the counterculture which had supported alternative comics was dying out. A lot of these middle-class kids who were part of the counterculture—as soon as they found out they weren't going to be drafted, that they didn't have to go to Vietnam—they just went on and became "straight" again. As a result, the alternative comics just didn't have much of an audience anymore. It was becoming difficult for me to get my stories published, so I thought, "What the hell?" You know?

I was at that time single, so I decided I would publish my own comic. So I saved the money to do it. I lived pretty frugally in those days, aside from spending enormous amounts of money on collecting records. I stopped doing that and instead saved up and self-published a comic book. That's what I've been doing ever since, until real recently, when I had cancer. I put out one a year from 1976 until 1991. I'll be doing them again, but this time through a deal with Dark Horse Comics.

CBR: How did you choose the curious title *American Splendor*?

PEKAR: Well, it was meant to be kind of ironic. *American* came from the DC comics I read as a kid that had titles like *All-American Comics* and *Star-Spangled Comics*. And *Splendor* was because most people would not think of my life as very splendid! [*Chuckles*] I also think I got that word from *Splendor in the Grass*, which I always thought was just a hilarious title for some reason.

CBR: The early issues of *American Splendor* were published during that transitional period between the demise of the undergrounds and the rise of the direct sales market. How did you weather it, financially?

PEKAR: Well, I just *assumed* I was going to take a loss. And I did! But I could afford it—I used to spend more money on records when I was an insane record collector than the loss that I took on publishing *American Splendor*.

CBR: After you achieved some notoriety for *American Splendor*, how did that affect your interaction with the people you encountered at work or in your day-to-day life?

PEKAR: True, the people I wrote about were mainly the people I had contact with. But even though they knew there was something going on—maybe they read an article about me—they just knew me as a guy who worked with them. They pretty much treated me the same way, although some of those who saw the comic said, "Why don't you write about *me*?" [*Laughs*] And I used to do that sometimes.

CBR: You achieved another kind of notoriety from your combative appearances on the network program, "Late Night with David Letterman." Did that change your life or career in any positive way?

PEKAR: Not too much, really. If it had changed my life, especially in a positive way, I wouldn't have found it so easy to stop appearing. There were people on the street who saw me and said, "Hi—I saw you on the David Letterman show." You know? Patients in the hospital where I worked would ask me what was he really like, or something like that. But I wasn't getting that much money from going on the show, and the sales of the comic didn't seem to be improving much.

I didn't quarrel with Letterman wanting always to be funny; I just wanted to be funny about more substantive topics. He just didn't want to have anything to do with anything that was serious. So I got fed up with the whole setup, and just wound up trying to, you know, sabotage the show. As it turns out, they wanted *me* more than I wanted *them*. Because after the last show, when Letterman and I got into a really nasty argument and I told him in front of his audience that he was full of shit, I thought they would never want me back. But after that show, they actually called me to come back on his show a couple of times after

ARCHBISHOP ROMERO REFUSED TO ATTEND THE NEW PRESIDENT'S INAUGERATION. I REALLY ADMIRED HIM FOR THAT. THAT'S WHEN I WENT TO SEMINARY SCHOOL.

(IN 1980, THE 63 YEAR OLD ARCHBISHOP WAS GUNNED DOWN IN A CHURCH WHILE SERVING MASS. HE HAD BEEN OUTSPOKEN ABOUT INJUSTICES TO THE POOR.)

BESIDES WORKING WITH CHILDREN, I ALSO VOLUNTEERED TO WORK WITH THE LEGAL AID OFFICE.

THIS IS THE WORST JOB OF ALL. WHEN SOMEONE REPORTS A DEAD BODY YOU WILL HAVE TO GO OUT AND IDENTIFY IT. THAT MEANS TAKING PICTURES AND DESCRIBING IN DETAIL ALL THE ABUSE THE PERSON HAS RECEIVED AND, OF COURSE, THE PROBABLE CAUSE OF DEATH.

ALMOST EVERY BODY HAS SEVERAL BULLET HOLES IN THE HEAD. MANY WILL ALSO HAVE AN ARM OR LEG MISSING. NOW THEY HAVE STARTED TO CUT OFF HEADS.

YOU WILL FIND THE HEAD HERE AND THE BODY THERE. MOST ARE TORTURED, BLACK MARKS FROM CIGARETTE BURNS AND ELECTRIC SHOCK...

...AND OTHER THINGS I CAN'T EVEN TALK ABOUT. I HAD TO DO THIS JOB EVERYDAY.

LOU ANN, DO WE USE THIS?

IT COULD TURN A LOT OF PEOPLE OFF...

DO IT! THEY HAVE TO KNOW.

FROM *REAL WAR STORIES* #1 © 1993 BY JOYCE BRABNER AND TOM YEATES & MARK JOHNSON.

that. But I just couldn't see any point to doing it, because it didn't even seem to be making me any kind of money or anything. Maybe in the long run it brought me some new readers. The issues of *American Splendor* with Letterman on the cover did sell a little faster than the average issue, but at the time I wasn't aware of the difference.

CBR: How did you get a mainstream publisher to collect issues of *American Splendor* as a book?

PEKAR: Doubleday came and asked me. They offered me money, and so now I've had three of these collections published by other publishers than me.

CBR: Do you strive to keep the individual issues in print?

PEKAR: My print run on these comic books has been 10,000 for every one. And I've never reprinted any of them. I never really thought about reprinting them, because it's always been enough of a hassle for me just to do one printing initially. If anybody else wants to reprint them, fine! But except under certain special circumstances, I'm not going to do it.

CBR: Since you're apparently not going to reprint the individual issues, has the mainstream publisher striven to keep the collections in print?

PEKAR: I don't fault my editor there at all. But the apparent policy is that as long as the book isn't selling like hotcakes, they're not going to keep it in print. For example, the second collection did sell out, but they just never printed it again. The publicity never seemed to work out right, either. They once had a publicist there who, when the Cleveland *Plain Dealer* did an article about me, called her up and asked for a comment. And she said, "Well, I guess that stuff is really real, but I sure wouldn't want to live in an apartment building with a guy like that!" [*Laughs*]

CBR: How do you select the artists for *American Splendor*?

PEKAR: Well, at first I worked with just about anybody I could because I couldn't afford to pay a lot. With Crumb, I was lucky. When I started

American Splendor, Crumb wasn't doing much work. This may have been due to the fact that when I was starting it, the undergrounds were losing their popularity. So he did a lot of work for me, you know? Then I met Gary Dumm here in town, and Gary's the only guy who has since worked on every issue of *American Splendor* from the beginning on.

Gradually as the book got kind of successful—when it got critical praise—people would hear about it and they would ask me if they could do artwork for it. More recently, I've been getting out a little more, and going to conventions, where I've met more artists. Or I'd get letters from people. Like Frank Stack wrote to me, and we started corresponding, and that's how I got Frank to illustrate my work. Now I don't feel embarrassed, if I see a guy whose work I really like, about asking him if he would illustrate my work. Whereas before, if they never heard of me or anything, I'd feel pretty funny about asking them to work with me.

CBR: Do you have any regrets about being best known as a "comic book writer"? Has that identification hurt you in terms of being taken seriously by the public in terms of what you have to say as a writer?

PEKAR: No—I'm really happy about going into comics. First of all, it's an ideal medium for me, because you can tell stories real directly, which I like to do. And you can have a lot of the background put in by the illustrator. So it's a real direct, economical way to tell stories. Another thing about comics that I find very exciting is that, even though they've been around for awhile, and cartoons have been around for centuries, there's really very little that has been done with them. So it's great to explore this medium which really has not been very well explored.

CBR: Do you ever feel your work is reaching a limited audience by being published in a medium where most readers are not going to be actively seeking the adult "mainstream" stories you tell?

PEKAR: The earliest readers that knew about me, usually didn't have the time for other comics. And the others who *did* have the time for comics, just didn't know about me. They were much more likely to know about Marvel and DC Comics, reading *Spiderman* or something like that. I've found the public either likes my work—or they're not aware of me.

CBR: We understand that there has been a theater production adapted from *American Splendor*. What was that experience like?

PEKAR: There've been *three* plays done based on my work by other people. One in Lancaster, Pennsylvania, in 1985, in Washington, D.C., in 1987, and in Los Angeles in 1990, '91. They were all different adaptations, though how they did it was fairly similar: they basically just used my dialogue and strung stories together. They would sometimes pick up on a prose piece I had written or an interview I had given and stick that in there, too.

BRABNER: You were also commissioned to do a stage adaptation of your work which was staged as a reading at Playwright's Horizon in New York, so that would really make it four.

CBR: Do you think comics translates readily into other mediums, most obviously—but not necessarily limited to—the theatre?

PEKAR: Absolutely! And it's very easy to see why. First of all, you can write a comic script just as well as you can write a play or a movie script. You have access to the same words that everybody else does, you know? You got the *whole* dictionary to work from, and you can make up words, if you want to. You know what I mean? In comics you can write as well as you want, as well as you *can*. Shakespeare could have written well for comics. If you're talented, you can write well for comics, just as you can for theatre, and for television, and the movies. Certainly the medium can be translated! Comics can be more easily translated into theatre, movies, and television than novels can.

CBR: Joyce, what led to your working in comics as an activist for social reform?

BRABNER: Well, I read comics when I was five or six years old—including *Mad* Magazine, which was my first exposure to political satire. I really wasn't that interested in comics after an early age because for the same amount of money I could get on the bus and go down to the library, but I did remember a lot of what I'd read. When I was living in Delaware working with people in prison, with kids in trouble, I was friends with two sometime artists who were very involved in comic fandom. It all seemed like a lot of fun. I was burning out working with the courts, with sexual abusers of children and so on. Tom Watkins was doing a lot of costumes for the Phil Seuling comic shows, so I began working as a costumer while continuing to work in the prison programs I had organized on my own. Although I didn't spend much time at the conventions or in the comic shop I eventually co-owned, it was a pretty good introduction to the business end of comics.

I was reading *American Splendor* and our store ran out of an issue, so I wrote to Harvey to get copies, and he wrote back to me, so we began to correspond. I was flying out to his part of the country on other business, and decided to visit him, and the next day we decided to get married!

In retrospect, people ask me what brought us together, and I have to say I really trusted his honesty from the start—the kind of honesty I find in reading his work. *American Splendor* gave me a worm's-eye view of what his other marriages were like, so that was it. How did I get into comics? I became a character in one.

CBR: Were you working together on the publishing of *American Splendor*?

BRABNER: I had a talent for publicity. *American Splendor* was losing money, and I had stopped working with the prison program. We also didn't know each other very well for our first year of marriage. So we started to have some fun, doing screwball publicity. I started cutting up his old clothes and making little Harvey Pekar dolls; just like the Shroud of Turin, they were made with clothing actually worn by the author, like some holy relic. They were these odd collectibles, and I carried these ugly little dolls around at our first San Diego con together and we picked up nine distributors for the book! After that *American Splendor* began to go into the black. One of the dolls ended up on "The David Letterman Show," and we were horrified to get a call from a Korean distributor the next day wanting to mass produce the damned things. I just make them now and then for charity auctions.

CBR: How did that lead to packaging books like *Real War Stories* and *Brought to Light*?

BRABNER: Lou Ann Merkle, who was an art student and activist living in Cleveland and knew about *American Splendor*, took a job in Philadelphia with CCCO—the Central Committee for Conscientious Objectors, which is a military and draft counseling organization—and found she needed a tool to reach teenagers with information about the military.

This was during the peacetime draft, when they were looking for smart white kids to sign up, and they had a very aggressive recruiting campaign around the time *Top Gun* (1986) was in the theatres. She thought they needed counterpropaganda, a way of presenting some of the things the recruiters weren't telling the kids about the draft. She paid a visit to Harvey, asking how much it would cost to do comic book stories that the veterans and people from El Salvador were telling to get them in the classroom, into the hands of the kids. She only had a budget for a black and white comic, but I felt that color was necessary if they were going to reach the kids. In the eighties, the military was getting to these kids by playing on their need for money; the kids wanted money and prosperity, and I knew it had to be a color book to appeal to *their* values. We were also up against the U.S. military, which has the largest advertising budget in the world. And here was this little organization trying to compete with these guys. It *had* to be a color book with popular artists and writers if we were going to get the kids, but it had to be realized with the integrity and honesty the undergrounds had. I felt I knew how to put that together, and CCCO agreed.

CBR: How did you package and distribute *Real War Stories*?

BRABNER: I had to find a publisher willing to deal with the printing of the completed book. We split costs with the publisher, recieved some grant funding, but some of the creators deferred their pay. Once the book was printed, the CCCO distributed the book in a number of ways. They sold them through donation telethons, and they got them into some schools and they were used in classrooms, enough to attract the attention of the Department of Defense and the Department of Justice.

CBR: Did they try to ban or prosecute the use of *Real War Stories* in the schools?

BRABNER: The Department of Defense has a clipping service, and a newspaper article brought it to their attention. In Atlanta, Georgia, the Atlanta Peace Alliance and CCCO were using the comic book during the high school "career day," so kids getting information on "Being All You Can Be" and earning money for college through military careers also had access to this comic book. An editor at a local newspaper lashed out against the presence of *Real War Stories* and related material at the school, saying there was no such thing as a career in peace in America, that it was inappropriate for these people to be invited where the military, on the other hand, offered careers. Local pressure led to different people from around the country, who at some point were joined by the Departments of Defense and Justice, forcing the superintendent of the school to give in and tell the APA and CCCO they *couldn't* be there, prompting the APA and CCCO to file a suit against the school board in order to have access to the school.

For the purposes of the hearing, the Department of Defense offered an expert witness who was asked a number of questions about military recruitment. At one point Lt. Col. Cullen was asked what he thought about the comic book and the information in it, and he said it was all made up. These were all autobiographical stories; I participated in all the interviews myself, and they were all carefully documented before being selected for the book. What was most disturbing people was Tim Merrill's story, who became a conscientious objector while in the Navy submarine service, realizing as a sonar technician he could one day be responsible for starting World War III. He went through the lonely and frightening experience of establishing himself as a C.O. while on a submarine, which is what the story was about. One of the things that helped clarify his thinking about his experience in the Navy had to do with this very brutal form of "hazing" of young recruits, which I was familiar with from my work in prisons: the guys who don't fit in are sodomized—in the Navy this is done with a grease gun.

What happened in the courtroom is that the military expert said this was all fabricated. We had military Naval court records on hand involving a female recruit who had this happen, and in court it had been established that this was a military tradition! Remember, this all happened before Tailhook. The military witness started backpedaling real fast, saying he was in the Army, not in the Navy, he didn't know anything about it, and our side cut them off on a couple more things. The case was continued, and at a later point CCCO got a letter from the Department of Defense essentially withdrawing the complaint. They had gotten involved because the comic was interfering with the recruiting process, so it was considered a "threat to national security." At this point they knew they were going to lose, and rather than hand a peace organization a win, they dropped it and avoided any real publicity.

We had been very careful while doing the book. We *had* to.

CBR: *Brought to Light* was another difficult project. That was originally a joint publishing venture between Warner Books and Eclipse Comics. What led to Warner pulling out?

BRABNER: The Christic Institute, which is a public-interest legal firm, best known at that time for its work on the Karen Silkwood case, had taken on a case that nobody else would in the United States involving the bombing of a press conference in Costa Rica. The American survivors who investigated the bombing found it involved much broader issues indicating covert operations, possible swaps of drugs for arms, a broader issue that for the purposes of bringing it to court became considered an act of conspiracy. Had they been able to go through the American judicial system in a more proper manner, had people in the Department of Justice really been willing to take a look at what they were doing, an outside organization like the Christic Institute wouldn't have been needed. But Christic became their only chance to try and bring some of this stuff to light.

The story that they told was *very* complicated. When you're dealing with a court case, there are things you can say you know as facts, and things you can allege, and things you can say are issues to be explored. The people at Christic had seen *Real War Stories* #1 and were trying to raise funds for this case, and asked if I could communicate this very complex story in comic book form. I found there were two ways the stories could be told. One was this very heavy legal deposition as filed by the institute, and the other was a straightforward look at the bombing. I decided to tell these stories in two different ways, as a "topsy-turvy" format comic book. A number of people in comics were too afraid to be involved with the project, but Alan Moore had a story in *Real War* #1 and I knew we could work together, and he took it on. I wrote the other.

Warner was interested in the project from the beginning, because it looked like they were going to get in on the ground floor of a book on the Iran-Contra Affair, which could be as big as Watergate. But they became very, very cautious when it became clear that this story was a lot bigger than everybody thought it was. I spent several miserable July days in New York City with one of two attorneys from Christic and libel attorneys from Warner, going over every single comma and period in the script and most of the visuals talking about all this stuff, which was all right with me because the idea was to check out what might be actionable. I was told at that time by Warner's attorneys that our sources were solid and our book would fly. I don't think that's what turned Warner off on it. I think they realized this wasn't going to be the enormous trial, or victory, they thought it would be, the plaintiffs were going to be ground down, so there was no reason to take a risk on something that wasn't going to be a real big story.

CBR: What is the current climate in the industry in terms of publishing this kind of confrontational material in comics form?

BRABNER: I am working on two books now, *Activists!* and *Cambodia, USA*. To publish non-fiction, public interest comics, I've had to go outside the world of comic book publishing. I continue to work with grant money. By and large, unless I bring in outside funding, comic book publishers don't want to touch me. They only want books that are "entertaining" or big box-office. At present, though I have funding in place, I cannot find a publisher willing to take on a reprinting of the *Martin Luther King* comic Al Capp Studios packaged.

Harvey and I are working with artist Frank Stack on a book about activism and cancer and being married and buying a house, about being sick at a time when we feel the whole world is sick—our cancer year.

PEKAR: It starts out with our realizing that we're probably going to have to buy a new house, so we're house hunting, and Joyce gets involved with what would have been *Real War Stories #3*, and my finding out I had cancer while she was out dealing with that. Frank is drawing the book, which we call *Our Cancer Year*.

BRABNER: We're writing it together from our different points of view, in the different way we experienced Harvey's illness, the radiation chemo-therapy treatments, everything. We began putting everything we re-membered of all these incidents on index cards, and worked with *how* we would tell the story. It was horrible, really, doing this at a time when we were supposed to be starting Harvey's postcancer life.

CBR: Has it been a healing process to do this together?

PEKAR: It'll be a healing process if we make a lot of money.

IV

INTERNATIONAL AMBASSADORS
The Worldly Storytellers

FROM "THE DETOUR." © 1993 BY JEAN GIRAUD.

11

JEAN "MOEBIUS" GIRAUD
Crack in the Comic Egg

The early to mid-Seventies nurtured a remarkable blossoming of the international comics medium, which quickly matured from its previous encystment of being considered merely an aberrant form of children's literature. The "mind-blowing" impact of the underground comix movement from the United States, the eruption from South America and post-Franco Spain, and the mini-Renaissance of comic art in France and Belgium is still being felt there  today. In France particularly, this period brought the expansion of the venerable *Pilote*, as well as the coming of *L'Écho des Savanes* and *Métal Hurlant*, clearly signaling the dawn of the new age of comics.

Métal Hurlant showcased imagery and dreamlike narratives that were rendered with breathtaking beauty—and often relentless violence and cruelty. The periodical was the maiden voyage for "Les Humanoides Associés," the offspring of four accomplished creators—Phillipe Druillet, Jean Giraud, Jean-Pierre Dionnet, and Bernard Farkas—who banded together to publish their own work (and that of their like-minded artistic associates) without the imposition of outside editorial control or interference.

Prominent in the first issue of *Métal Hurlant* was the particularly vivid artwork (including the cover portrait of a yowling alien sitting alone on a barren rock—a particularly apt image for the magazine's often primal intensity) of an artist who signed his work with the singular name "Moebius."

Moebius's distinctive vision was first introduced to American audiences in 1977, with the debut of the "Adult Illustrated Fantasy" magazine *Heavy Metal*. He was, of course, already known to the international professional comics community for his work (as Jean Giraud) on the classic Western strip, *Lt. Blueberry*. He had also been one of the few European artists to receive both a special award from the National Cartoonists Society as "Best Realistic Artist" in 1972, and a Shazam from the short-lived American Comic Book Association in 1974.

Working through his own American company, Starwatcher Graphics, Giraud has since 1987 supervised the repackaging of his complete *oeuvre*. These definitive editions are essential reading, featuring new translations (by Randy and Jean-Marc Lofficier) and with many presented in color for the first time. His books are presently offered to American readers from a variety of publishers and imprints, most predominately from the Marvel/EPIC line.

Giraud's influence is profound and truly global, having reached far beyond the parameters of the comics medium alone. In 1974, Giraud, along with Chris Foss and H.R. Giger, made the groundbreaking crossover from the graphic arts into designing for the cinema when recruited by director Alejandro Jodorowsky (with whom Jean later worked in comics) for an intended production of Frank Herbert's *Dune*. Though the project ultimately collapsed, it did establish the important contributions comic book artists continue to bring to many prestigious films (including *Star Wars, Alien,* and *Blade Runner*). Jean Giraud still designs for motion pictures, most recently in the United States on *The Abyss* (1989).

With his expansive vision and tender heart, "Moebius" is prominent among the spiritual fathers of the comic book rebels.

(Portions of this interview are excerpted by permission of Starwatcher Graphics, Inc.)

COMIC BOOK REBELS: Have you any memories of where your intense love for drawing began?

MOEBIUS: It's very difficult, because everybody has a period of time when they draw as a child. It's the discovery of making lines and curves, so it's fascinating to everyone. I think it's part of our development as human beings, just as when we first discover music or song. And if in one of those moments there's a connection with our emotions,

THE MAN FROM CIGURI BY MOEBIUS © 1992.

THE MAN FROM THE CIGURI CONTINUES IN CHEVAL NOIR #33.

that period of discovery can become a major direction in life. For me, it was that way.

When I discovered drawing, it was in a period of my life that was very important because my parents were splitting up. My mother was alone, so she put me in my grandparents' home. I don't remember exactly, but I'm sure now that it was a very strenuous time. But at that time I was also discovering drawing.

I'm not sure it's true, but I think it's the reason why suddenly drawing became for me a major way to escape confrontation. And it was also a way to communicate with others, and to have back a feeling of having some power in my life. No matter what happened in different periods of my life, I always had that possibility of drawing. Sometimes when I was alone, sometimes when I was with my friends at school, drawing was always a possibility of not only power, but of self-understanding and amusement. Contentment. Anything could be discovered through drawing—even pain.

When you draw, you always give yourself pleasure. But it's a small pleasure. Yet when you start to try to do something with a project, it not only stops the pain but gives you a greater pleasure. So I became an addict to that process in my early days. I also, early on, saw the possibility of my work being seen by others . . . by girls. But not very successfully at first! [*Laughs*] Because girls are not impressed by artists unless they have had some success. But you know, the way my success acted within me gave me a sense of self-confidence. I had that way of thinking, "Okay, I'm not very good at many things, but I am good at drawing."

CBR: Do you recall the moment when you first believed you had that "success"—that self-confidence—within you as an artist?

MOEBIUS: I remember I was drawing in the woods close to my grand-parents' house. A voice came from behind me, and it was a girl's voice. When I saw her, she was absolutely *beautiful*! She asked me what I was doing. It was the first time that drawing gave me that self-confidence to talk to her, and we became very, very close friends—and lovers—after that. I was fifteen years old. And it was discovering that connection between art and self-confidence, because the reason she asked what I was doing was because *she* was interested in art.

But even if I don't talk about it, art stays within me, and gives me serenity. It's always there. When we are good at something on any level, we *know* that, and it gives us an inner strength.

CBR: Do you recall the very first drawing that ever satisfied you?

MOEBIUS: The first drawing that ever satisfied me in an emotional way was a drawing I did when I was very, very young—maybe three. *Everything* comes from that drawing. I was very, very small, but I remember very well the drawing I did. It was a big boat, with a chimney on it. And I was in the back of the boat, waving bye-bye to the people on shore with a handkerchief. And I drew my grandmother, and she had her hair in a bun, and I drew that bun very well. And she recognized herself from my drawing!

She was amazed, and she showed that drawing to everybody in the family—and in the neighborhood! You know? So I had my first success. I became addicted at that point. It was my first "convention"! [*Laughs*]

CBR: Do you think more children would become interested in the arts if so encouraged by their families at such a tender age?

MOEBIUS: No—it's not just encouragement. It's a *spontaneous reaction*; it's not because someone says, "Oh, how nice!" It depends on the needs of the individual, and those needs are always mysterious. The questions of the universe cannot be answered by the people, the answer comes from something much more mysterious. It's the universe that wants your art; it's not my grandmother! You know? She didn't do this with any sense of education or to "be good" to me; it was purely innocent of the woman to completely fulfill my needs.

I was a very solitary child, often alone because I had no brothers or sisters. My grandparents' house had few children around. I would spend many, many days playing by myself, which was good; I was very happy because I was always doing something. But this is not really a good situation for a young child. In fact, I was desperately lonely, but I didn't know it—we imagine our happiness when we're young.

CBR: Yet you knew even then that you wished to be an artist! What kind of encouragement did you get when you decided you wanted to become a professional, to have a career in the arts?

MOEBIUS: After thinking I should do art as a professional, I spoke with my family, and everybody was okay with that idea. So I was in a good situation; I did not have to fight with anybody. They did not understand exactly what I wanted to do, but they trusted me enough to let me go to school. It was an art school in Paris. But the first year I was there I did not have enough money to be a young student in Paris. I started to have a taste for movies, and had other new interests. So my first work was not in comics, but by doing art objects—handicrafts. They're all gone now. It was not a good way to make money, though, spending time selling them in the streets. I was shy! [*Laughs*]

Very, very quickly I realized that comics were more applicable to my needs.

CBR: You spent a good part of your career working on the *Lt. Blueberry* strip, which was serialized in *Pilote* beginning in 1963, and subsequently worked on it for a decade. You obviously have a deep and abiding fascination with the American Western genre.

MOEBIUS: *Blueberry* was *whooooah!* It took *all* my energy; I had to stop doing anything else. For me, it was the most difficult challenge of my career. To do a modern comic for a teenager, but with *all* my imagination. And *all* my dreams about Westerns, about movies—everything. When I started to do this project, I had the idea that it was possible to capture the flavor of this period. But to catch the spirit, you have to know the details. The spirit is made by the details. Though if I had been living in the United States, or had been American, perhaps *Lt. Blueberry* might have been much better . . .

Many things about it are not bad, but a little twisted! I am very clever—I can give the *feeling* that it's real. You know, this is the secret of our profession in comics: You give to the audience the feeling that everything is in the picture. You can give the feeling that two thousand bad guys are riding upon you. But when you count them—only sixty! [*Laughs*]

CBR: What was going on then in your community of artists, that led to their later bonding together to conceive *Métal Hurlant*?

MOEBIUS: The older generation of artists had the feeling that it was a lowering of their dignity to do comics, and had an aristocratic self-vision. But during the sixties a new generation of artists was coming in, confident of doing comics and with a very good general culture, who were graduating from the art schools and universities. And they were very self-aware.

For example, I may realize I might never be on the level of a Michelangelo, but we are of the same *family*. We are in the same tradition. There is no separation between the arts. No separation between literature and comics. When writers think about story, they naturally put themselves in the community of Molière, Proust, Joyce, Miller, or any major writer. We don't think: Those writers are Olympians, and we are nothing. Nobody thinks that way anymore: *everybody* has access to genius. The connection between the movies, literature, poetry, avant-garde, history, psychoanalysis, the personal expression of the moment—this was the tradition that suddenly arrived into the comic book field like a sunburst.

The second influence was the American undergrounds. Because the first to dare to do all this was the Americans. Nobody appreciated completely the importance of the American undergrounds in the artistic community. They were very, very important, and really beautiful. These artists were pioneers! They were visionaries! Crumb, of course. Bode. Spain. Wilson. Rick Griffin, Greg Irons. Great artists! Great artists! They completely blew our minds with their work. And this influence in the sixties was not just in the small area of comics—it was everywhere! It was the Revolution of Youth.

CBR: In 1973, *Pilote* was at the apex of its success when you, Philippe Druillet, and Jean-Pierre Dionnet left to create your own magazine, *Métal Hurlant*. At the same time, Gotlib, Mandryka, and Claire Bretecher left to create their own, *L'Écho des Savanes*. What happened? Weren't you happy at *Pilote*?

MOEBIUS: We were all in the situation as children in relation to their parents, the parents being the publisher, Dargaud. It was even more complicated because *Pilote*'s editor-in-chief, Rene Goscinny, behaved like a father, but his role was very ambiguous. We never really knew if he was on the side of the artists, or on the side of the publisher.

At the time, some of the artists, including myself, didn't know if *Pilote* was a magazine of political commentary, social satire, or simply a magazine geared towards exploiting the teenage audience. It was unpleasant for us to see our more relevant strips, which were literally screaming against that form of exploitation, cohabit with strips that were in effect the ones pandering to the teenage market which we were condemning. It was an ambiguous, and ultimately unacceptable, compromise.

That a part of the magazine was devoted to true, artistic expression didn't happen suddenly. It took several years. For a long time, throughout the sixties, we were kept within very inflexible formats where you could only express yourself in certain ways—like adventure comics, Westerns, nice, harmless humor, etc. The first artists who broke away from those formats were, of course, the humorists. Gotlib, Mandryka, and even myself with the story *The Detour* (*Pilote* #688, January 1973), which was a humorous story. We took themes that had been taboo until then and made fun of them.

And, progressively, this caused the whole edifice to collapse. For example, Gotlib realized that he had used all the themes that he could possibly use in *Pilote*. He had lampooned all the classic comics themes and, by so doing, he'd killed them. Now, he had no choice but to go forward. But he couldn't do that in *Pilote*, at least as it was then. So he had to leave.

CBR: But *Pilote* continued after you all left?

MOEBIUS: Yes, but it was dead. They just didn't know it. When they realized it, they began changing the magazine until it became just another version of *Métal Hurlant* and *L'Écho des Savanes*. It was incredible, because the traditional pillars of *Pilote* were *Asterix* and *Lucky Luke*, and suddenly they didn't have their place in it anymore. They had to be published in another magazine. Once that break had been recognized, it was no longer possible to publish that kind of strip alongside the other material.

CBR: So how did the idea to self-publish arise?

MOEBIUS: It had never before happened that a small group of artists got together and pooled some money together to create their own publishing company. We'd been talking about it on and off for years. After the weekly editorial meetings at *Pilote*, we all went to have a drink, and someone or other always said, "What we should do is what the Americans are doing, self-publish."

We meant, of course, the undergrounds, which were our model. We could see that, even though they weren't all actually published by the artists themselves, they were still published by small companies, artisans. The publishers themselves were like artists, they invented new structures, new formats, new covers, new ways of reaching the readers. The artists were tapping into cultural references that came from outside the small, traditional comics culture, such as psychedelics, the Vietnam War, etc.

Some of us were more interested in the purely structural, or material, format of things. They saw the creation of a new system of publishing comics. Others only saw the freedom that it would give the artists, whatever the format or structure. This is a very important difference. Mandryka, for instance, was more in tune with the former. He saw he could use underground comics to breathe new life into French comics. He wanted to borrow the format itself. Gotlib and Bretecher, on the other hand, were mostly interested in the possibility of expressing themselves, without any restrictions being placed upon them.

In the case of *Métal Hurlant*, it was the same thing. From the start, the magazine looked slicker and more professional, because Jean-Pierre Dionnet was a professional and wanted it to have that very sharp look. We didn't want to simply parody the undergrounds. We wanted to publish a real professional magazine, but one where the artists would be totally free to do what they wanted—which is a very scary concept!

The style Jean-Pierre and I gave to *Métal* was an immediate success. The very tone and look of the magazine became so influential that any magazine which came after was unable to ignore it.

So we had these two different motivations: One was to create a new tool, a new medium; the other was just searching for freer ways of expression. I was part of the latter myself. I was in a euphoric state, because I could create freely, without being at all responsible for the magazine, even though I owned twenty-five percent of it! In fact, once in a while, people who would disagree with Jean-Pierre's style would come and see me to try to convince me to stop him, but I said, "Look, he leaves me totally free to do my comics. I should leave him free to run his magazine."

CBR: But, technically, it was as much *your* magazine as it was *his*.

Moebius: Yes, but, although we were creative partners in the magazine, I never truly felt like an owner. I wanted it to be that way, so that I could reap the creative joys without having to bother with the responsibility of running the company.

To be a self-publisher, and wanting to run the company yourself, can be something very dangerous. After Gotlib left *L'Écho des Savanes* to create his own magazine, *Fluide Glacial*, his creativity suffered, and he always blamed it on the fact that he felt responsible for *Fluide*, although in reality, he had Jacques Diament to manage things for him. I don't know whether the same thing would have happened to me if I had chosen the same path, but I think it's very likely. Those kinds of things exact a price from you. There's no such thing as a free lunch, as they say.

I never really tried to develop that kind of control over the business aspects of my career, until more recently, because I felt that I wasn't good at that kind of thing. I'm too irresponsible a person. I think that, to develop such a side of myself, I would need to kill another side, at least in part—that is, my creative side.

To self-publish and be in control of your career as if it were a business can certainly have a huge impact on your creative life, because in essence you become a parent, either to others if you have colleagues or collaborators, or even to yourself if the only thing you do is self-publish. You become your own parent. You can't help but take over the parental role in regard to other artists, distributors, etc. You can see it creeping into your own language: You start talking about responsibilities, money, etc. It's very dangerous, because it can be in total contradiction with the principle of being an artist.

You can even assume that role regarding yourself. You start treating the creative part of yourself as you would a child. And sometimes you can abuse that child, so that you become your own victim and your own torturer.

I'll give you an example: When I took over *The Silver Surfer* (Marvel Comics, 1988), I acted as a publisher, as a parent who is sending his child—the creative part of myself—into an area where he is going to feel miserable. And, even though you tell the child that it's for his own good, he still suffers.

CBR: How did you reconcile your two roles in *Métal Hurlant*: that of owner, and that of artist?

MOEBIUS: Let me say that I have a very high opinion of the role of a publisher. If he does his job well and honestly, a publisher is the artist's best ally. When we began *Métal*, I specifically asked Jean-Pierre not to treat me better than the others, or to give me perks or bonuses that might endanger the company, just because I was one of the owners. Yes, we wanted to change the system, but on the creative end. So it was an extraordinary situation, because I was asking my own partner to look at me with a publisher's cold and calculating eye. Of course, I didn't need to ask Dargaud to do this because we always assumed that's what he was doing anyway.

CBR: You mentioned other artists. We gather that part of the reason you went into self-publishing was also to open the field to new talents who couldn't be published in the regular magazines at the time?

MOEBIUS: Very much so. That was our intention from the very beginning. Again, it comes from the American undergrounds, where big names like Robert Crumb and Gilbert Shelton helped sell lesser-known artists. At the very beginning, *Métal* was quarterly, and we foolishly thought we might be able to fill it all with just the three of us, but we quickly realized that it would never work.

As soon as #1 came out, people came to see us because they wanted to be part of our experiment. There were also people who said nothing, either because they were too intimidated, afraid, or because they didn't understand what we were trying to do. And of course, there are ego-related problems, especially with artists. When we used to all be part of a tightly knit community, where nobody was upsetting the apple cart, it was different because, even though some were more talented than others, there was a feeling of a comfortable hierarchy, where everyone knew his place.

But when a small group secedes from the community and they start doing something truly new and different, people begin feeling uncomfortable. Some people start to wonder about what's happening and whether they're being thought stupid or out of it because they haven't been invited to join. Others will swallow their pride and hop in. Others will absolutely refuse to have anything to do with it because they're either genuinely not interested or because, deep down, they're scared.

It's an implacable mechanism. When there's a revolution, you're either part of it or not part of it. It's like a train. You're either on it or not on it. You can't be halfway on it. Some people might be able to catch up with it at a later station, but it's never the same thing.

CBR: That was almost two decades ago. What's happened since then?

MOEBIUS: It was interesting. We saw the publisher-author coupling reform, but under different conditions. *Métal Hurlant* eventually became a respectable and major publisher, although it went bankrupt several times. I lost quite a lot of money, but I'm willing to take responsibility for this, since it was my own decision not to involve myself with the company's management. Furthermore, I think it wasn't entirely a bad thing, because it shows the artist that a publisher is not some kind of eternal institution that you can join the same as you would if you went and worked for the Post Office. Publishers are something alive, and therefore they can die. It makes the artists more responsible.

I think that we learned that our audience isn't something that is owed to us, as was sometimes the case under the old system. We're entertainers and subject to the same rules. We're on stage and, if the public loves us, all is fine, but if they hate us, they throw vegetables at us. We should never forget this. One can push the relationship with the public to its limits in terms of intimacy, but no further. It's like if you were whispering on stage, it's more difficult than doing slapstick. But they've got to believe you, otherwise you fall flat on your face. And for that, you need to have some magic.

So the same mechanisms that freed the artists ended up creating new publishing houses, which grew and sometimes died. But what is important is that the global scene changed. Comics were no longer what they used to be. The creative landscape was totally new.

Now, we have an incredible amount of freedom in terms of personal, artistic expression. To me, this is the fundamental difference. You can come in and see a publisher with a completely crazy idea, something never done before, and if it's really good, they'll publish it! If it has that magic I was mentioning before. We're getting closer and closer to the real world of literature. We're almost there, in fact.

CBR: Then you see the benefit of the experience was in the *creative* arena rather than the structural one?

MOEBIUS: Yes. The relationship between author and publisher, and their respective powers, didn't fundamentally change because, primarily, I believe that it must be the result of a personal work that the artist must do upon himself.

An artist is by nature someone very sensitive who expresses with talent the pains that he suffered. He uses art to replace the true communication that he didn't, or doesn't, have with others. More artists were sensitive children, often introverted, and suddenly they discovered that there is a big demand for that very same expression of their sensitivity. They discover that, in our harsh world, there's a small oasis for dream makers, and you even get paid for it.

So, this is incredible to them and they go there, but they're still not alone. They're still surrounded by, say, sharks, and they must learn to defend themselves and fight with the sharks on an equal level. The sharks are not simply the publishers, they're also the colorists, the letterers, the inkers, the friends, the colleagues, the media, the kids, the mothers-in-law, etc. You must learn how to deal with all these people, and determine what kind of relations you should have with them. This is the personal work of the artist. He and he alone is responsible.

I'll take an example. My relationship with some of my publishers has sometimes been one of conflict. Naturally, the goal of the publisher, or that of the managers who work for him, is to maximize the profits, and therefore reduce the costs, which is sometimes done at the expense of the artist. The artist is an easy prey: he works alone, at home, he doesn't know what's going on. But the publisher only does what's natural for him. It's up to the artist to get his act together, or find a business partner. Of course, it's easier if you're a star, but even young artists can group together and form a studio and hire an agent.

CBR: What is your perception of North America's comics industry today, where constant change seems to be the current state of affairs?

MOEBIUS: Everything happens faster in the United States, but at the same time, it doesn't have the literary tradition that we have in France. Here, the book publishers seem to be very bestseller oriented, and serious literature is quickly categorized and relegated to a small niche. There is a risk that comics will end up being treated in the same fashion.

CBR: The most obvious form of such categorization in the comics market as it *does* exist in the United States is the commercial dominance of the superhero genre. Do you think today's young artists will be able to extract themselves from their present cultural referential system, which is still primarily comic-book oriented, to really express themselves in more open ways?

MOEBIUS: That is another question to which I don't see any answers yet. The child isn't born yet. Comics must learn to express personal, internal universes, deal with social or political themes, or truly original visions.

It is important to reach a public that doesn't let itself be trapped in genres and categories. To me, adolescents who are stuck in a single genre, like superheroes, are already old people. To me, to be young is to be free of prejudice and preconceived ideas. It is a fact that artists can't do anything unless they have a public. So what we're also looking at is a global evolution of society.

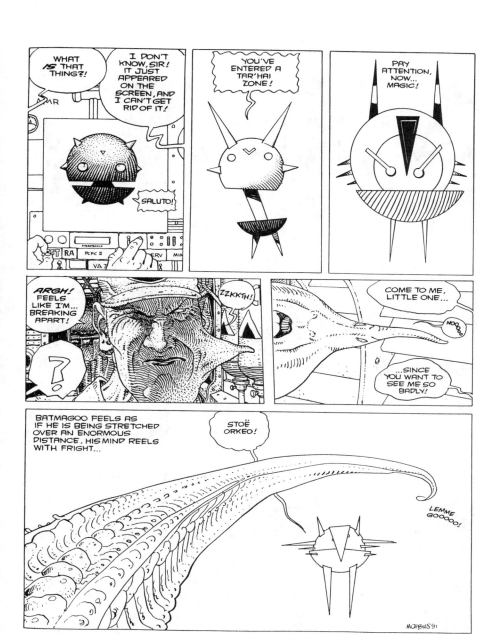

THE MAN FROM CIGURI BY MOEBIUS © 1992.

FROM *FROM HELL: VOLUME ONE* © 1993 BY ALAN MOORE AND EDDIE CAMPBELL.

12

ALAN MOORE
Bard of the New Order

Within the context of the industry and its history, there have been many comic book writers who have left their mark. Alan Moore, however, is perhaps unique in that his work as a writer has organically enlivened and wholly elevated what is possible in comics as a form of literature. For he is not just an exceptional comic book writer; he is an extraordinary author who *chooses* to create, first and foremost, in this medium.

Moore's superb writing earned him international prominence in less than a decade—in an industry where usually only graphic artists (and fictional characters!) are ever acclaimed as "superstars." Moore is a revelation: contrasted with the discursive shallowness of most mainstream comic scripts, his style and content is rich, profound, and complex. His collaborative efforts with a procession of fine artists have in turn brought forth the best work of those artists.

The writer's earliest efforts for the British weekly comics yielded at least two masterpieces: the strangely moving "The Reversible Man" (*2000 A.D.* Prog. 308, 1983), and the ingenious "Chronocops" (*2000 A.D.* Prog. 310, 1983), a science-fiction black comedy deliberately drawn by Dave Gibbons in the style of *MAD* Magazine's Will Elder. His subsequent work for *Warrior* (1982–85) laid the bedrock for the dramatic revisionist superhero strip *Marvelman* (reprinted and continued in the U.S.A. as *Miracleman* by Marvel, from 1985 to the present), and the dystopian epic *V for Vendetta* (reprinted and completed in the U.S.A. by DC Comics, 1988–1989).

On the heels of British artist Brian Bolland, Moore spearheaded "The British Invasion" of the American comic book scene with his adventurous work on *The Saga of the Swamp Thing* (1983–87). This prolific period of work with DC Comics culminated in Moore's and Dave Gibbons's ground-breaking *Watchmen* (1986–87), which, along with Frank Miller's *Batman: The Dark Knight Returns* (1986), largely redefined the parameters of the superhero genre. Moore subsequently abandoned the archetype, until playfully returning to the idiom in early 1993 with *1963* for Image Comics.

By 1987, however, Moore shifted away from the mainstream arena to pursue more personal projects, prompted primarily by his disgust with the industry's amoral business practices and his desire to transcend the commercial restraints imposed upon the medium itself. Cofounding Mad Love Publishing in 1988, Moore launched the as yet incomplete *Big Numbers* graphic novel, and a body of political work that includes the self-published *Aargh!* (1988), as well as significant contributions to Joyce Brabner's *Real War Stories* #1 (1987) and *Brought to Light* (1988).

The scope of his most recent efforts is just as remarkable, ranging from the dark historical novel *From Hell* (from 1989 to the present), in which he and artist Eddie Campbell dissect Victorian society in the orbit of the Jack the Ripper hysteria, to the more intimate concerns of the erotic *Lost Girls* (from 1992 to the present) with artist Melinda Gebbie. Perhaps his most personal effort to date is *A Small Killing* (1991) with artist Oscar Zarate.

Wherever he chooses to let his literary talents take root, Alan Moore's work sets the standard for others to try and surpass.

COMIC BOOK REBELS: Why does the comics medium still interest you the most as a writer?

ALAN MOORE: Mainly because it's the medium which has been the least explored.

What it comes down to in comics is that you have complete control of both the verbal track and the image track, which you don't have in any other medium, including film. So a lot of effects are possible which simply cannot be achieved anywhere else. You control the words and the pictures—and more importantly—you control the *interplay* between those two elements in a way which not even film can achieve.

There's a sort of "under-language" at work there, that is neither the "visuals" nor the "verbals," but a unique effect caused by a combination of the two.

A picture can be set against text ironically, or it can be used to support the text, or it can be completely disjointed from the text—which forces the reader into looking at the scene in a new way. You can do this to some extent in film, in terms of striking interesting juxtapositions between the imagery and what the intent of the characters may be, but you cannot do it anywhere near as precisely as you can in comics. Here the reader has the ability to stop and linger over one particular "frame" and work out *all* of the meaning in that frame or panel, as opposed to having it flash by you at twenty-four frames per second in a cinema.

Also, in the way in which we order our minds, in the way in which our very *thinking* is constructed, it would seem to me to be in a balance of words and images. These are the two representational forces that most shape our thinking as humans. And I think that goes all the way back to our very earliest written languages; if you look at the ancient Chinese ideograms, the word for "hut" actually looks like a hut! The Chinese sentence was almost like a comic strip: a sequence of images that could be decoded by the reader and would then have meaning. This strikes me as something very primal which, partly because it's got a very low position on the cultural totem pole, has been underexploited.

People tend to think this language is beneath them, and thus serious artists, generally speaking, have not explored this medium. It's still pretty much virgin territory, and that's why—to me—it's probably the most exciting art form of them all.

CBR: Do you think that the critical low esteem for comic books was due to the generally juvenile level of writing that has been the standard for decades in America and England?

MOORE: What we're mainly talking about here is a set of commercial considerations that have held the comic book back. There *have* been great writers, but they've been marginal throughout, because commercial considerations have meant that the comic art form has been dominated by comics as an *industry*. The industry mines a juvenile market, and it more or less imposes juvenile restrictions on its creators—or at least it has done so until relatively recently. But by and large, it's on the comic book industry where the blame must rest.

To some degree, this has resulted in a creative problem as well. When you have generations of creators grow up having to accept the limitations forced upon them by the industry, inevitably you're going to get a set of lowered horizons from those creators. They're not even going to be able to *imagine* comic book stories which go beyond those fairly juvenile concerns. During the Sixties and Seventies, that was particularly true; with a few notable exceptions, you had this sort of *malaise* which not only suggested that this was the way comics were, but that was the only way comics *could* be. It wasn't until the underground movement started to point creators into different directions that you started to get the comic book renaissance—for want of a better word—that happened in the Eighties.

CBR: What conscious goals did you bring with you in deciding to work with various American publishers after your notable success with the British publications *2000 A.D.* (from 1977 to the present) and *Warrior* (1982–1985)?

MOORE: Well, since it was the work in *Warrior* that attracted the American publishers, I assumed that they wanted me to write stories that were as extreme. So I figured this was my opportunity to take these same radical techniques and approaches, and to utilize them in a much bigger country, with a much bigger audience. And therefore have a greater chance of substantially changing the way that comics were seen and perceived by the readers, the critics, and by the creative people working in them.

America was like a huge playground—full of all these great, quaint old characters that were left lying around by the publishers. And color! The idea of comic books in color was an incredible luxury to somebody who had worked their way up through British comics. The idea of telling stories that were longer than eight pages—that seemed incredibly luxurious!

There were all sorts of new possibilities in America. Working on *The Saga of the Swamp Thing*, for example, was an incredible experience. It was like having practiced swimming in the local municipal baths, and then being suddenly given the entire Atlantic Ocean to play in. All of a sudden I could start structuring stories in twenty-four-page lengths, which allowed me to do some fantastic things I never even thought of doing before—because the opportunity simply wasn't there. Beyond that, I could structure saga-like narratives that ran from issue to issue, which again gave me the opportunity to build up characters like never before. *Swamp Thing* was a great learning process; that was the comic which really took the manacles off me, to a certain degree.

CBR: Did you ever tailor your writing style on a project to fit the style of a particular artist?

MOORE: I think I've always done that. It's one of the skills which is difficult to explain or to teach anybody. The idea of working in comics, in a collaborative capacity. There's a certain quality of *empathy*—or something—which is almost intangible, but is still the most important factor that there is between writer and artist. When I was working, for example, with Dave Gibbons on *Watchmen*, I had to think my way into the sense of Dave's lines, into his sense of composition, into what sort of pictures I could imagine looking really good in a Dave Gibbons story. Consequently that allowed me to do things in *Watchmen* that I probably could not have done with any other artist.

That was for Dave Gibbons. Working with Steve Bissette, John Totleben, and Rick Veitch on *Swamp Thing*, what really kicked it into gear were these copious letters to Steve and John, and realizing that in their artwork there was this lavish, insane, phantasmagorical berserk psychedelic quality that could be brought to the comparatively staid adventures of Swamp Thing. I couldn't have done *Swamp Thing* with Dave Gibbons; Dave's style is so clean, it would have lost that beautifully rotten "messy" quality that perfectly summed up the overgrown, fetid beauty of the swamp. Just in the same way Steve and John and Rick could never have done *Watchmen*.

I was being inspired, in all of these cases, by the artist.

This is really a *major* difference between writing prose fiction and writing comics. There is something so solitary in writing prose fiction: you're creating a world entirely out of your own material. It's as rewarding in some ways, but it's . . . different. The aspect that I most enjoy working in comics is the meeting of minds and the meeting of sensibilities. It's like some kind of cultural sex for me; to grasp what someone else is feeling is thrilling in an intellectual and creative way. This cross-fertilization between different imaginations! And the key to making that work, in my own experience, is the empathy the writer has with the artist, of thinking in pictures that *they* might have created.

FROM *FROM HELL: VOLUME ONE* © 1993 BY ALAN MOORE AND EDDIE CAMPBELL.

Think less on tommorrow's work, boy, and more upon today's

The lord has his own plans for each of us, and 'tis vanity to speculate

The scriptures ...ung... The scriptures say "what doth the Lord require of thee, but to do justly, and hurp.. to love mercy, and to walk humbly with thy God?"

Yes, father

you are right.

UWP.

Father? Is it vanity to hope the Lord may choose for me a task most difficult?

No that would seem a worthy Christian attribute, so long as it were not for Glorys sake.

Oh no.

Though I should have a task most difficult, most necessary and severe, I should not care if none save I did hear of my achievement.

Only the Lord and I shall know

And that shall be sufficient

So the person that I'm working with shades every aspect of my scripts. They define to a large extent what I am doing.

CBR: In terms of "cultural sex" partners, didn't you take on a riskier group by engaging in *Lost Girls, From Hell,* and *Big Numbers*? In other words, wasn't this more risky, both creatively and financially, than going back and developing, say, new volumes of the *Watchmen*?

MOORE: No shit, Sherlock! [*Laughs*] Yes, these are the "high risk" projects! I've just put a condom over my word processor. [*Laughs*] But it's true. Yet I'm now going after more exotic flavors, and that's not said to the detriment of any of the people I've worked with before. But each of these new artists that I'm working with is a very extreme artist in his own way. All the artists I've worked with have had their own degree of extremity, but working with Mark Beyer on "The Bowing Machine" (*Raw*, Vol. 2 #3, 1991), that's about as extreme as it gets!

I mean, it's a way of extending myself. I tend to use artists, to some degree, as a series of weights for working out with. That's a clumsy metaphor, but it's something I'm very conscious of when I'm working with each different artist. Each one suggests different stories, different possibilities of language. What I have been looking for, and what I'm always looking for, is an edge to throw myself over. Too far . . . it's the only place to go! To seek out what seems to be the most extreme elements, and then try and stretch myself to the point where I can relate with it creatively—that's what keeps me going.

CBR: Then why did you choose to throw yourself off the edge in terms of renouncing your ever working again with the major comic publishers? You instead formed your own company, Mad Love, and went on to work with smaller, independent creator companies.

MOORE: The aesthetic decisions and the business decisions have always been connected in my career. Back when I was working for *2000 A.D.* and *Warrior*, there were no royalties at all, there was no creator's control of copyright. Now this is obviously not the best incentive to doing good work. As ridiculous as this might seem in retrospect, at the time DC was a much better proposition. Because at least they were giving creators royalties and even though they wouldn't allow you to own your own work, they were making noises and moves in that direction.

But the two seemed to go hand in hand: if you've got creative freedom—which is also a business consideration—then you're going to do better work. You're going to follow that extremist ideal I was talking about in aesthetic terms. I started by working for *2000 A.D.* and British Marvel. I then worked for *Warrior* because the business deals seemed to be more ethical, and because, hand in hand with that, there seemed to be more potential for creative growth. I went to work for DC for reasons that were very similar.

But eventually your ambitions outgrow the particular playpen that you're in. When you've had a taste of the satisfaction that comes with owning your own work, eventually you become less and less satisfied with work for hire! Less and less satisfied with just pouring your heart and soul into the bottomless pit of a corporation that doesn't really care about you a great deal.

After *Watchmen* I reached something of a turning point in my career. I mean, *how* do you follow *Watchmen*? It's a big problem. Do you do something that's an even more complicated superhero book? (Which I'm sure is what DC would have loved me to do.) Or do you do something that just repeats the Watchmen formula over and over again? Or do you do something else? And if you do something else—*what*?

It suddenly struck me that the topics about which I really wanted to write were quite . . . marginal subjects. [*Chuckles*] You know? Crime and murder. Sex and pornography. Normal life and normal people. And I couldn't see DC overly enthusiastic about a project like, say, *Big Numbers*. I imagine if I proposed it to them, they might have made some thoughtful cooing noises, and then gently suggested that I might be better employed doing another Batman graphic novel. I really couldn't see DC going for any of the more extreme ideas that I had.

So I figured the only real way that I could guarantee that I had the space to continue to expand creatively was to be in control—in a business sense—of the entire process. So that there was nobody above me who could say, "Well, we really don't feel this is going to be a very popular title. We'd rather you do superheroes." The only way I could see of getting that room was to enter into self-publishing and to align myself with other creative publishers.

CBR: Then what led you to returning to superheroes, specifically in your recent project for Image Comics, entitled *1963*?

MOORE: Besides the fact that Steve Bissette called and asked me?

[*Laughs*] But it's a number of things, not the least of which are the financial considerations. As has been pointed out, the subjects explored in *Lost Girls* and *From Hell*—Jack the Ripper, Alice in Wonderland in Austria in 1913, a shopping mall being built in Northampton—these are probably *not* the most commercial ideas I've ever had in my life! Now I've never been able to consider working again for DC or Marvel in any capacity since turning my back on them all those years ago. I will only work with creative publishers, and ones that will allow me to own my own work. And although my aesthetics are different than theirs, I admire what the people at Image are doing. They've shaken up the industry in a very brutal way, and I think probably shaken it up for the better.

But when they approached me, I didn't know whether I had any interest at all in doing superheroes again. I simply wouldn't do a superhero book again unless there was something in there that I could find interesting. Because even though I said money was a consideration, I have *never* ever done anything purely for money. You know? If I can't find a way to enjoy the project, then I won't do it.

Now this presented a problem in that after *Watchmen* and *Miracleman* I had become pretty thoroughly sick of superheroes. I had become particularly sick of the postmodern superheroes that followed in their wake. It seemed to me that postmodern comics were like viewing a distorted mirror at a fun fair, where you go in and see these grotesque-looking things, and you think, "My God, that's me!" That was the feeling I got reading some of these comics: I could see stylistic elements that had been taken from my own work, and used mainly as an excuse for more prurient sex and more graphic violence. I had essentially a nasty time getting through them. And you do get the impression of saying to yourself, "Oh, my God, I wanted to make comics a better place to visit."

But now everywhere I turn there're these psychotic vigilantes dealing out death mercilessly! You know? With none of the irony that I hoped I brought to my characters. And I felt a bit depressed in that it seemed I had unknowingly ushered in a new dark age of comic books ... You know? Where there was none of the delight, freshness, and charm that I remembered of the comics of my own youth. It struck me as a terrible shame.

CBR: So with *1963* you set out to recapture the charm that you found in the superhero comics of that period, a time that coincided with your own youth?

MOORE: What I enjoyed about comics as a youngster wasn't just that adolescent male power fantasy element. That's true to a degree, but they're not *just* boys' power fantasies. Sure, it would have been nice to turn into the Hulk if you were getting bullied, and I suspect that a lot of kids will admit to that element in the way they appreciated the comic books of their youth.

But more important than that, the biggest element for me was the world of *imagination* that comics opened up! It was not the fact that Superman could push planets around that impressed me, but that he had a Fortress of Solitude, and possessed a bottled city, and he could travel back and forth in time and get involved in all sorts of strange time paradoxes, and that the planet he came from had a gold volcano and a jeweled mountain. And this was incredible, fantastic stuff that took my mind into all sorts of interesting places! It was the same with the early Marvel Comics: it was the wonderful concepts, not the superhero's muscles, which gave me the biggest charge.

But when I look at postmodern comic books, I don't really see any of that "sense of wonder." I see it now as being largely replaced with wall-to-wall fight scenes between characters who have unlikely—and not terribly imaginative—powers.

There's also a question of morality here. I was talking to a friend recently, and we both came to the same conclusion. That, however silly it might seem, if I had to look back to the biggest single factor that shaped my moral code as a child, it wasn't my parents—who didn't give a great deal of moral instruction—it wasn't the school; it wasn't the church.

It was Superman.

Superman had a code of morals that was expressed repeatedly and quite clearly. It wasn't very sophisticated; it more or less amounted to, "Don't lie. Don't kill anybody. And always try to help other people out if they're in trouble." Which is naive and simple, but as a basic code of morality, it'll do until you can grow up and can shade in some of the more subtle areas. So that was true of me, and I think it was true for a lot of people in our generation; that we learned our morality from these simple, silly-ass superhero books.

Now I have to wonder, in a world of Punishers and Wolverines and Lobos, just what kids *are* learning today? That worries me! There is now this sort of nihilism in comics. Which is all right if you're a smart, cynical adult: you can chuckle at that violent behavior. But if you're a nine- or ten-year-old, I wonder what sort of values that opens up?

Particularly in a world which is already permeated with Arnold Schwarzenegger films, and tough killer commando movies? It just makes me wonder. So I basically decided it might be fun to attempt to recreate a more innocent age of comics, going back to 1963, which seems to me to be a vintage year. And to try and create a line of imaginary comics—as they would have been in 1963! With all that innocence, and all that naiveté intact.

I would also create the comics in a way that was consistent with the way that comics were created back then: rather than do a very detailed, and well thought out script, I would give the plot descriptions and panel descriptions to the artists, who would then draw the pages, and then I would dialogue them. Which is a very speedy way of working—and totally foreign to the way that I've worked before. *1963* has been a great deal of fun. It's given me a great burst of energy that has been very refreshing in the midst of my more demanding projects. It's a bit like customarily working in a symphony orchestra, but playing in a bubblegum band on weekends. And it's plugged me back in to some of the reasons why I became involved in comics in the first place.

CBR: Do you feel the potential of comics has yet to be fully realized?

MOORE: There is an *endless* amount of untapped potential in the comic medium. And the further I get into it, the bigger it seems. In just doing the first four or five issues of *Big Numbers*, I've managed to think of three or four entirely *new* things that have not been done in comics before. And this is just me—this is just *one* person following their own individual ideas. Yes, it gets progressively harder to think of new ways to use the language of comics, but that doesn't diminish in any way the fact that those new ways are still out there. I can easily imagine the younger talents who aren't so hollow and jaded as myself who will be able to unearth some real gems along the way.

I think there are possibilities for the comic medium that have yet to be *imagined.* Comics are an ancient language, going back as I said earlier to the Chinese ideograms, and what we're doing here is establishing the most basic grammar and vocabulary. I hope that later generations will be able to use this grammar and vocabulary to compose magnificent works. We've barely scratched the surface of what can be done! I mean, when you've got the whole world of words and pictures in conjunction to play with, then you've got *everything* at your disposal.

There is *nothing* that comics cannot do. There is nothing that has been attempted in any other artistic medium that comics could not, eventually, equal or better. It's up to the people who are alive at this time to explore the language as thoroughly as possible, to find their own themes, and to follow their own individual, quirky paths.

And follow them relentlessly.

At the house there's a new entourage and they're all going off to a Campaign for Nuclear Disarmament meeting.

Georgette gets changed

Won't you be too warm?

One has to suffer for these things.

Why so glum, Alec? Help yourself to some beer.

If we left you any.

Janey's making more beer. I feel that I've behaved badly so I run home some 3 or 4 miles to get the extra sugar that's needed.

So now we're in the pub.

Your letter made me angry

Alec, if you pursue Georgette you're headed for heartbreak.

You're underestimating me. I know I'll get nothing from Georgette. Alec loves Georgette, so he bought her a hamburger.

That's not love. I don't think you know what love is

You don't even know me. You've never tried to "touch" me...

I love Monet's Waterlilies but I know I can't take them out of the Tate Gallery.

13

EDDIE CAMPBELL
New Bottles, Vintage Wine

Since the mid-Seventies, Eddie Campbell has eloquently etched his fascination with the ebb and
flow of the human condition into the parameters of
countless comic book pages. Many of his tales are
peopled with the associates, friends, lovers—and
the occasional imaginary fellow traveler—in the
orbit of Campbell's pen-and-ink *doppelgänger*,
"Alec MacGerry." The sensitivity and candor of his
work breathes fresh air into the international comics
arena.

His travels have taken him from his Scottish homelands to the shores of
Brighton, England, and on to his current home in Queensland, Australia,
where the cane toads reign. Every step of the way, Campbell's comics told
his travels of the heart and mind, and the people—real and imaginary—
who crossed his path.

Campbell's unique comic tales first surfaced in the British "stripzines" (independent photocopy or small-press comics). His friends Phil Elliott and Ian
Wieczorek founded one of the earliest stripzines, *Elipse*, in the early Seventies,
and Campbell was on the scene with the creation of the most vital of the
self-published stripzines, *Fast Fiction*, in 1982. *Fast Fiction* became a catalyst
for a new generation of comic artists who began to create their own

photocopy comics. Campbell soon graduated to the pages of *Escape* and publishers like Harrier Comics, beginning his reach into international markets without ever compromising his own delicate and humane vision in the process.

The *Alec* stories (1984–88) remain his most personal and readily accessible body of work to date. *Doggie in the Window; Alec MacGarry Bares His Teeth—Among Other Things* (1986), *Alec: Alas, Poor Alec* (completed 1988, published by Eclipse Comics in *The Complete Alec* (1990)), and *Graffiti Kitchen* (Tundra Publishing, 1993) are mesmerizing meditations upon life, death, love, and sex worthy of Henry Miller.

In contrast to this remarkable body of work is the equally compelling *Deadface/Bacchus* series (from 1987 to the present), a twilight confection in which the surviving mythological Greek deities carry on with their squabbling and powerplays in the modern world as paranormal businessmen and superhuman barflies. Mention must also be made of his collaboration with British writer Alan Moore on the dark historical fiction *From Hell* (from 1989 to the present), along with an imposing multitude of collaborations, anthologies, and one-shots from a number of American and British publishers.

Moore once wrote of him, "Eddie Campbell thinks he can see across the world and hear babies sleeping, and I think he can, too."

We think he probably can, too.

COMIC BOOK REBELS: You're acclaimed, first and foremost, as a storyteller. What was the reason for your choosing comics as the medium to tell your stories?

EDDIE CAMPBELL: I *knew* that was going to be the first question! [*Laughs*] I don't believe them when people come out with a formalized reasoning for why they choose one medium over another. I think the apparatus is there, and you use it, you know?

CBR: You've reportedly stated that you're not all that keen on drawing; that if you could spend your days sitting in a pub telling your tales to strangers, that would be just as satisfying?

CAMPBELL: That's true. I think one of the greatest storytellers in the world is the Scottish standup comic, Billy Connelly. He just stands on stage and jabbers away for a couple of hours. He's a master of timing; it all seems to come out of him spontaneously. His material all seems to be unprepared, which is part of the art of storytelling, to make it *appear* so natural.

CBR: The same can be said for your comic work, which on the surface appears to be very organic and "unplanned."

CAMPBELL: Yes, which is kind of odd because my favorite kind of art, in the entire history of art, is classical Greek sculpture, you know? Which is the most formalized and impersonal form of art there is. See? I knew you were going to try and rationalize what I do!

CBR: Given your declared admiration for this formal, classical art, how do you compare it against your "deliberately unplanned" and "sketchy" approach to art?

CAMPBELL: Well, there's a classical discipline. A formal, organized discipline behind everything that I do. That spontaneity you see . . . it's a ruse! It's a game. Not only in the drawings, but in the actual telling of the stories. Even when I go off on a tangent, I know precisely what I'm doing. To use that "organic" metaphor, I suppose it's like exploring the branches of the same tree.

The thing that annoys me with comics nowadays is that everyone uses the same term, "storytelling," but it doesn't mean *telling a story.* You know what I mean? They use "storytelling" as short for "storytelling technique." Everybody's obsessed with storytelling technique, but the genuine art of telling a story has gone out the window! It's been lost.

CBR: Is that what you look for primarily when reading other comics? Those which have the ability to tell a real story?

CAMPBELL: I don't read a lot of other comics. I confess I'm becoming one of those boring old fogies who believes that the comics of today aren't as good as when I was a kid. And I read a lot of the Marvel Comics of the early Sixties, especially.

I used to look at *Nick Fury,* the way Steranko drew him, and noticed the trim and immaculately tailored suits that he would always wear. And I used to think, "One day I am going to get me one of those three-piece suits!" Now I pick up a new comic from Marvel, such as the first issue of *X-Factor,* and you know that in the entire comic there were only two ordinary, everyday people in suits! One of them was Nick Fury, and the other was the President of the United States! And the suits were horrendously drawn!

I mean, drawing a collar on a suit is very difficult, because it moves from one pictorial plane to another across the back of the neck. It's a very difficult thing to draw. Our generation of artists can't draw things like that. We can draw muscles upon muscles, but we can't draw a simple collar on a suit!

CBR: Perhaps, but you work with a number of talented creators whom you do respect and who do get you excited, such as Phil Elliott, Glenn Dacon, and Ed Fentus. How do you tailor your talents to work most effectively with these other stylists?

CAMPBELL: I'm kind of a Dr. Jekyll and Mr. Hyde. I don't have a single style. In fact, I have three styles. When I do my egocentric, auto-biographical comics, where I draw myself, and I am the most important figure in that universe. Then I'm doing this costume drama, this Victorian piece called *From Hell*, and I do that in this sort of old, turn-of-the-century pen technique. And then I do my *Bacchus* style, which is my attempt to go the superhero route, where people beat the shit out of each other, with muscles drawn upon muscles.

CBR: But when you work with another creator, you seem to tailor your talents specifically to match that particular project. It would appear you have a fourth, fifth, and sixth style by now.

CAMPBELL: Yeah, but I've kind of turned away from working like that. I don't work like that anymore. I don't collaborate any more, with the exception of *From Hell*, which was started four years ago. Now everything I do is done in my office here. And if somebody else works on it, it means they come in here to be my other pair of hands, because I find it too difficult to collaborate in the old sense anymore.

Claude Monet once said, "You can't paint a picture unless you have it in your head first." Do you follow me? Miles Davis once said, "I'm only playing the music that I'm hearing in my head." Which is constantly developing and running ahead of him, so he's chasing it, right? And while Miles Davis was making one album, he was already starting to hear the next one playing in his head. He hears it, and then he makes it concrete. He makes it exist. Just as Monet would see it in his head, then

Back in my little room I am only half aware of Jane telling Danny about my pal Harwood being a nihilist and they're disagreeing about the pronunciation.

Pages turning up like that has caused a sublimely mischievous idea to form in my noodle...

Next day I find that Georgette has become even more unreachable. She has an entourage now.

This young guy Gerald is a budding photographer and is now on the scene.

George has become his muse or something.

It is clear to me that rampant foolishness is to be the order of the day.

I will empty all the separate jars and bottles of my life into one big pot and cook them all up into a stew.

I'll take all the characters from my other book and put them into this one. It'll be a great big cross-over.

It's time to reintroduce the KING CANUTE CROWD.

he would paint it. The funny thing about this great Impressionist painter is that his work looks so spontaneous, as if he was making it up as he went along, dropping the paint on the canvas. But he was the one who said you cannot paint a picture unless it's already in your head first.

I mean, if I have a comic in my head, there's no point in my writing it down and sending it to somebody in another country! Which I have done in the past. Because the only way I can really explain to him the comic in my head is by drawing it for him, you know? At which point, why work with someone else? When I work with other people now I say right off, "Look, this is what I want. Can we do this?" If it's started, and it's not working, it isn't going the way I see it, I'll say, "Let's try it another way until we can get it right." But I enjoy working with other people because they can bring in the qualities that I haven't got to a project. Sometimes you see something in your head that you know to be beyond your own abilities, you know?

CBR: So you believe it makes more sense to work with someone else at that point rather than trying to expand your own talents?

CAMPBELL: Say you're making a movie, and you need someone to speak Italian in the movie. Rather than go out and learn Italian yourself, it's easier to hire someone who knows Italian and say to them, "Can you translate this into Italian?" You know what I mean? It's got to a point where it's simply too late in life to go out and learn each new discipline that you need to use on a project. It's easier to bring someone in who has that talent at the time you need it, because by then you're already on to something else where your strengths are needed. If I can compare my collaborations to music again, I guess you could say I'm the fellow who hears the music in my head, and employs others to help me orchestrate it. That's the way of putting it, yeah.

CBR: We understand you have someone who helps you with the perspectives on the buildings presented in *From Hell*?

CAMPBELL: Yeah, I've got a fellow who comes in on Mondays and does my perspectives. How it works is that I'll draw a fellow walking out of a building, but I don't draw the building! I've got a guy who comes in and draws the building. But he doesn't draw the bricks, because I've got a guy coming in on Tuesdays who draws the bricks! But then you get into demarcations disputes . . . ! [*Laughs*] Walt Kelly did a continuity once for his daily comic strip *Pogo* where there was this demarcation dispute about *breathing*. And he resolved the matter by having half the characters only breathe in, and the other half would only breathe out! Kelly was one of the great geniuses of the comic strip.

CBR: Some of your earliest work appeared in the underground publication *Fast Fiction*. Can you tell us something about those formative years?

CAMPBELL: There was something always going on in comics in England, but back then it was sort of a mainstream thing. Then *2000 A.D.* came about, and even though it was a daring and dramatic departure for a comic, it was still rehashing many of the old themes, and it was still a comic book company hiring people and assigning them various tasks, you know? It was still an *industry* that calculatedly produced a comic that became a popular sellout; that's how many of us perceived it.

I'm not saying I'm down on that, but I was doing comics that I had nowhere to go with them. I did a series of comics back in '78, '79, called *In the Days of the Ace Rock 'n' Roll Club*. They were great little stories, and they were genuine short stories that I thought, "One day there'll be an audience for these, but the time is not right." But in 1981 there were a lot of these dissident voices like myself hanging about, and a fellow called Paul Gravett organized a sort of outlet for all these mavericks. Because we had no markets then; we were sending the material to each other in the mail! Know what I mean? And what can you hope to do by sending your comics through the mail? You might have twenty friends who'll read your stuff through the mail . . .

But he organized an outlet where he put everyone in contact with each other. He called it the "Science Fiction Service," which was a brilliant idea, and it became sort of the basis for our New Wave movement. He didn't create the movement—it was already there—but it was just that before him everybody was laboring on their kitchen tables in obscurity. He was able to produce a regular bimonthly market for comics and collectors of this "junk." And it was completely against the whole mindset at the time of what comics were all about. Paul was very interested in what was happening with European comics, especially in France, and Italy, and even in Japan. When people need to know what's happening with comics in the rest of the world, they still go to Paul. Suddenly the whole operation acquired momentum, and this small press became much bigger than anything we'd ever imagined it would become.

Fast Fiction began in August of 1981, and by May of 1982 it already had become some sort of authority, where it bestowed recognition upon certain things, and became in itself a thing to be challenged or kicked over. But by May of 1982 Phil Elliott was producing a little science fiction magazine, which was just a little photocopy magazine of 500 copies. Basically it was me and Elliott turning in stories, with other people coming in and out. But the magazine eventually ran for twenty-four issues, I think. And it became like a roll call for anyone who did anything of value in the small press. If you had a collection of them, you could look through it and be surprised, "Oh, yeah—that's where he started . . . !" You know what I mean?

But when we were doing these little photocopy booklets, we were fighting against a *terrible* conservatism in the comics field. People would look at our photocopied efforts and say, "Oh, I'm not paying a dollar for that!" You know? "It's black and white!" So we'd do these crazy things like hand-color the covers! You know? We'd run off three hundred copies of these photocopied booklets, and we'd hand-color *all* of the covers! Just so we could be in good competition with the regular comics with the color covers! It was crazy!

I came across one of my little comics with the hand-colored cover the other day, which I originally sold for a dollar—fifty pence in England—and there they were at the San Diego comic book convention selling for twenty bucks! Four or five years after the event, after we'd made it, the fans now regard them as art objects. [*Laughs*] I suppose we could have pushed them as "art objects" in the first place, but we just wanted to find a way of selling two hundred for fifty pence!

CBR: You then did work for *Sounds*, a music magazine. Did that publication allow you to reach a much wider readership?

CAMPBELL: Me and Phil Elliott held down a spot in there for two years. Alan Moore had done for them a story called "The Stars My Degregation," which he won't allow to be reprinted anywhere. But Phil and I did a series we were both quite pleased with, and would be happy to see reprinted today. *Sounds* was a rock magazine, but we were doing things that had nothing to do with rock music—we were doing a very pure, kind of cartoon thing that had come out of the small press movement. But eventually we got clamped down on. After eight months the editor called us and said he didn't understand what we were doing—could we do a proper comic? So we switched to a horror story and did lots of lavatory humor. But even then he thought it was too intellectual.

CBR: You're presently best known for your *Alec* stories. Alec MacGarry seems to be your alter ego; just how autobiographical is the series?

CAMPBELL: My idea was always that comics was an art. An art like any other form of entertainment that should be out there, competing in the marketplace with every other form of art. I have in my files a review from an art magazine where *Alec* was reviewed among all these other forms of art, such as architecture, which was great! You know? And there it was, right against these other serious articles. On the other hand, I was on the radio—on an arts program—and some serious playwright was on before me, and he was asked about his themes and his techniques.

But they asked me, "What made you want to draw comics?"

Which is why I hate that question! Why does an interview always have to start with that: "What made you want to draw comics?" So from doing photocopied booklets to being interviewed on the radio talking about them was for me quite a journey.

CBR: The question remains: just how much of you is Alec, and vice versa?

CAMPBELL: Oh, *Alec* is the truth. The whole truth. But the truth encompasses many lies as well, as you know. Sometimes to get across the truth of the matter you have to lie a bit. What do I mean by that? I mean sometimes the concise use of symbols can do the job. You can sometimes throw the whole piece of business, because even though it's word for word the truth, you can get your whole message across with a symbol. Which may not be literally the way it happened, but it conveys the truth of the matter in a more concise and entertaining way. You haven't subjugated the honesty of what you are saying . . . you've merely changed its underpants. [*Laughs*]

CBR: When *Bacchus* first came out, it seemed a radical shift into fantasy from the stark realism we had been accustomed to through your *Alec* series. Why the leap into fantasy at this point?

CAMPBELL: There is sort of a connection there. I kind of simplified with this larger than life symbol the relationship I had already tried to depict in the word for word, truthful autobiographical stories. I took it and made those truths into these larger than life stories. On the face of it, *Bacchus* was supposed to be a superhero comic, but it became much more philosophical. Its original title was *Deadface*, but the paradox is that Bacchus, the god of wine, is this huge, life-affirming symbol.

But getting back to the storytelling business, I don't see a difference between the "real" and the "fantastic." To me, it's a qualitative difference, not a quantative difference. For some reason, people have thought I was "against" fantasy. But even in *Alec* there are little bites of fantasy running throughout.

There was also this idea that I was espousing "literalness." And I used to argue, "If your story is convincingly real, and you've got a guy sitting in a bar on a chair, you can draw the chair as a ripened tomato without breaking the spell! If you're clever enough in your narrative and your storytelling abilities, you can introduce completely off-the-wall, wacky, and fantastical elements into the picture. And the reader so wants the reality to remain intact, that he will dismiss it as an artistic bit of nonsense. Know what I mean?

CBR: Besides avoiding a distinction between realistic and fantastic fiction, you also seem to avoid consciously placing your work into any specific genre. Why is that?

CAMPBELL: I can answer it more simply by getting back to that business about seeing the picture in the head before you begin to paint. And I've never actually "seen" a comic or a story as genre. I've never seen a story in my head as "in genre." I think I've been lucky enough to be able to make a living by devoting my time, to a large extent, to just depicting the stories I see. Do you know what I mean? Here I've been thinking about how incredibly lucky I've been, and then I just remembered all those years when I nearly starved! [*Laughs*]

So the simple answer to this is that I don't think of genre, it just never comes into my head. Sometimes people call up and say, "Would you like to write this? Would you like to do that?" And I think, "Well, I could probably write a single issue of whatever it is, a licensed DC Comics character or whatever, but then I think to myself, "Oh shit! I'll probably have to read all the issues in which that character previously appeared!" And I couldn't force myself to do that! [*Laughs*] It would be terrible! Can you imagine having to read every back issue of *Wonder Woman* just so you could write an issue?

CBR: What was your motivation for finally moving over to the American publishers, such as Dark Horse, Eclipse, and Tundra?

CAMPBELL: Well, it's like water finding its own level. It seemed like the easiest route to go with these publishers. In an ideal world, I think I would just write a newspaper column every day, in the way it was done in the 1920s, know what I mean? Just fill up newspaper space with whatever was in my head that day. That would be my ideal. But I guess it's easier working with these new comic book publishers than trying to change the newspaper industry.

CBR: Out of curiosity, what kind of comic book industry does Australia support?

CAMPBELL: Australia has *no* comic book industry. One way of explaining my situation is to state that you wouldn't believe how good my assistants are. Most artists' assistants are there just to sharpen your pencils. Yet because there is no work here, I get people drawing my backgrounds who are extremely clever and competent people. People keep trying to do magazines, and for some reason they just don't work. Australia is very good for political cartoons, however. And there is a great tradition of cartooning, leaning heavily towards political cartooning. It's gotten to such a way that if you say you're a cartoonist here, people will automatically say, "Oh! Can you do me a sketch of the prime minister?" Most people simply don't understand the concept of comics as comic books here. The newspapers are filled with the American comic strips. In fact, they think most of the strips are Australian; the average citizen really thinks *Peanuts* is Australian. I'm sure he does. And the American comic strips *are* better, so they remain in power.

But there is no industry here; there's nowhere for anyone local to go. Last year I made my income in five different currencies, including Swedish and Spanish. But I only made $200.00 from working in this country—and that was by doing a lecture at the nearby university.

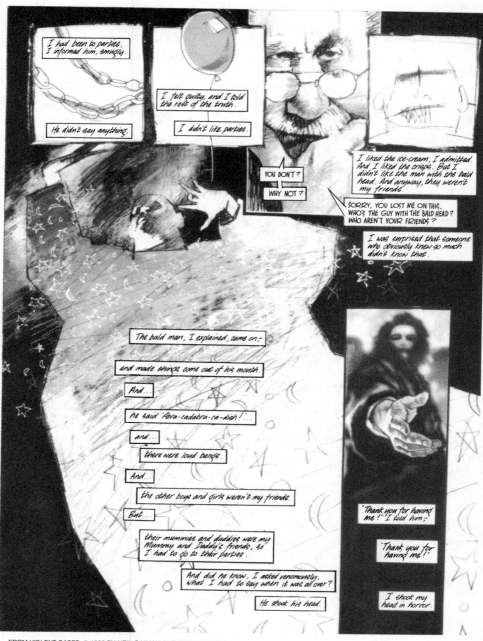

FROM *VIOLENT CASES*. © 1993 BY NEIL GAIMAN AND DAVE MCKEAN.

14

NEIL GAIMAN
A Man for All Seasons

Most of the creators identified herein as "comic book rebels" have bucked the status quo of how comic books are published and the role creative people are relegated to in the traditional business structure of the industry. Yet Neil Gaiman continues to regularly work with established publishers like DC Comics. How, then, is he a "rebel"?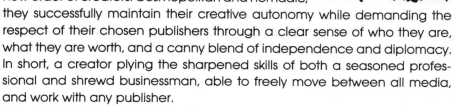

Gaiman was chosen as being representative of a new order of creators. Cosmopolitan and nomadic, they successfully maintain their creative autonomy while demanding the respect of their chosen publishers through a clear sense of who they are, what they are worth, and a canny blend of independence and diplomacy. In short, a creator plying the sharpened skills of both a seasoned professional and shrewd businessman, able to freely move between all media, and work with any publisher.

Born in 1960 in Portchester, England, and growing up in Sussex, Gaiman left school purposely to become a writer. His first professional work in the early Eighties was as a journalist, meeting and interviewing many authors and cartoonists whose work he admired. Alan Moore showed him the rudiments and structure of how comic scripts were crafted, and in short order he chose to abandon his early company-owned comics work to collaborate with artist Dave McKean on their first graphic novel, *Violent Cases* (Escape, Titan, 1987; reissued in color by Titan/Tundra, 1991).

Soon after, Gaiman and McKean completed the painted comic *Black Orchid* (1988) for DC, prompting an invitation to write a monthly title for the company. Resurrecting the name of a character created for DC by Joe Simon and Jack Kirby in the Forties—but completely creating his own incarnation rooted in the Dream-lord of myth and folktales—*Sandman* was launched in 1988 and continues as one of the finest mainstream comics ever created. He was Alan Moore's choice to continue *Miracleman* (Eclipse, from 1990 to the present), and his other comics projects include a number of short tales for anthologies like *Taboo* (SpiderBaby/Tundra), and the graphic novels *Signal to Noise* (Gollancz, 1991, U.S. edition from Dark Horse), *Mr. Punch* (Gollancz, 1993), with Dave McKean, and *Sweeney Todd*, a work in progress with artist Michael Zulli. Outside the industry, he has authored or coauthored several books, including the best-selling collaborative novel with Terry Pratchett, *Good Omens* (1990). He is presently developing a television series for England's BBC–2.

So how is he a comic book rebel? Gaiman grew up seeing how previous generations—and his own peers—allowed themselves to be badly used by the industry. Along with others of his generation, he is determined to take better care of himself. Just consider *Sandman*, which is owned under work-for-hire law by DC Comics. Gaiman's accomplishments and negotiations after the first year of its run led to DC's granting an historically unprecedented (and retroactive) creative coownership and share of the character and title, including all licensing and foreign sales—rights and revenue DC had always denied creators. Having already alienated key creators like Alan Moore, who had at one time earned considerable money and prestige for the company, DC has finally begun to realize it is in their own best interest to nurture better relations with certain creators. Very quietly, a revolutionary change in how business is done has occurred, a vital precedent set for this and the succeeding generations to come. While working within the existing system, Neil Gaiman continually expands the possibilities of both the industry and the medium.

COMIC BOOK REBELS: What were the building blocks as a reader that brought you to comics as a creator?

NEIL GAIMAN: The main one was that I never discriminated—in the racial sense of the term—between comics and anything else I read. I was a voracious reader as a kid; I read anything and everything. And one of the things I read was comics. I couldn't understand why there was any kind of prejudice against them; why we weren't allowed to bring them to school; why was it something everyone sort of frowned on? Books were considered cool, and yet there was as much thought and artistry in a lot of the comics that I was reading—some of Archie Goodwin's work, some of the early DC horror comics. So I never discriminated; I never felt that comics were in any way a ''lesser'' medium. They seemed to me a *more* exciting medium: I always figured I would be a writer when I grew up, and one of the things I always wanted to write was comics. And here I am.

CBR: With your ability to now pick and choose between various mediums of prose—from short story to novel to screenplay—why are you still apparently most enamored with this medium?

GAIMAN: As a creator, I get more of a buzz from comics than I do from anything else. I cannot go back and look at a short story or a novel that's come out with pleasure. Rather I look at it and think, ''Oh God, I should have fixed that.'' Whereas I can look at a comic I've done and get a real buzz off it and have a real feeling of pride. It's always a feeling of surprise to me when something that I wrote as a script comes out and it actually *works*. And it's a very pleasant surprise because I didn't really do it—all I ever did was *write* it. Knowing that the script for a comic is *not* the comic. The comic is the comic.

CBR: *Violent Cases* and *Signal to Noise* are driven by memories and meditation, *Sandman* by dreams, and even your work on the superhero title *Miracleman*, in a genre traditionally composed of larger-than-life actions is by nature intimate and reflective. Do you find comics an inherently introspective medium for storytelling?

GAIMAN: I don't think comics are an introspective medium. *They are a medium.* That's all. But, by nature, I *am* an introspective writer. My stories tend to be as much about what goes on inside people as what goes on outside people. I don't want to sound naive, but I'm telling *my* kind of stories.

CBR: But don't you consciously reject the traditional comic book exploitation of action and violence in your work?

GAIMAN: *Black Orchid* is very much a conscious rejection of the traditional approaches to these themes. In *Black Orchid* I wanted to do a pacifist fable in which acts of violence did occur, but were unpleasant—a fable in which meditation and beauty played a very important part. *Black Orchid* was sort of a look at all the things I *didn't* like in comics, and then do the kind of comic I would like to be out there.

In a completely different sense, it was the same reason I did *Violent Cases*. *Violent Cases* was something we did for people who don't read comics; *Black Orchid* was something that we did for people who do. But having said all that, I don't think anything I've done since then has been done as a "reaction to" what's out there. What's been done since then has been done mostly as a combination of terror and desperation to find the way to the next panel or to the next word or to the end of that story. And there was never anything in *Sandman* where I said, "Okay, now I'm going to do a comic book like nobody else has ever seen!" It was much more of, "Okay, *that's* where the story went," so I followed.

I figured sooner or later DC would turn around and say, "You know, you really can't do that," and they never have.

CBR: You're currently best recognized by the public as the writer on *Sandman*. Considering you own most of your comic book material, why did you initially agree to work on a character you did not create?

GAIMAN: But *Sandman* very much *is* my own creation. Is it my own ownership? No, that's due to strange antediluvian business practices of a gigantic Engulf & Devour style corporation. But is it my own creation—sure! The idea that I'm probably best known for it has more to do with the fact that one gets known for the largest and most easily followable body of work. And if you line it up against everything else I've done, *Sandman* is very obviously the largest body of work.

CBR: You've said before that *Sandman* for you is a finite story. How is DC handling that, since comic book companies never allow a commercially successful character to be purposely taken out of circulation?

GAIMAN: This has been already dealt with, pretty much to everyone's satisfaction. About two years ago, I raised the issue with my editors at DC, and each of them went pale and said, "Well, this has never been done before, um, maybe, no, um . . ." But they've had a chance to let the notion sink in, and now realize that when I'm done with *Sandman*, that *Sandman* is done. But just because it may be the end of *Sandman* as a monthly comic book, it does not mean—as far I'm concerned—the end of Sandman. There are stories outside of the monthly continuity that I would quite like to do. There's a story that begins before *Sandman* #1, which would be the storyline for *Sandman* #0. There're a number of myths and legends I want to write that I'll probably do in a few years time. So there are a number of *Sandman* stories yet to be done. Basically, I've agreed to come back to the character so long as DC leaves it alone in the meantime.

CBR: Any downside to the acclaim that *Sandman* has brought to you? Creators often get pigeonholed to keep working on the same series, or at least remain in the same genre.

GAIMAN: I don't know; there is a level that I tend to get pigeonholed as a horror writer. But, then again, anybody who knows anything about my body of work knows that isn't *all* I do. And *Sandman* isn't even particularly horror. So I can't really think of any way it's affected me adversely. It generates an interesting body of fans, ninety-nine percent of whom are quite wonderful. And one percent of whom take it all a little too far and assume that I am privy to a body of wisdom denied to the commonality of mortals. Now that's a little difficult to deal with . . .

CBR: You've worked with an impressive procession of artists—particularly on *Sandman*—but your most frequent collaborator is Dave McKean. What is the bond, and how do you work together?

GAIMAN: Dave is one of my best friends in the world, and simply put, a remarkable artist. He's also a remarkable writer, as his own series *Cages* demonstrates. It's been a very interesting and rewarding relationship; comics is just one of the many things we do, and there are things we do apart. We work with other people, but we still ring each other up every day. I love the fact his mind works differently from the way mine does. He sees things I wouldn't see and I tell him things he wouldn't think of. By now, we must have worked in every conceivable way that's possible to work in collaboration.

With *Violent Cases*, I wrote it essentially as a short story and handed it over to him and said, "Okay, now run with it." With things like "Hold Me" [*Hellblazer* #27], or the story I wrote for *Outrageous Stories from the Old Testament*, they were written as formal scripts. You know, "Page one, panel one." While *Black Orchid* was scripted like a movie, and *Signal to Noise* was written in some strange bastard form that only myself and McKean could understand a word of. The script would be completely meaningless to anyone else, because they would ignore the fact that we'd been talking on the phone about this for a month and a half, and are, in a way, telepathic.

It's a relationship in which we trust each other implicitly. That's why I love working with Dave on the covers for *Sandman*. I trust him. What he wants to do is okay by me.

CBR: You mentioned *Violent Cases* being written in short story form. Any plans of adapting your short stories or novels into comic book form? Clive Barker, for example, has done quite well with the adaptations of his prose work into the comics medium.

GAIMAN: Mostly I would look at the material and say, "Well, I already wrote it once. You know? Why should I write it again?" If somebody came to me and said, "We would like to adapt *Good Omens*," I would say, "Okay, here it is. Go do it. Have fun! Send me the comics when they come out."

I'm not convinced that you can simply transliterate something from one medium to another. I remember when I was watching the stage play adaptation of *Violent Cases*, which was incredibly faithful—and didn't work. The dramatic highs and lows were all in the wrong places. They took the words of the comic book, but in terms of theater, the one bit of theater magic they did was during the sequence where the character is talking about the wonderful light in the sky. And at that point the director flooded the stage with this wonderful light. Which means that became the central image, and so became the center of *Violent Cases*— which it isn't! So the stage adaptation became kind of mushy and soft-centered, and the center in *Violent Cases* is about Al Capone beating these guys to death with a baseball bat while a birthday party's going on, which is something which was covered in two lines of dialogue on the stage—pretty much as a throwaway. It was at that point I realized that faithful adaptations very often miss something.

You need to recreate your story, you need to retell it.

What is interesting is that I did "A Murder Mystery" for the publication *Midnight Graffiti*, as a short story. And about twenty-five percent of the people who read it noticed that there was one incredibly obvious story, and beneath it, one much, much less obvious story going on at the same time. And a lot of people don't even notice that there's anything beneath the surface story to read! Whereas I know that if I did it as a comic, there would be two or three little visual clues running through it, which would have meant that perhaps ninety-five percent of the readers would have picked up on the other story.

That's why I find comics so interesting. The way that people read comics and the way they read prose is a different experience. I believe a lot of people don't read prose with the amount of attention and effort that they give to comic books. In a comic book they will read *every* picture, and *every* word, and be forced by the juxtaposition to look at how these things relate to each other.

CBR: What was the experience of adapting *Good Omens* into a screenplay? Was that an enriching experience?

GAIMAN: Not particularly, for a number of reasons. First time we tried to make the book into a ninety-minute movie, and it didn't fit. You remember the old story about the guy who goes into the tailor to be fitted for a suit? And the tailor fits him really weirdly, so the suit hangs on the guy with the arms being four or five inches too long? So the tailor says to him, "Just raise your arms." And then the guy says, "Well, look at the way the back hangs." So the tailor says, "Fine, just curve your back and hunch over." And then the guy complains, "Well, look at these trousers!" The tailor says, "Fine, just lean that leg forward." Finally the guy walks outside, looking like Quasimodo, and this man comes up to the guy and demands, "Who's your tailor?" And the guy asks, "Why do you want to meet my tailor?" So the man says, "If he can fit somebody like you, then he can fit *anybody!*"

Which is sort of like the process of writing a film script from a novel. You're chopping off limbs, and trying to put things in that fit. So that aspect of it wasn't a particularly pleasant experience.

CBR: In other words, "Screenplay by Procrustes."

GAIMAN: Exactly! On the other hand, it *was* a pleasant experience to take everything that I've learned from doing these adaptations of *Good Omens*—the one I did with Terry Pratchett, and the one I did on my own—and using it for developing this TV series for the BBC. It has the working title of *The Underside*. So that was very interesting because I was working on something that was *meant* to be filmed, and meant to have actors floating around a sound stage. And I could do all sorts of neat things that I never would bother doing in comics. For one thing, rather than an artist drawing word balloons, here I could see actors speaking my words, and using their own expressions.

CBR: You touched earlier upon the concept that people literally have to read comic books more intensely than prose. In what sense?

GAIMAN: People skip when they read prose. People skip words, they skip pages, sometimes they skip thoughts. Or they flip through pages. Or they read it faster and less attentively than they read other sections. A writer has no control over how somebody reads. In comics, you have a lot more control over the experience of reading. Over what and how the person reading it reads. You are doling out pieces of information to them with an immediacy that they otherwise might not have.

CBR: You often draw upon world mythologies to either deliberately dissect them, and/or build upon them. Do you have a conscious game plan for using mythologies in the comic medium?

GAIMAN: No. I remember speaking to a woman who had been a friend of Joseph Campbell, and she said that Campbell believed that super-heroes are the mythologies of the twentieth century. I don't actually think they are. Mainly because they don't have stories attached to them—they are simply characters. You've got this strange division in twentieth century mythology right now, in which you've got stories floating around with no people attached, like the urban legends: the vanishing hitchhiker, the death cars. And you have characters like Tarzan and Superman and Batman—but with *no* stories.

I think all I wanted to do was to create people with stories.

I love and am fascinated by religion. And I love and am fascinated with myths. I love and am fascinated with history. So all of these things come out in my fiction. Were I someone interested in physics, hard science, and bioengineering, you'd be getting hard science fiction from me. But those are the subjects which fascinate and obsess me: myth-ologies; how people see the world, how the world sees people; what stories people create to allow them to cope with and interpret the world. Myths are almost like the rules of the game. They tell you rules and truths, even if the truths are not necessarily what they ought to be. Which is the same function that has evolved for the urban legends.

Myths are my favorite subject. I think if I wasn't writing comics there probably wouldn't be a career for me. Unless somebody came up with Personal Religion Designer. You know—people would come up to me and they'd say, "Hi. I'd like something that was strong in the sin department. I'd like a whole pantheon, and I'd like really neat holy days, and a great creation myth." And I'd say, "Okay, that'll be $20,000 and five percent of your poorbox takings." I could do that.

CBR: In *Violent Cases* and the serial killer story in *Sandman* you explore violent American lore, while in *Mr. Punch* and *Sweeney Todd* you draw from murderous archetypes of European folklore, as if exploring both sides of the same dark street of human nature. A darker side than *Sandman* chooses to explore.

GAIMAN: Well . . . yes. [*Pauses*] *Sandman* is an entertainment. It's a delightful entertainment, even though I've had to work harder and longer and it's given me more headaches than anything else I've had to do. But I think it's something to do with choosing your targets, who your audience is. And yes, my audience is me. That is, at the end of the day, the person I'm writing most to please is myself.

But *Sandman* represents to some extent my preoccupation and fascination with America, with a sort of mythic take on American cities and institutions. The New York in *Sandman* is probably not the real New York, but the one I remember seeing on my first day there. With these magical manholes spouting steam, and this mad old woman rushing past me going "Fuck! Fuck! Fuck! Fuck! Fuck!" And standing before these buildings that just went up forever . . .

Violent Cases was a way for me to talk about America as well as violence. It germinated from the fact that a lot of the incidents in the first few pages are, in effect, true. It is quite true that my father sprained my wrist when I was about four, grabbed my arm trying to get me to go to bed and something went. He took me to a gentleman who, I was informed a few years ago, had been Al Capone's osteopath. That much is true. But other than that, the rest is not. Beyond that, I've always been fascinated by America. I always figured America was kind of like Oz—it was a country where, for only ten dollars, you could buy your own submarine and set it up in your bedroom! I knew we didn't have anything like that in England, so America has always been a "myth" that I've been fond of, and a myth I like building on and newly creating.

Your statement about there being a difference between my American work and my British work is partly to do when you think of the old saw that in England a hundred miles is a very long way, and in America a hundred years is a very long time. I have this theory that you can find anything in America. Absolutely *anything*. You just have to drive far enough. Sooner or later you'll find the guy with the seven-foot-high ball of string. Or the guy who makes furniture out of cheese in his garden. You just have to go far enough.

In England, you just have to look far enough back. And whatever you're looking for is going to appear sooner or later. So *Mr. Punch* and *Sweeney Todd* are looking back, if you will. It's significant that in *Violent Cases*, the osteopath character is European. He went to Chicago, and then he came back. In *Mr. Punch*, you're looking again at a childhood incident that happened to me around the age of seven or eight, partly real, partly imaginary, built up from family myth and from the inside of my head, and from Punch and Judy.

The patterns in *Mr. Punch* go back to the medieval mummers' plays and possibly before. It's buried in that. *Sweeney Todd* goes back to the mythical founding of London. That is the starting point for *Sweeney*, to some extent where the story will lead and end. Someone once explained about the "desks" of London, saying, "Well, about twenty feet down are Roman times." It's true: civilization *is* lower. You can calculate the time periods from the strata, how the ground has risen and so forth. *Sweeney Todd*, and to some extent *Mr. Punch*, involve just getting in there with our spade, and digging in particularly bloody ground.

CBR: How do you think your work in comics has changed the field?

GAIMAN: There is a level of work being done today that is more graphic in violence and sex. Yet I don't think that has very much to do with anything truly significant; it's a superficial "pushing of the envelope." The only way I can really reply is to remember what it was like when Alan Moore was doing *Swamp Thing*, and that was the mythical archetype around which *everything* revolved, coming out of the monster cycle. And you look at the comics that never quite got into it even that far. Yet, for example, there were no gay characters in *Swamp Thing*. There were no nipples, as I recall. Now mainstream comics have both. But these days, somewhere in all that, we've since come to think we have done something.

I think *Sandman* #6 to some extent is a watershed. Because it went farther in terms of extreme and graphic horror and sex than anything anybody had ever done previously in comics that I can think of. *Sandman* #8 was a watershed because it went farther in "nothing happens in this issue" than anybody had ever done in mainstream comics to date! But other than that, I don't know. I can't see a huge influence that I've had on the field. I confess that if I have had an influence, it's probably not anything you'll see for at least ten years. Well, maybe eight years . . .

But what I'm now interested in is the thirteen to fifteen year olds, who are reading their *Sandman* and *Black Orchid*, and who are sitting in class and arguing with their teachers. Saying, "Look, look—see this? This is literature! It's every bit as good as the literature you've been teaching us! When I grow up, this is what I want to do for a living."

CBR: Which of your series are you personally most satisfied with?

GAIMAN: I have individual favorites. One of my favorites is *Miracleman* #19, the Andy Warhol issue. And *Miracleman* #22, which ties earlier episodes together. I love *Sandman* #14, "Midsummer's Night Dream," because that was such hard work. And I'm really proud of it. I'm proud of the fact you can't see me with my desk, covered with tiny pieces of paper, trying to keep the action backstage, frontstage, back of the audience, front of the audience, and the play, all moving along in three dimensions, and getting it all down saying everything I have to say. I'm terribly proud of *Signal to Noise*.

CBR: Any major encounters with censorship along the way?

GAIMAN: No, not really. I had one script about a serial killer in *Sandman* where I was asked to change a McDonald's into a Burger Joint. Things like that. I was told I couldn't use the word "masturbation" in my serial killer script. Having said that, I probably could use the term today. But I have been relatively uncensored in the industry.

There *was* one story I decided not to write. It would have been sort of a little complement to "Dream of a Thousand Cats." It would have been a story about fetal dreams. It would have made a lovely story. Had it only been published in England, where abortion is not really an issue, I would have quite happily written it with no problems. But I chose not to write it, because I suddenly thought there would be some fifteen-year-old girl who's been raped and wants an abortion. And somebody would come up to her and show that story, and say, "How can you even *think* of getting an abortion after you read that story?'' So I decided not to write it, which in a way tears me apart.

I know I had enough people come up to me and say that *Sandman* #8 got them over the death of their child, or the death of a best friend or someone like that. But you know that your stories *can* change people's minds, and hearts. So that was a case in which I decided to censor myself; I didn't want to be responsible for the consequences of a living soul. But for the most part the censors leave me alone, for reasons not adequately explained.

Sweeney Todd is about Manners, and Mirrors, and Meat. It's about razors, and women, and men. It's about death, and about London.

It's about the past, and about the legacy from the past that we carry with us forever.

You never know what you'll find when you go looking for something. *Sweeney Todd* began for us as a small, elegant chance to retell a familiar tale, and has grown and shifted with each new jigsaw piece until now it squats monstrous and dark and still, waiting to be told.

FROM *CAGES*. © 1993 BY DAVE MCKEAN.

15

DAVE MCKEAN
Citizen in a Village of Endeavor

Though British comics enjoyed the pioneering color work of artists like Frank Hampson (painting the adventures of *Dan Dare* in *The Eagle* throughout the Fifties), the American comic book industry rarely moved beyond the parameters of the cheaply printed four-color comic book format until the past decade. Painted comic book covers were *de rigueur* for some publishers, but the narrative form was limited by the comic book printing pro-cess itself. Everything changed with the importation of the lush European color graphic albums and the emergence of full-color work by Richard Corben and others in the underground comix. The mainstream comic book publishers' tentative adoption of more expensive (and expansive) printing methods allowed painted comics to proliferate in the Eighties, wherein artists like Bill Sienkiewicz, Jon J. Muth, and others further defined and refined the raw potential.

British artist Dave McKean is a prominent member of this current generation of comic artists working in the industry at a time when experimentation with the printed medium can be almost taken for granted. Painting, collage, constructions, sculpture, and more can be wielded with a sense of abandon that was unimaginable to prior generations of comic book artists, and

McKean's first published comics work proved he was one of the most imaginative and facile practitioners of the expanded palette.

His striking painted comics work with author Neil Gaiman on *Violent Cases* (Titan Books, 1987; U.S. edition 1991, Tundra Publishing) and *Black Orchid* (DC Comics, 1989) and with writer Grant Morrison on the best-selling Batman graphic novel *Arkham Asylum* (DC Comics, 1989) set new standards for illustrative graphic novels—standards which McKean questions and, in many cases, rejects in his subsequent work. The most seductive printing and painting techniques are secondary to the *heart* of the work itself, and McKean knows this. Uninterested in simply applying his talents to a procession of popular comic book characters, McKean has chosen instead to build upon the challenging and wholly original *Violent Cases*. His collaborations with Neil Gaiman have continued, yielding *Signal to Noise* (serialized in *The Face*, June–Oct. 1989; revised U.K. book edition from VG Graphics, 1992, U.S. edition from Dark Horse, 1993) and a new graphic novel, *Mr. Punch*, along with the occasional short comic narrative.

Compelling as his work with Gaiman is, it is McKean's own synthesis of his writing and art in the ten-issue series *Cages* (Tundra Publishing, 1990 to the present) that ranks him with the most adventurous and distinctive creators working in English-language comics today. McKean unveils the lives of the tenants of a London apartment building in a beautifully orchestrated tapestry of the mundane and ethereal, realized throughout with an eye and ear for character both loving and wryly sardonic. Among the many creation myths that frame *Cages* is the statement, "If you overrefine, you get lost in the music. If you underrefine, you get lost in the experience. Either one results in going away from who you really are."

It is clearly a credo Dave McKean lives by.

COMIC BOOK REBELS: Does your work as a freelance commercial illustrator and artist doing book covers, record and disc jackets, and so on, give you an anchor for your work in comics?

DAVE MCKEAN: I always like just doing "stuff"—all kinds of stuff. Some of it is music, some of it is writing, or painting, drawing comics, whatever. It all just sort of filters out and finds its place roughly.

One of the nice things about doing a lot of illustration work is, I don't feel the need to do illustrations in comics anymore. I *love* illustration. I love the traditions of it and a lot of illustrative work; I'm not sure if it's really appropriate for the comics work I've done. For the covers, maybe, because that's an illustration, but not necessarily for the actual storytelling.

I dearly love illustration and want to continue doing it, so the fact I can do record covers is a nice way of satisfying those urges, without having them slop over into the comics. The one thing comics hasn't got is a soundtrack. I still play a lot of music and want to keep that going, and doing record covers is tremendous for that, it's my favorite kind of illustration work. Even if I hate the music. I can still respond to it somehow; I always get a lot of heavy metal bands, and I'm not a heavy metal fan, but if you whap it up to eleven on the hi-fi and do a painting, you get a response. You certainly do a painting that you wouldn't have done, and that's great.

CBR: Do you consider yourself part of an artistic movement, in the classical sense of the term?

McKEAN: Probably not in the way that you mean. There's a collection of work that doesn't really include any comics that I've seen, but it's a lot of different work: some filmmakers, some illustrators and painters, animators, and music, all very much influenced by each other, that feed off each other. It comes from a few key people. I don't feel like I'm a part of that yet, because I haven't been at this very long, but I really feel a great affinity with that. Every time I see somebody who is a part of that world, I can recognize it and feed off that.

Certainly animators like the Brothers Quay and Jan Svankmajer, filmmakers like [Andrei] Tarkovsky and [Werner] Herzog, a lot of great poster designers in Poland and Czechoslovakia—really, from the 1900s onward, you can trace this remarkable stream of work. I mean, [artist Egon] Schiele is a great guiding light, as is a composer named Arvo Part; Tarkovsky certainly is. There's a sax player called Jan Garbarek who comes from Norway, and he says—it's a lovely quote, it's my favorite, he says it well—that his work is part of a village of endeavor, but the village is scattered geographically all over the world. It's an aesthetic community of people that recognize each other from this small village.

CBR: Doesn't your affinity with that "village of endeavor" allow it to finally manifest itself in comics?

McKean: A little, yes. Certainly people like Lorenzo Mattotti, a wonderful Italian artist who recently did *L'Homme à la Fenêtre* [*The Man in the Window*, 1992], José Munoz, people like that. Over here there's Kent Williams and one or two others. But they're just scattered around the place, from all over.

There're a number of things I admire very much, which are not so much influential—they just give me a kick in the bum, really, make me get on and get my thoughts in order. Things like *Raw* and [Art] Spiegelman's work—while admiring it like anything, though. I don't really relate to it very closely because it very much comes out of the American underground, cultivated by the Manhattan art scene, neither of which I have anything to do with at all. I'm not of an age where underground comix meant anything to me and I don't live in America.

CBR: Do you maintain personal contact with the artistic community you *do* feel a part of?

McKean: Oh, certainly. I'm friends with Mattotti, and Munoz I see occasionally, usually in Europe. Kent Williams, [George] Pratt, Jon [Muth] and that bunch I see and talk to all the time, and the Spanish guys like Raul Fernandez and Federico del Barrio and like that. There's a little group of artists out of Madrid who're part of a magazine called *Medios Revueltos*, a great bunch. There's the *Mocha* group out of Belgium, again a great bunch.

There're these little groups of people, often almost self-publishing or scraping away, trying to get their books into print, and occasionally they'll have a run. *Medios Revueltos* got backing from the Spanish government, so they managed to get six issues out and a special, then the government changed and it all collapsed and they're back to scraping around to get published again, but that seems to be the way of things. There's enough around to keep things bubbling away. Until recently in America, it seemed to be bubbling away, but it seems to have gone off the board a bit—it's a cyclical thing.

CBR: Do you see anything presently galvanizing or focusing that body of work?

McKean: I hope it's not just going to "bubble away." It's such hard work, apart from anything else, just constantly starting from scratch again and trying to get things off the ground. I'm hoping that the

FROM *CAGES*. © 1993 BY DAVE MCKEAN.

interest from book publishers and the interest from book stores may build bridges between this odd little goldfish bowl world of comics and out into a wider audience. It has happened in a few countries in Europe much more than America and England. Hopefully, we'll get to that cross-pollination. Certainly, *Raw* is a great gauntlet thrown down to everybody.

CBR: *Violent Cases* was your first published work. How did that project come together?

McKEAN: Neil [Gaiman] and I were both doing strips for a comic that never happened, called *Borderline*. It would have been an anthology of about five or six books originally, with a major strip in the front of them and one in the back. I was writing and drawing two strips for that, and Neil was writing three strips, I think, all of which collapsed. As we got going, talking to distributors, it seemed that anthologies were not the right way to go.

By then, Paul Gravett's *Escape* magazine in England was the real focus of an alternative way of doing things. England's really been overshadowed by *2000 A.D.*, the whole *Judge Dredd* thing, which I was never into; that was the way to get in, the only place to be, the only place to go (Marvel U.K. doesn't really count). *Escape* was a great, enthusiastic focal point. Paul Gravett is just infectious. So, we were going to do a five-page strip for *Escape*, and it turned into a forty-four page novel, *Violent Cases*.

CBR: *Violent Cases* was unusual in that it was a reverie, a meditation, though its title and "gangster" subject matter suggested a more traditional use of the medium to portray action and violence. That introspective quality made it a revelation to many readers.

McKEAN: It always struck me as odd, that, really. Leaving aside (you can't really leave it aside, but *try*) what has been done in comics so far, the concentration on action-adventure, what you've actually got—what the form *is*—would lead you completely in the opposite direction.

If you were actually going to produce something that would use the form to its best advantage, it would be a one-to-one experience. It's very much like a novel in that sense. It's not like sitting in a movie theatre, where you're hit with the experience. Everyone laughs together and it's a big community, which would lead you in the direction of trying to elicit even bigger laughs and bigger frights.

Comics is a very intimate, one-to-one experience. It's even more intimate than a novel, inasmuch as a novel has no visual intimacy, it's cold, hard text on paper. What could be more intimate than the one-on-one experience of a drawing? It's very much like a postcard or a letter or something like that, it's that intimate.

So it seems to me to lend itself to very introverted stories, rather than these very extroverted things. I'm not quite sure why it went that way, because I've always seen it much better used in other ways. A lot of comics, like movies and books, are there to entertain, and that's fine; they go down that route, as a medium of entertainment like a candy bar or something. They have nothing to do with comics as a unique language, an actual medium in and of itself, separate from all the others. The comics medium is not just a submovie, or a heavily illustrated text, where the text and illustrations are *separate* things, not working together. If you take away the narrative, you've got pictures in a gallery, a book of portfolios. If you take away the static quality of the imagery, you have a submovie; I think if you rely too heavily on the cinema for your language, you have a storyboard for a movie. When it becomes a unique language, the text and illustrations are *fused* perfectly, and it's static imagery—nonspecific, nothing in particular, not necessarily a drawing. And it is a printed form, I think.

Let me add that I used to think that any kind of imagery would do, that you could make a comic out of any kind of imagery, and I still sort of think that, in principle. It's infinite. But it just seems to me so obvious that *some* kinds of imagery don't work.

CBR: Such as?

McKEAN: Well, such as a lot of the things I did. The heavily finished, highly illustrated stuff I tend to think doesn't work so well—*Black Orchid, Arkham Asylum*, things like that.

I think it comes down to the amount of time invested in the making of the images, compared to the amount of time you're expected to absorb and read them. If that can be done in a closer relation, it just seems to work better. Really, at the moment I'm just floundering around trying to find things that work, and then when I have a few things that work, I look at them all and see there are common threads here that I can build some definition of comics out of.

I'm not saying that painted comics don't work. I am saying that the painted comics I've done so far haven't worked very well, and I'm trying to find the reasons for that; I think it's that heavy illustration, the heavy reliance on photographs for the images. I had reasons for all of that. I wasn't doing it arbitrarily, but at the end of the day I just don't think they work very well.

CBR: Is there any aspect of that work you still feel *is* valid?

McKEAN: The one thing I did like about *Violent Cases* was the link between a photograph and a memory, and the link between collage and the way memory works. I think that might have some miles to go, and I might be able to do it better, and clearer, in *Mr. Punch*, which I'm currently working on. It's another one of Neil's memory books.

CBR: You still use photography and color photocopying in your work. Do these techniques expand your conceptual, as well as technical, palette?

McKEAN: Well—for example, I've been messing around with color copiers a lot for *Pictures That Tick*. Color copiers seem to be an ideal tool for making comics. You have four scans, so you have time built into the thing immediately, just by moving things around on the surface. You have that time built into the image. You have four color scans—yellow, cyan, magenta, black—which have very particular emotional connections themselves. Maybe with the different scans, different words or different pieces of text or images can be assigned different emotional values, with the colors you scan.

All that seems to be an ideal and legitimate way of using a device like a color copier, whereas using a color copier just because it produces great beautiful ''whizzy'' images is probably a similar attitude to the way I use paint, yes? [*Laughs*] It's *not* a legitimate way of using a color copier.

Photographs, as well, are great for comics. It's *real* time, you know? I'd like to do some real-time comics. Setting up a scene that has all the information of a story within it, and then go around it and take photographs of that scene where the narrative is built in the sequence of the photographs; all these are just basic principles that I've been playing with.

CBR: In *Cages* you work with a very wide palette, utilizing line drawing, painting, photography, and so on, with such an intensity of purpose—have you arrived at a balance you've been seeking?

McKEAN: Yes, I'm much happier with it, along with the painted stuff I've been doing for my other book, *Pictures That Tick*. That seems to be going *right*. I'm spending a lot less time on the pictures; they're done much quicker. I paint them *on* photographs, very quickly, the speed is in the picture.

It comes down to this idea of comics working best when they're like something handwritten, like a postcard. It has that immediacy, it has the personality of the person. I see the personality in a drawing, but in the traditional method of doing comics, by the time a pencilled page has been inked and colored, I keep seeing the personality being *lost*. The personal contact is lost. When I made a drawing for *Arkham Asylum*, sometimes there was personality there; by the time I'd spent ages texturing it and sticking things on, painting it and layering it and repainting it, sure, it may look quite pretty, but the personality is *under* there somewhere. I only realized it when people seemed to respond to the slick surface and not the drawing. I just thought the *drawing* was important, the techniques applied were just the conveyance of it, but obviously it was getting lost. I saw that as a real fault of the books, not the fault of the readers at all.

CBR: So you're striving to strip away the veneer to arrive at the core of the drawing and the medium?

McKEAN: It also has to do with what I think a good drawing is, which is not necessarily what is accepted in comics as being a good drawing.

I always thought it would be obvious, what would be considered a good drawing, but I often find people in comics talking at cross-purposes. It's clearly a matter of personal taste. I like [Egon] Schiele very much, because you *see* those lines going down absolutely for the first time, *bang*, and very occasionally he'll make the wrong line, but there's no fussing about with it: he just makes the *right* line next to it. That degree of personality is as much in those lines—you take that line out of context, and just look at the line on its own, and it's *filled* with emotional content and value that relates to the imagery.

All that is what a good drawing *is* as far as I'm concerned. Whereas, since comics have been largely linked with illustration, the style and the slick finish is what's valued, and that's of no value to me. So when I say it comes down to doing these quick drawings and paintings, it has to do with making sure the personality is there, unencumbered by style.

CBR: Was *Signal to Noise* an important step in that change of attitudes? It seems to be a thematic companion to your subsequent work on *Cages*; *Signal to Noise* concerns creativity faced with mortality, whereas *Cages* thus far seems to be about creativity struggling with creation.

McKEAN: *Signal* was half my story. My half was the lead character being a film director, because these retrospectives and tributes to [Sergei] Eisenstein were being broadcast to commemorate his death forty years earlier [in 1948], and I was working on something for that. One of the tribute programs about him had somebody saying that he knew he was going to die at fifty, and he did. That seemed to me a key to something—I didn't know what, so I started working with that idea. Also, it actually tied in with some other things I'd been working on, because my father died at forty-nine, never wanted to get to fifty: he just had a thing about fifty. So that hit home as well. Those ideas never went anywhere, so I brought that along with me to Neil to discuss what we were going to do for *The Face* magazine, where *Signal* was first serialized. Neil wanted to do this story about the year 1999, the shift in the millennium, so we made that the film this fictional director was working on.

Cages is going to talk about death, being caught up in mortality, as well, in its final stages. *Signal* still feels very much like a bridge book, between *Black Orchid* and *Arkham Asylum* and the more focused stuff I'm doing now.

CBR: What made *Signal to Noise* such a bridge? Was it the opportunity to reassess and rework your art between its serialization in the British pop magazine *The Face* and the collected edition?

McKEAN: Yes, that's true.

It's also because, instead of constantly moaning that we didn't feel like we were reaching our potential audience, this wasn't going to be the fact. This was going to be in *The Face*, reaching 80,000 readers who knew about comics or read about comics, a completely different audience, so we *had* our potential audience.

That certainly kicked us into rethinking the strange values that we'd absorbed while working at DC Comics for a year or two.

CBR: Could you define those values, in terms of the industry?

McKEAN: I'm sure Neil would have a completely different view. For me, it was just such a friendly world. I wanted really to belong to something, and when DC came along, I came over to America to meet everybody, and I'd always read DC Comics as a kid; I just thought, "This is great! This is wonderful. It's what I always wanted." I fit and I belonged somewhere.

And then, just a ways down, you realize that the value systems are very different, what you feel is good and worthwhile is *not* what the mass market of comics does. Just the fact that I did a comic like *Black Orchid* and then would come in, having reassessed it a few months later and worked on new stuff, and would say to editor Karen Berger, "I'm going to be really embarrassed to see it out, I think it's really poor." This seems to them a strange thing, that you'd actually dislike the work that you're doing, or you've done.

CBR: Is that because the industry wants the consistency of a craftsman? The more adventurous artists are always going to be pushing at the parameters of what they're doing, which leads to that dissatisfaction, that sense of restlessness.

McKEAN: Yes, it's a very sort of self-congratulatory bubble.

I've noticed there's a strange little ritual that you have to go through when you meet somebody, you have to say something nice about their work, and then they have to say something nice about your work, and then you can talk. I didn't get this, didn't notice this for a while, and then I realized why things were so awkward! Once you're aware of it, you can try to hedge the conversation a bit or whatever: I can deal with that. I didn't even know what was happening before. That was a strange thing. That seems to be an archetype of everything that goes on.

I think it's because it's such a fragile little thing, it's such a little pond. I get the feeling that if everybody looked up just a little bit and saw the real world for too long, the whole thing would just collapse because the foundations are so weak. It's so reliant on this direct distribution system, the publishers rely so heavily on their figurehead characters—they're very strange and ethereal things to grab hold of.

It seems like a lot of the artists and writers grab on to people who were working thirty years ago, and seem very reluctant to criticize them. I think also it's the problem of working with something you loved as a kid, there's just something about that that brings out this strange behavior: you don't *want* to question the values, which again always struck me as being odd.

If something really makes me feel great, I really want to know *why* it works and take it apart, find out why it's affecting me that way. A friend of mine who is a lecturer told me the reason he loves to do that is, there might be the meaning of life in there. You never know—go to the next one, it might be in *there*. That seems to be a wonderful attitude, one that will move you forward and keep your brain working. This feeling that what happened thirty years ago is perfect and just be retained and reiterated constantly, pay homage to that and keep the grand tradition going—I guess you're right, it's a craft attitude, the craftsmen originated this mold or this chair, and you keep the tradition going by remaking the chair.

I can certainly understand it, it's just not something that moves me.

CBR: Do you ever see yourself going back to the realm of company-owned characters?

McKEAN: I honestly hope, never. Although I loved that stuff as a kid, it's not one of the things I liked as a kid that I have a soft spot for now. They would only be things like the *Flash Gordon* serials, which I love, and for some reason there's something about the old Sean Connery James Bond films, I would *love* to do a James Bond film! The urge only lasts for about ten minutes, you know, but when I hear that music I want to do that—but there's certainly nothing about the comics I read as a kid that I'm really interested in any more.

It's *just* the *medium* that I still love, there's not really anything about those comics that I want to re-present or work to bring those feelings back.

CBR: What foundation have you found for yourself at this stage of work in comics?

McKEAN: I've found a foundation in myself, in just focusing and trying to be very honest, trying to recognize all my faults and the things I've done wrong, and trying to put them right.

The hardest one is the fault of being derivative of other people's work. Every time I get the urge to "put those clothes on again," I say, "No, just keep them in the closet." It's the ideas that I value, so I have to try and stay away from just copying other people's ideas. If I have a direction I want to go, I try to speak in my language instead of other people's. It's very tricky because a lot of those things go very deep, and often I can't see it too clearly; it takes other people to make me aware. I have a few friends that I trust implicitly and if they say, "That was derivative of that," I have to look honestly at it and try to see why they're saying that, not just put up barriers immediately. That's one thing.

I have a foundation of friends I've already talked about, and broader than that, I have a foundation in this group of work that I really respond to and feel a part of, in a very small way.

I want to add to that.

CBR: Of your current work, what do you believe *does* add to that larger creative community's body of work? Does *Pictures That Tick* aspire to that?

McKean: There's a strip I've done called "Lilly" in *The Residents' Freak Show* comic (Dark Horse, 1992), that I'll probably reprint in *Pictures That Tick*. There are a few things.

I'm hoping to make *Pictures That Tick* "pure" in the manner of "pure" and "applied" maths, that sort of thing, trying to make it pure uses of medium. I'm not really interested in doing a dry textbook on what I think comics to be, a set of laws or instructions—if anything, I'd rather take the rules away. It's going to be a book of examples, more than anything else; various things, different directions, all of them trying not to be subversions of other media. Secondly, I'm trying not to be derivative of other people's work, which is very difficult, because almost everything is to a degree. There's the principle of it, with no boundaries at all.

THE NEW
INDEPENDENTS

Pass the Ammunition

FROM *SIN CITY*. © 1993 BY FRANK MILLER.

16

FRANK MILLER
The Mean Media Machine

Though he is among the most celebrated of contemporary American comic book creators, Frank Miller's hard-earned fame doesn't seem to mean too much to him. "It's as fragile as a soap bubble anyway," he tells us. "Some of the greatest artists in comics are considered those who routinely can't sell."

Like many who choose to enter the mainstream comics industry, Miller moved to New York City in the mid-Seventies, hoping to get his foot into the door. "I literally went around and sat in lobbies and bugged people—it wasn't a field that people were entering that much," Frank recalls. "I hung around Neal Adams's Continuity Studios a lot—he had everything to do with my starting in the business. In teaching me the basics of the craft, he was extremely generous with me. When I was first starting out, I would just come in with an absolutely terrible bunch of samples, he would tell me they were absolutely terrible, that I should go home, and when I didn't, he would teach me." After a series of pencilling jobs for Gold Key mystery titles and DC war comics, Frank gravitated to Marvel Comics and was assigned the pencilling chores on one of the company's least popular characters, a blind vigilante called *Daredevil*. The rest, as they say, is history.

With his early success as the Young Turk writer and artist who resurrected Marvel Comics' *Daredevil* (#158–191, 1979–83), Miller gained the prestige necessary to convince DC Comics to publish his own creation *Ronin* (1983–84) in a new format and apart from the standard work-for-hire terms. An ambitious experimental blend of dystopian science fiction and splashy *manga*-inspired samurai adventure, *Ronin* reinforced Miller's stature as one of the industry's cutting-edge mainstream talents, and marked his first collaboration with artist Lynn Varley, whose striking color work became an integral complement to Miller's bold style. Though it was quite successful (reprinted around the world and still in print in the U.S.), Miller chose to build his next project around a proven comic book icon. *Batman: The Dark Knight Returns* (1986) was a more cohesive work, representing yet another experimentation with design and format that became an incredible commercial success and a standard for the industry.

Never one to rest on his laurels, Miller continued to experiment and test himself. After *Dark Knight*, he began a series of collaborative efforts writing for an eclectic procession of cutting-edge artists, including David Mazzucchelli (*Daredevil* and *Batman: Year One*, 1985–87), Bill Sienkiewicz (*Elektra: Assassin* and *Daredevil: Love and War*, 1986–87), and Walt Simonson (*Robocop Versus Terminator*, 1992–93). Miller also made the leap to Hollywood, scripting *Robocop 2* (1990) and the upcoming *Robocop 3*. Along with his latest work with Lynn Varley, *Elektra Lives Again* (1990), these were all work-for-hire projects, though his collaborations with Geof Darrow (*Hard Boiled*, 1990–92) and Dave Gibbons (*Give Me Liberty*, 1990–91) were original works coowned by the creators.

Frank Miller continues to challenge himself anew with each undertaking. *Sin City* (1992) strips his script and art to its most primal essence, and the result is devastatingly impressive.

COMIC BOOK REBELS: From your first comics in the fan APAs to *Sin City*, crime fiction seems to have been a primary influence on your work.

FRANK MILLER: Well, back when I was an amateur, and through to this day, the bulk of my fiction reading has been old crime novels. As a kid growing up in Vermont, I was always really enchanted with the notion of big cities, and with the romance that came through in Raymond Chandler and Mickey Spillane and the others that fall into that list. The crime fiction from the 1940s and '50s remains my favorite, the era that, in many ways, Dashiell Hammett started and Chandler refined, along with Jim Thompson, James M. Cain, Charles Willeford, and Spillane. So as an amateur, the comics I did generally were crime stories: tough guys in trench coats and spooky urban landscapes.

The main reason I moved out of that was because when I first started working in comics, the only kind of comics you could do were super-heroes. But mostly, my work reflects the stuff I'm a fan of. I did grow up reading superhero comics, I just hadn't read them a few years before I started working professionally. I found the more fantastic stuff was actually very liberating to work on. For instance, by doing the near-future stories, you can write about the present without libeling any-body. I've read a fair amount of science fiction, but haven't retained an interest in it. A lot of the stuff I've done, including arguably the super-hero stuff, could generally be classified under science fiction. I didn't come into this field intending to do science fiction, and I don't regard myself as being at all a true science-fiction writer: I haven't read enough of it, I don't know enough about science. What I believe I am is a fantasist, and to me technology represents a very scary and wonderful paradoxical element. It's all I have a use for from science fiction.

With *Sin City*, I've come full circle in a way. I'm back to the kind of material that I most wanted to do when I first started to work at being a comic book professional. When I was fourteen years old I thought Mickey Spillane's stuff would make some *great* comics. Even though it took me twenty-one years to get around to it, I still hadn't felt that it had been done in the meantime.

CBR: Do you still find the industry's pervasive orientation to genre fiction—specifically superhero fantasies—a problem?

MILLER: One of the things I've been hung up on for years now—since *Ronin*, really—is how comics have been so genre-limited for so long that there are still a lot of avenues to look for: places to find, things that comics can do that generally they're not used for. I figure there're another million kinds of different comics to do out there, and so rather than finding all the corners to find in one genre, I want to take this form and explore every other genre possible.

CBR: What interests you more, reworking classic characters or creat-ing entirely new ones?

MILLER: Right now, without question, creating new ones. Working on Batman and the Marvel Comics characters, I really got to play with all

my childhood icons. For the present, at least, I'm much more interested
in creating characters that are new. The traditional comic book characters have gotten very, very old.

I also enjoy creating a world for *my* characters to inhabit that reflects
my own observations about things, my own ideas about what would be
fun to draw or write, rather than adding to an immense canon of
previous material—which is what my whole career is built on.

CBR: Your first series work was on Marvel Comics' *Daredevil*. It was
unusual for such a young artist to be allowed to take over the writing of
a series as well. How did you manage that?

MILLER: With *Daredevil*, I had the advantage of working on a title that
wasn't selling. As it was with *Batman*, there's no better opportunity for
somebody who wants to do subversive superhero stuff than to find a
character who's dead in the water. So there was a lot of leeway on what
could be done with *Daredevil*. Entranced by Will Eisner's work and
really still wanting to do crime comics, I did everything I could to pull
the character over into a crime world.

I felt there was kind of a "wascally wabbit" quality to Daredevil that
would pit him against such a massive, powerful, networking type of
villain, like the Kingpin; that the hero would actually be the force for
chaos, and the villain for order. I was in my twenties, a very rebellious
age, and so my heroes had to be rebels.

I think heroes by their nature have to be challenging the status quo. I
think heroes are much less interesting when they are a force *for* the
status quo.

CBR: You created the character of Elektra in *Daredevil*, under work-
for-hire conditions. Elektra is owned completely by Marvel Comics,
and yet their policy is very much "hands-off" unless *you* are doing it.
How did you manage this?

MILLER: Some of that was simply a matter of a handshake agreement.
I've had enough continuing interest in doing the character, and she's
been popular enough when I've done her, for the arrangement to be
justified. It's a verbal agreement, it was never formalized in writing.
They own the character lock, stock, and barrel, and can do whatever
they want with her.

FROM *SIN CITY*. © 1993 BY FRANK MILLER.

CBR: In the final issue of your *Daredevil* work as writer-artist you did the story "Roulette" [*Daredevil* #191, 1983], which at the time seemed a pretty conclusive meditation on the whole vigilante archetype with nowhere left to go with the genre. How did that lead to *Dark Knight*?

MILLER: That story was in a way the last throes of liberal guilt wrestling with vigilante hero. Doing that story, I think, freed me up to look at the myth itself for what it was, and define it as something where the hero no longer needed to be *my* fantasy proxy, and could be something truer to itself—in Batman. *Daredevil* was very much a vehicle for "what if *I* were heroic?" Batman was more like another person to look at, not just another person, but a myth. I don't know if I'd want to have dinner with him, but his adventures were really exciting.

The entire *Daredevil* run that I drew was done in a real burst of violent creative energy, and I didn't find along the way very much to articulate. But people had begun talking about heroes and superheroes, and the field at the time was struggling to articulate what it was we were up to. So my stories started reflecting that before I'd really started consciously thinking about it. But after that and before *Dark Knight*, I had a period of going off by myself and studying the material and coming to my own conclusions about what it was, and they all paid off in *Dark Knight*.

CBR: In all your key work you strip your characters down to their primal essence. Was this a conscious agenda from the beginning?

MILLER: It's much more conscious now. When I came into comics I did recognize that people were hung up on the details, and had lost the main thrusts and appeal—or terror—of the characters. I wanted to strip the stuff down to its basic material and use it for all the power it was worth. I've always loved characters of tremendous force and a sort of Wagnerian stature, and at the time I came into comics people seemed to be lost amid the continuities and details, the choreography of these gigantic complicated universes filled with so many good guys you would step on one whenever you turned around.

A real turning point for me was when I saw the Fleischer Studio *Superman* cartoons as an adult. I'd seen them as a very young kid, but I saw them again as an adult in a rep house in New York and all of a sudden it seemed so *simple*, not just with Superman but with all the other characters. I saw them shortly before I'd conceived *The Dark Knight*. I knew I'd wanted to do *Batman*, I knew I wanted to make him tougher, I knew he seemed kind of silly in such a benevolent world. This guy dressing up like a bat and throwing criminals through windows when everybody was so *nice*, so ordered, just seemed kind of irrelevant. I knew that *that* character could only work in a world that was pretty terrible, a world that justified his presence. I think one of the reasons I tend toward a less benevolent world in my stories is because my work is so centered on a powerful protagonist, if not a hero, and there's not much need for that in Utopia. The censorship in comics with the Comic Code and all created a world that at least a McCarthyite would call a Utopia.

CBR: Why do you feel the need to be so brutal in your work?

MILLER: Part of the thrill of fantasy is that it does push to unrealistic extremes. In writing and drawing fantasy, I find that it can be *more* than real. I think it was Alfred Hitchcock who once remarked that melodrama was real life with all the boring parts taken out. I think it's a natural function: part of what gives fantasy its punch or thrill is that it will terrify you by going beyond things you ordinarily see.

To get the emotional response I'm after, I believe the violence is necessary, depending on the story. I've always loved horror, and I'm kind of a "genre mixer," and one of the things I greatly enjoy doing in a story is replacing catharsis with horror. The way it is in movies and most adventure comics, catharsis is essentially a very satisfying, happy conclusion: the Death Star blows up, or whatever. Making that moment terrifying is something I like to play with, so it no longer leaves you feeling all is right with the world.

CBR: Between *Daredevil* and *Dark Knight*, you completed *Ronin*, which was a dramatic departure for DC Comics, as the publisher, and the marketplace in general in concept, design, and format. What was the genesis of the project?

MILLER: There were two fronts to fight there, one was creative, and the other was business. That was back at the time in comics when there was talk of a guild, where the arguments had begun about royalties, and DC Comics had taken the historical step of offering royalties paid on comics. It was the first chance any of us had to move beyond the way things had been in this business for decades. It was early in my career, and with *Daredevil* I could see there was a sense that the audience was starting to recognize individual talent. I thought this was the most important thing that had happened, because that way we could each start carving out our own way.

When DC opened the door to royalties, I had done enough research to know the royalties they were offering were quite low, but the *principle* had been broken. A precedent established. So I negotiated with Jeanette Kahn [at that time publisher of DC Comics], and set what I thought was a more proper royalty in exchange for me bringing them *Ronin*. DC wanted at the time to become (to use that horrible term) the "creator-friendly" company, so they were willing to break some of their own precedents in order to get me.

I was given complete autonomy to do whatever I wanted to, and I had a million things I wanted to do. The handcuffs came off, and I just went nuts, you know? At the time I was in Upstart Studios with Walter Simonson and Howard Chaykin, who had helped expose me to what was going on in Europe, and I'd been exposed to what was going on in Japan, particularly with [Kazuo Koike and Goseki Kojima's *Kozure Okami*, U.S. title:] *Lone Wolf and Cub*.

The way I came up with the story of *Ronin* was to synthesize all this stuff. I couldn't stay in one style with the book because there was so much I wanted to do. Before working on it, I'd met Lynn Varley, and saw the work she was doing in paint. So all these factors were in play at the same time I got my freedom, and I charged into *Ronin* like crazy. It was a very, very difficult book, but very rewarding.

CBR: What was the reaction to *Ronin*?

MILLER: The reaction was twofold. At the time, people seemed mostly shocked. They were expecting an extension of *Daredevil* rather than a total departure, and though much of it had a high level of violence, it was very different from *Daredevil*. So I got very mixed mail, mixed reaction from professionals, and from my perspective at the time it felt very much like a failure.

However, since then, reaction to it has gotten historically much more positive, and I hear people speak of it as a very worthy work.

CBR: Given the attitude at that time that *Ronin* had been, in some way, a failure, did you *need* Batman, esthetically and commercially, in the wake of *Ronin*?

MILLER: To a certain extent, yes. I think for one thing I had flown into *Ronin*, it was a very explosive piece of work, and *Dark Knight* was really the beginning of a much more conscious approach to the craft.

Taking all my ideas and wrapping them around Batman was a very good way to bring a new level of discipline to my work. *Ronin* was like a shotgun blast, just exploding and it kept on exploding until the foldout at the end, and *Dark Knight* was a much more conscious piece of work. I outlined it; it was when I started outlining my work much more carefully before working on it. Between those two projects, I really felt that I'd built a level of skill that was able to propel me into the newer work I've done.

CBR: Part of the new work you were doing at that time included writing for other artists. What kind of changes did that necessitate, and how did it fuel your own work?

MILLER: Collaboration is a real blast, when you're dealing with another intellect and talent. When I'm working with somebody, I study what they've done before, and it helps form what I'm going to do with them. In the case of David Mazzucchelli with *Batman: Year One* in particular, I knew that he would be able to bring an amazing quality to very mundane situations, so I was looking to strengths he had that I didn't feel myself having, and concentrating on grounding the stories.

I've learned things from all my collaborators. From Dave Gibbons and David Mazzucchelli in particular I've learned to concentrate more than ever on the three-dimensionality of the panel. The strength of having characters grounded on a floor, in a room with the right things in it. My inclination was always to just make my point and run, and those two artists are such impeccable storytellers that all the right little pieces meant the stage was "full."

A good example is in *Sin City*. I'd always been nervous about drawing certain mundane things. I've always done a poor job of them. But I'd just been working with Geof Darrow writing *Hard Boiled*, whose art takes the mundane into the bizarre and draws it beautifully. He and I are friends, and I came to learn some of his working methods. He introduced me to the wonderful value of three-dimensional reference. I'd mainly worked from photographs; when possible, from life, but mainly from photographs. It's because of Geof that I now have a shelf covered with die-cast metal cars and I've got large combat boots sitting in my studio. All of a sudden I found the things I'd tried to avoid drawing for so long would give the page so much more strength. Now I love drawing cars and I love drawing footwear and all kinds of things.

Bill Sienkiewicz probably stretched me more than anybody as a writer. The work was so absurd and extravagant that it tested me in terms of writing comedy, and in terms of storytelling. Bill's work was such a barrage of imagery, often without any coherence, that the script had to be doing much more of what the art traditionally does in storytelling. So it was a wild opportunity, but it was one bitch of a job! [*Laughs*] I had to rewrite every script. I gave him full scripts, and then I'd get this barrage, I'd feel like the astronaut in *2001* confronted with the future, sitting there wide-eyed looking at the pages, then I would reconceive the script.

CBR: Is the process of drawing or writing more satisfying to you?

MILLER: I think I'm a lot better company when I'm drawing. I find that when I'm writing, I feel like a little ogre at the keyboard, and I often find myself envying the artist I'm working with. Not that I would want to draw, say, the issue of *Liberty* I just wrote, but I would find myself getting the urge to draw the characters in it. The other part of the envy is that when I get pages from (for the sake of comparison) Dave Gibbons, I wish *I'd* drawn them.

Drawing is much more physical. I can do it for twelve to fourteen hours and feel fine and happy, whereas half that time in writing and my brain is boiled.

CBR: Your comic book notoriety aside, why do you think Hollywood so readily accepted you as a screenwriter?

MILLER: It gets down to one producer, Jon Davison, who took the initiative of calling me up and asking me to write *Robocop 2* because of *Dark Knight*. I think *The Dark Knight*'s influence on the first movie was fairly obvious, and he really liked the book, and thought he'd give me a shot at it—although I imagine he was biting his nails before I turned in the first draft, and wanted to be certain the pages were right-side up [*Laughs*]. That was the main thing, also there was a general momentum in Hollywood that Jon was ahead of the rest on, which was that comics had been "discovered," particularly with *Dark Knight* and *Watchmen* and a few other books.

Hollywood all of a sudden discovered that "us jerks" working in this backwater little field were doing stuff that was a lot more interesting than what *they* were doing. I really believe that has everything to do with the fact that in comics, the stakes are so much lower. Artists work with so much more autonomy. Whether our stuff is trashy or juvenile or not, we really are having a ball and it really shows. I think to a great extent, in Hollywood people aren't having as much fun as comic book artists are. The stakes are so much higher in a movie, there're so many more people involved, that before a screenplay can get into production it's often been through such a gauntlet that things tend to lose their freshness. Everything's been triple-checked through so many times, run by demographics tests and all.

CBR: In hindsight, what did you learn from the experience with the *Robocop* movies?

MILLER: One, there's a great vast number of things I can't cover in the course of an interview that just have to do with the knowledge accumulated. It was the best film school you could ever go to. Encountering all the problems, seeing what worked and what didn't, and the main reaction is, I'm very, very glad I solved it.

As far as observations on a much more general level, I would say that on future films, beyond seeking more creative authority—namely, by directing it—I would spend much more time by myself making up my mind what movie I wanted to make *before* dealing with other people. Then, while trying to keep my ears open, I would essentially be forcing my point of view down everybody's throat. That's the way good movies are made. What I hope to do, and what I hope other cartoonists can do, is bring their single-mindedness with them. Be tenacious as all hell. Yes, you have to listen and you have to learn from them, to adapt to all the many different forms, to make use of the advantages and lose what doesn't work. Good movies most often are made because one person, at the heart of them, has the movie he wants to make, pushes for it, and doesn't stop. It's amazing how much tenacity is required simply to stay on a project, let alone to see it through in the form you want it to be in.

CBR: In your dealings with DC and Marvel, you initiated dramatic change in how the mainstream comics publishers would deal with individual creators. Do you think further change is possible from within the mainstream comic book publishing companies today?

MILLER: I think the main change is happening *outside* the two major companies now, and I think that's an understatement. Things have changed to the point where there's *one* major company, Marvel, and where DC is fighting off a herd of competitors at this point in terms of who's in power in the industry. But I don't really think the change is going to take place within Marvel Comics, or even within DC Comics, where it might be more likely. Marvel's riding too high for one thing, they're just making too much money to change their ways. Beyond that, I believe on a profound level both companies are so dedicated to work-made-for-hire that they would sooner go out of business than change their ways. Work-made-for-hire is the main thing, on a business level, that's been holding comics back.

I've got to say that I do believe the opportunities have opened up, and now much more than before. The onus is upon the artists to produce work that will lead to a real renaissance. I see a lot of good things happening, but I don't see an overall change in the air, especially now that so many people are seizing on the advent of Image and Marvel's success.

CBR: What do you find in the comic book industry that exists for you nowhere else?

MILLER: Freedom. I appreciate this even more now that I've been working in Hollywood. The ability to take an idea from start to finish without having anybody holding authority over you.

CBR: And what do you find the most debilitating?

MILLER: The self-contempt of the field. This is a field that doesn't understand its greatest virtues. We should enjoy the fact that we're outlaws right now.

One of my worries these days is that comic books seem to want to be more like Hollywood, and with that comes a tendency to lose our outlaw status, which is a very precious thing. Comics has always been this disreputable little field with a massive inferiority complex. Now we're starting to see comics break into the mainstream, and everybody has this desire to turn into Hollywood or into rock stars, and try to get so big that we'll just end up compromising body and soul just like all those other fields out there. I think that's an aspect of self-contempt that dates back to at least the 1950s.

I'm feeling much less like being a crusader in the political sense in comics these days and much more like enjoying the good fortune I've got to be able to *do* the stuff I want. I'd rather show it on the pages; I think I'm much better at making comics than I am running for office. All this doesn't make me want to turn the clock back, because things have improved, but to reestablish us as being on the *edge* of culture, not the center.

FROM *A DISTANT SOIL*. © 1993 BY COLLEEN DORAN.

17

COLLEEN DORAN
Bringing Home a Distant Soil

In an industry that feeds so voraciously on youth and fresh talent, Colleen Doran has not only held her own for over a decade, but against all odds, has thrived. Her experiences are particularly telling, because she originally brought her talents to independent publishing in the direct sales market, the "promised land" of opportunity for artists and writers who wished to retain full ownership of their work. Even so, she found herself engulfed in a nearly soul-  crushing battle to retain creative control and legal ownership of her own creation.

Her often difficult journey of discovery began with her first professional work for an advertising agency at the tender age of fifteen. Overtures from comic book publishers soon followed, none of which interested her until an editor from the Donning Company Publishers asked whether there was a story behind a group of her drawings that were particularly evocative. As Doran explains in *A Distant Soil* #3 (1993), "There was—it later became known as *A Distant Soil*. The publisher of the company thought I was too young to take a chance on. He was right; I was underage and would not necessarily be bound by any contract. So the editor decided to show my work to another company, WaRP [Wendy & Richard Pini] Graphics."

Founded in 1979 by *Elfquest* creators and self-publishers Wendy and Richard Pini, WaRP debuted *A Distant Soil* as a backup story in *Elfquest* #16 (1982). *A Distant Soil* was launched as its own title the following year, running nine inconclusive issues.

A Distant Soil has been Doran's anchor throughout a very stormy career, and a fascinating mirror of its creator's trials, triumphs, and professional maturation. What began as a teenager's fantasy—extraterrestrials seeking allies in their rebellion against powerful invaders, and their involvement with young humans who possess latent psychic abilities—soon blossomed into an intriguing series with a compelling cast of characters.

Even as the scope of Doran's epic tale expanded to embrace Arthurian legend, the intrigue *behind* the scenes of *A Distant Soil* was exacting a terrible toll on the series and its creator. Her undeniable youth and relative inexperience in the field initially prompted the imposition of an older writer upon her creation—a situation Doran found completely intolerable. After leaving WaRP, she gravitated back to Donning Company Publishers, rewriting and redrawing the *entire series* as two full-color graphic novels. Regrettably, the compensation for her efforts was miniscule, and the promotion of the two books was "nonexistent." When the company's graphic novel line perished, Doran was left to sort out a complex knot of legal entanglements with both of her publishers before being finally able to reclaim her creation as her own.

Throughout this process, which perhaps may be better described as an ordeal, Colleen Doran has honed to a razor-sharp point both her artistic and business skills. Currently engaged as a much sought-after freelance artist for the mainstream publishers (Marvel Comics, DC, and Disney Comics, among others), she began self-publishing new episodes of *A Distant Soil* in the fall of 1991. She does not intend to look back ever again.

COMIC BOOK REBELS: *A Distant Soil* has seamlessly blended the science fiction genre with elements of traditional fantasy, particularly when Sir Galahad was introduced. What were the original inspirations for the series?

COLLEEN DORAN: Would you *really* like to know? [*Laughs*] It was this really awful animated television series called *The Young Sentinels*, or something like that! Actually, *A Distant Soil* started off as three different books which were being worked on at the same time. One of which was a fantasy novel. Also, I had been reading about King Arthur since I was a child; I must have a hundred books on King Arthur in my library by now—I just read about the subject voraciously. Anyway, I eventually noticed that different characters in my assorted books were actually the same person, especially Liana. So I figured out a way to get them all into one story, though it took about ten years for the series to get to that point! I guess I was a real strange ten- or twelve-year-old when I started it all.

CBR: Besides Liana, Jason remains a key character in the series. Yet there were several issues in which Jason was literally in a coma, and didn't come back to life, so to speak, until you regained control of the series with issue #6. Was Jason a fictional barometer of what you were going through as the set-upon creator of the series at the time?

DORAN: Oh, absolutely! And if you were to look at the art for the series up until that issue, you'll notice that everyone—especially the men— were really *thin*. Emaciated. And extremely androgynous. The funny thing is, I didn't draw that way before that time period; if you go back and look at my earlier work, everyone was a little on the plump side, or had just normal body weight. But I was so unhappy at the time! My stress counselor told me what I was basically trying to do was emasculate every man that I had control over. And the only men I had control over in my life at that time were these fictional characters. Later, when I got control of my book back again, I was able to make them more likable people, and they stopped being so hyperandrogynous, and so skinny and delicate.

CBR: Yet it wasn't just your problems with losing and regaining control of *A Distant Soil* that have shaped your career. You've had less than pleasant encounters with other publishers, haven't you?

DORAN: My early years in publishing were just awful, period. I mean, I felt that if you didn't go to a comic book convention with a baseball bat, some old weirdo was going to jump you. My mother chaperoned me for years, everywhere I went, but then they hit on *her*. It was so ridiculous. It got to a point during that time period where I just wanted to kill every man I could get my hands on. So I basically spent about six issues of *A Distant Soil* torturing the men in *it* instead! Which is a terrible thing to say—but my work didn't improve, it actually got worse while I fought to regain control of my book.

CBR: Growing up, did you have any idea that you would encounter such a rocky road in pursuing a career in comics?

DORAN: I had a pretty sheltered and protected childhood. I mean, I was basically . . . spoiled. My parents loved me. In fact, everything was great until I got into this business. And then it was just unbelievable. I'm sorry, but the comic book industry seems to me like one big dysfunctional family. And the way they treat women in this business—and children, for that matter—is appalling. I can't stand the way some people carry on at conventions; I think it makes conventions a very unwholesome place for kids. I would never have children go to one.

But, yes, I have spent a lot of time in this industry getting harassed. For a several year period, this one man would just fly across the country to harass me in person. I think that, even though I was in my late teens and early twenties, I was very childlike because I was very sheltered in my youth. And a lot of people in this business would give me a lot of crap because I traveled everywhere with my mother. So for a while I went to conventions on my own, because I was led to believe I didn't need her to travel around the country anymore—yeah, right! God! So I travel with her now—even though I'm now all grown up.

It was really awful. I still get so angry about it . . . ! I could give you one instance which illustrates this situation really well, though I could just as well give you thirty. Very early in my career an editor called me up and said, "Would you like to go to such and such convention? You are our new artist now, and we will send you all expenses paid." I thought this was great. Publishers wine and dine you, and send you to exotic places—like Cleveland. Where you can sit at a nice table and sign autographs for people. And I thought this was really super.

But when I got to the convention, I go up to my room, and my editor is already there. And I asked him, "What are you doing in my room?" And he says, "Well, we're going to have to share the room." I'm not going to go into the gory details, but I was broke, absolutely broke, and I could *not* stay in that room with him. So I ended up having to spend the weekend in the bathroom of the hotel lobby, because I had no money for a room. I had just thirty dollars to eat on, and to get a cab back to the airport.

There was another guy, who still works in this business, who was stone cold crazy. He's married, and very successful, and he would fly— on his company's account of course—to my home. And he would tell me, "I'm going to take you to dinner." And I would tell him no

FROM *A DISTANT SOIL*. © 1993 BY COLLEEN DORAN.

repeatedly, but it got ridiculous. I was going to school at the time, and he would show up at my school! This went on for several years, and it scared the hell out of me. He simply would not take "Go to hell!" for an answer. At that time, I wasn't the kind of person who could even say that, but I am now. I kept on trying to be polite, and kept telling him that this wasn't the right thing for him to do.

I remember I once had a job in a library, and he showed up at the *library* looking for me. And he called me from the library, and said, "Why aren't you here?" And I said, "Oh, I've had an accident. And I don't really feel well, so you're just going to have to go back home. Don't come over." So of course he insisted on coming over. And I thought to myself, how am I going to prove I had an accident? So I took a Coke bottle and I hit myself in the face to raise bruises so he wouldn't touch me. And you know what? It didn't stop him.

That's how bad some of these guys are, and there are plenty of them.

CBR: Do you find their business tactics as predatory as some of their personal harassments?

DORAN: Yes. At least. At least.

CBR: Is it because you're a "struggling young artist" that some unscrupulous publishers attempt to take advantage, or is it because of sexism you're perceived as a "helpless young female" in what is predominately a male-dominated industry?

DORAN: Both. I think it's a double whammy on women professionals. First of all, as creators we're naive. We're malleable. They think we're idiots—I never met a publisher who didn't look down on creators. And as a woman . . . oh, my God, they don't think we even exist as human beings. I'll go to conventions and people will say, "Who did this great work?" And I'll say, "It's my work." And they'll say, "Oh—*you* couldn't do that."

At the time, I thought it was just me experiencing all this grief. But it wasn't just me. I kept my mouth shut for years, but I eventually found out it was very common, and the men I had had problems with were doing this same exact thing to a legion of women. They'd do it to fans, they'd do it to professionals.

I know one woman who had shattered her knee in an accident, and was on crutches at a convention. And a publisher went up to her and said, "Oh, gosh, it's such a hard trip going up and back into town on the train in this condition—why don't I take you home?" And she thought, "Oh, what a nice man!" Well—he took her to *his* home! Talk about taking advantage! My God, I just don't get it.

In my entire career, I've only met one woman who has said she has never had any problems. Only one! But every other female professional I know has had problems. From being chased around the office desk, to being grabbed and being groped. And molested. You name it. It's just awful. Now I'm getting the reputation as the "Bitch from Hell." But I would much rather be thought of that way, because in some ways it's easier to just yell at them so they'll back off. But some of them it doesn't affect at all.

They *just don't get it.*

They don't understand that you have a choice in the matter as a professional. Because they're real candid about the fact that they'll give you this job or they'll give you that job if you give them "something" in return. It's real bad. It's like if you don't have a man—a husband or a boyfriend—who is standing right there to protect you, you're just a target.

CBR: Can you tell us how you were able to reclaim *A Distant Soil,* after losing control of the series?

DORAN: We settled out of court, so I can't tell you how I did it. But I *did* it, and that's the important thing.

CBR: In more general terms, then, could you offer some advice to anyone who is concerned with retaining copyright and legal control over their creations?

DORAN: My advice to any creator from the word go is to get a good arts and entertainment lawyer. From the very beginning. So you have someone there to explain to you what publishers are legally entitled to, and what's going to happen when things go wrong. Contracts aren't there for the good times—the contracts are for the *bad* times! When people break up and go their separate ways. And in terms of collaborating with another writer or artist, unless you go into the project knowing you're going to share fifty-fifty forever of the profits, don't do it. Don't let anybody tell you they're going to "do you a favor" by helping you out now. Absolutely avoid them—like the plague. They will come back later and you'll find out that "favor" carried a great big fat price tag.

CBR: Given the state of the current marketplace, how are you able to afford to self-publish *A Distant Soil*, in terms of both your finances and time?

DORAN: It makes a profit. It doesn't make a huge profit, but enough to make it worth my while to do. But it doesn't make a profit to support me in the style to which I've become accustomed: food, lights, a roof over my head. [*Laughs*] So one must do what one can. So if I want to advertise my book, I've got to do work for Marvel. If I want to travel to conventions to promote my book, I've got to do work for DC. I really don't have a choice. If *A Distant Soil* was selling approximately twice what it does now, I *would* have a choice.

CBR: You are doing a considerable amount of mainstream work at this point in your career. How do you pick and choose what is best for you as a fulltime freelancer?

DORAN: There are two factors: one, whether or not I'm going to have a good time. And two, what the deadlines are. (I already know I'm going to make money from the project, from knowing what the page rate is, going in.) But I have to know if I'm going to have any fun. There are some books I find just miserable, and even if it were to mean regular work, I would be miserable working on them. Whether it was working with the creative team, or whatever. Nothing personal—but it just might not meet whatever purpose in my life it was supposed to meet.

Deadline considerations are equally important. I'm trying to avoid— even though I know I probably should take on—a regular assignment. And even though taking on work with a regular title would be very good for my career, and give me greater visibility, I'm reluctant to take on anything that would interfere with my self-publishing plans any more than it already has. So I try to take on titles that have flexible deadlines, or are limited issue runs. Something finite.

CBR: You mentioned earlier the sexism you've found so pervasive in this industry. Does that sexism ever carry over in terms of the specific titles you're offered?

DORAN: Well, they wanted me to do *Wonder Woman*! [*Laughs*] I get a lot of that. It was really irritating for a while. For example, I was really looking forward to doing *Shade, the Changing Man*. And when I had my chance, that was when the Shade had a sex change (#27–29, 30–32, 1992)! [*Laughs*] It's so bizarre! They give me the great sex-change issue of *The Legion of Superheroes*. They wanted me to do *Dr. Fate* when Dr. Fate became—a woman. So I get the "fantasy" issues for these characters. Sure!

CBR: You've done a fair amount of work in the horror genre. Is this out of a personal interest in dark fantasy, or has it been simply a case of horror has been where the steady work is?

DORAN: I like horror. And even if the particular issues of *The Sandman* (#20, 1990; #34, 1992) that I did happen to have all female characters (why does this keep happening to me?), people don't think of the fact that it was an "all-girl" issue. People just think of it as a horror story. But I enjoy horror, and I read it all the time.

CBR: Beside your personal work, your mainstream work runs the gamut from superheroes to Disney characters to the undead. How do you tailor your style to such a variety of markets and titles?

DORAN: Oh, I just—*change*. There's this little switch in my head so that when I sit in a chair and close my eyes, I'll tell myself to "draw like this" now. And then I sit down at the drawing table and I draw—like that. For example, when I was working on *Beauty and the Beast* (1991) for Disney, I was also working on *Clive Barker's Hellraiser* #14 (1991). You don't get any more different in styles than that—those two projects really got to me. I got such migraines.

But I don't really have that much of a problem with switching styles. I think that if you can draw at all, you ought to be able to be versatile. Like an actor. As you move from book to book, you switch from role to role.

Superheroes require a certain dynamic that I don't use anywhere else. I actually don't find it a very attractive dynamic on the whole. But when I do superheroes, I figure I might as well study the best. So I'll often immerse myself in what Frank Miller did for *Batman* and *Daredevil* because Miller was so good at everything. And of course I try to think a lot about testosterone. [*Laughs*] I think big! I think power! I think overdone! And underdressed!

CBR: Do you find the constant shifting of gears between the volume of mainstream work you take on and your own self-published work invigorating or frustrating?

DORAN: It's draining. I like moving from one project to the next. I don't like working on many different projects with very diverse styles at the same time. Which is what I usually end up doing. When I was working on *Beauty and the Beast* and *Hellraiser*, I was also working on Anne Rice's *The Master of Rampling Gate* (1991), and *A Distant Soil*. And they all must be done in completely different styles, so they all look completely different. I did not enjoy that experience at all.

But if I can work on them in succession, what I normally do is take a little time out between books. Just a few days to do nothing but *think* about what I'm going to do. And then I can sit down and do it straight through. But I find if I have to do more than one job a day, I find that I lose at least an hour between the jobs as I shift my gears. So I normally work this way, but I don't like it very much.

CBR: The majority of your work has been of a fantastic nature. Are there any plans to adopt a more realistic approach to any future stories?

DORAN: I definitely do. I've been working on an autobiographical piece, which I think will take from about four to six issues. We had a wacky childhood, growing up on a farm. My dad was a policeman, and he taught us all about forensics when we were kids.

CBR: Forensics?

DORAN: Yeah! My dad was a wacko! [*Laughs*] No, he had a great sense of humor. He was studying for his master's degree, and he would have to study these autopsy files to learn about how people decompose, and wonderful things like that. He would show us pictures of autopsies, and we learned a lot! My most vivid memory is of the drowning victims. There is nothing *uglier* than a drowning victim. If somebody just dies, then they're just dead. But a drowning victim is so over the top, I just couldn't deal with them! You know—they blow up, and turn green . . . ! He would also teach us how to identify a homicide from a suicide. And he would hold up a picture and ask, "Can you tell me? Is this a homicide? Or a suicide?"

CBR: Then we don't have to ask where your interest in horror originated. Seriously, have your trials and tribulations in this industry permanently scarred you, or have they only strengthened your resolve as a creative individual?

DORAN: Oh, they've definitely strengthened me. I almost dropped out of the business a couple of times. Working in mainstream comics is something that is an awful lot of trouble for something that I could be doing on my own. Okay, maybe nobody would ever see it, but drawing and telling stories in this medium is the thing that I enjoy most. But the problem with this industry is that you really need a buyer to be a storyteller. If you want people to see what you're doing, you have to produce.

The fact is, if those publishers hadn't pushed me away so hard, chances are, I probably would have stopped fighting to make it a lot earlier. I'm just naturally ornery: I was starting to take it very personally. I would say to myself, "Nothing would ruin your day more than to see me a success. Oh, boy! I'm really going to ruin your day!" And that's precisely what I've done.

UMM, 'SCUSE ME? UM, WE WERE WONDERING IF YOU'D HEARD ANYTHING YET?

FOR THE TENTH TIME, MR. WALLACE HAS YOUR SAMPLES. IF HE WISHES TO SEE YOU, HE'LL CALL YOU IN.

UMM, YOU DON'T THINK YOU COULD ASK HIM IF HE'S LOOKED AT THEM YET, OR...

KID, WHY DON'T YOU GO HOME AND CLEAN UP A LITTLE? WHAT'S THE MATTER, THEY DON'T HAVE SHOWERS WHERE YOU'RE FROM?

UH... UH, NO. WE HAVE A BATHTUB. I TOOK ONE THIS MORNING, I...

MAYBE WE'LL JUST WAIT.

I'M BEGINNING TO THINK THIS IS A MISTAKE, JOE. COMIC BOOKS AREN'T IN THE SAME LEAGUE WITH STRIPS LIKE FLASH GORDON OR PRINCE VALIANT

MAYBE WE SHOULD KEEP TRYING THE SYNDICATES?

BUT THEN, WE'VE ALREADY BEEN TURNED DOWN TWICE BY EVERY ONE IN THE COUNTRY...

AND I'VE GOTTA' GET SOMETHING GOING NOW. MY OLD MAN'S PUSHING ME TO HELP WITH HIS BUSINESS...

IF MY WRITING DOESN'T START MAKING MONEY SOON, ALL MY HOPES AND DREAMS WILL BE TRAPPED IN THAT TAILOR SHOP.

I WOULDA' GIVEN UP A LONG TIME AGO IF IT WASN'T FOR HIM! I JUST DON'T UNDERSTAND WHY PUBLISHERS CAN'T SEE HIS POTENTIAL!

YOU THINK MAYBE HE NEEDS A MASK?

NO, NO! A MASK IS ALL WRONG FOR SOMEONE LIKE HIM.

HE STANDS FOR TRUTH AND JUSTICE. HE'D NEVER HIDE HIS FACE BEHIND A MASK.

NOT TRUE-MAN!

58

FROM *THE MAXIMORTAL*. © 1993 BY RICK VEITCH.

18

RICK VEITCH
The New Breed of Hero

Rick Veitch's thirty years in the comic book industry have spanned everything from underground comix and *Heavy Metal* to *Swamp Thing* and the *Teenage Mutant Ninja Turtles*.

He was first enticed into the underground fold by his older brother Tom, whose own collaborations with artist Greg Irons remain seminal works. The two brothers did complete one rough-and-ready masterwork, *Two-Fisted Zombies* (Last Gasp, 1973), before leaving the underground comix scene to go their own separate creative ways. Veitch subsequently enrolled in the Joe Kubert School of Cartoon and Graphic Art in Dover, New Jersey, and was a member of the school's very first graduating class. He then quickly established himself as a low-profile but highly accomplished writer-artist.

Veitch's fertile relationship with Marvel Comics' *EPIC Illustrated* magazine and the EPIC Comics Line had him working with legendary editor Archie Goodwin, who offered Veitch the blend of guidance and creative freedom he craved. This period yielded the serialized novel "Abrasax and the Earthman" (1982–83), an ambitious fantasy drawn in part from Herman Melville's *Moby-Dick*, and the subtly complex series *The One* (1984–86; later collected by King Hell Press). Notably, both "Abrasax" and *The One* laid significant groundwork for his eventual "Heroica" line of revisionist superheroes.

In 1986, Veitch left the pastures of creator-owned independence to till the soil broken by Alan Moore, Stephen R. Bissette, and John Totleben with their reinvention of DC Comics' *Swamp Thing*. (A character originally created by Len Wein and Bernie Wrightson in 1971.) Initially assisting on, and then penciling, various issues, Veitch eventually took over the art chores for the final year of writer Alan Moore's tenure on the title. Though filling Moore's shoes seemed a Herculean task, Veitch later did just that—becoming the writer-penciler for *Swamp Thing*, and admirably extending and reinterpreting the spirit and specifics of Moore's seminal work. However, DC Comics' policies and nefarious business practices took their toll on Veitch as they had with the others before him on the title, and he left the series in 1989 due to management's refusal to publish *Swamp Thing* #88. (After the script had been accepted, and guest penciler Michael Zulli had completed all but the last three pages of the issue.)

Disgusted with the industry's work-for-hire practices, Veitch returned to creator-owned and controlled projects, launching his own publishing company, King Hell Press. In association with Tundra Publishing, King Hell launched the "Heroica Universe" with the controversial *Bratpack* (1990–91), which gleefully exposes, lambasts, and deflates the terrifying subtexts of the superhero "teenage sidekick" conventions. First in a number of interlocking miniseries, *Bratpack* successfully lead to *The Maximortal* (1992–93), and in collaboration with John Totleben, *Hellhead* (1994). Like the rugged, take-no-bullshit superheroes in his cutting-edge Heroica Universe, Rick Veitch is not what most people expect a talented and successful comic book artist to be like, either.

COMIC BOOK REBELS: What started this almost obsessive, lifelong romance with the medium?

RICK VEITCH: I know that comics were read to me as a very small child; I actually learned to read from memorizing what words looked like that were told to me in comic books. As I grew older, and was in the first or second grade, I noticed my older brother Tom—who is ten years older than me—was drawing his own comic book. This was absolutely *enthralling* to me. You know how it is when you have an older brother: Everything they do is really cool! [*Laughs*] I tried to emulate him, and the passion just stuck.

Comics became part of my life in a very organic way. Instead of sitting in front of a television set, I'd go up to my room with a clipboard and a piece of white paper and draw out my fantasy stories in my own comics. I put out monthly comics all through grade school and through high school until the underground scene hit.

CBR: Your professional career goes back to the underground comix, with the collaborations you did with your brother Tom on *Crazy Mouse* and *Two-Fisted Zombies*. What brought you from that era into working for the major mainstream publishers?

VEITCH: Probably the Joe Kubert School. I had always read mainstream comics as a kid, and if you look at a lot of my underground work, the Jack Kirby influence is pretty obvious. But after doing *Two-Fisted Zombies*—and watching the whole San Francisco publishing scene collapse—I moved back into the woods. I got married, had a kid, and gave up trying to have a career in cartooning. I was still drawing comics for myself, but I just couldn't make the business end of it work, either through the undergrounds or through the mainstream. After two or three years of that, I realized that I still really wanted to draw comic books and that I needed to go to art school. Basically I was running on the energy of an adolescent, in terms of my art, and I needed to reformulate it, and to learn new things.

Completely penniless, I somehow got the money together to go to Joe Kubert's cartooning school, and that, more than anything else, allowed me to break into mainstream cartooning. For one thing, it put me into the New York metropolitan area, which was where mainstream cartooning was happening in the late seventies. I also got to work on a day-to-day basis with professional cartoonists, people who had been doing this for twenty or thirty years. Up to that point, drawing had been something I did whenever I felt like it, or was bored. But when you hang around a human dynamo like Joe Kubert, some of that energy rubs off on you! Drawing then became much more integral to my life, and I started drawing *continually*.

CBR: After graduation from the Joe Kubert School, you first attempted to break into DC Comics during the great implosion of the early Seventies. Your career almost ended before it began.

VEITCH: While in school, I had done a number of stories for DC under the tutelage of Kubert, and the feeling was that we were kind of being groomed to start our careers there. But it was just at the time of graduation that the implosion happened, and I believe they canceled anywhere from a third to nearly half of their titles. So I went up to DC and basically got the door shut in my face. It was traumatic at the time, but it actually turned out to be a wonderful twist of fate. Because of course where do you go when DC shuts the door in your face? You go to Marvel. And in fact the door was wide open there, and it was doing much more progressive types of comics, such as *Epic*.

CBR: You worked for Marvel Comics throughout the Eighties while still maintaining creative autonomy and even ownership over most of your material. Simply put, how did you "get away with it" for so long with one of the major companies?

VEITCH: I was just in the right place at the right time, when Marvel began their *Epic* imprint, apparently responding to the brand new direct sales market and the then just-being-born independent comics such as *Cerebus* and *Elfquest*.

I had taught myself how to run an airbrush, and was working with Steve Bissette on a number of color projects. Together we evolved an interesting illustration style using colored pencils, Dr. Martin dyes, and collage, which worked really well with the new reproduction techniques that *Heavy Metal* and *Epic* magazine were kind of pioneering in the comics. Their contract was terrific; they only purchased one-time North American rights, which was unheard of in those days. And Archie Goodwin was the editor. Just about everyone in the business would crawl over broken glass to work with Archie! So it was great while it lasted, and it left me with a really large body of work that I'm very proud of, and which someday I hope to reprint.

CBR: It was at Marvel you began your first series of revisionist superheroes, especially with *The One*, your final series for *Epic*. How did *The One* come about?

VEITCH: What lead to *The One* was my belief that there was a depth and an importance to the genre of superheroes that had never been plumbed.

I can remember talking to others at the Kubert School about superheroes, and saying "if only a more literary and honest approach was taken, then something *really* interesting might be created." I had a

BUT I DON'T WANT YOU BOYS TO LOSE ANY SLEEP OVER MOVIE DEALS.

THE IMPORTANT THING IS TO DEVELOP THIS GUY BY DOING THE BEST COMIC BOOK YOU CAN.

WE'LL WORK FOR NOTHING IF YOU'LL TAKE A CHANCE ON US, SID!

ARE YOU KIDDING? ANYONE WHO WORKS FOR ME GETS OUR TOP RATE! FIVE WHOLE BUCKS A PAGE!

WWOWW!

AND WE ALSO MAKE SURE YOU'RE PROTECTED-- RIGHT FROM THE START...

...WITH A CONTRACT! HOW OLD ARE YOU?

WE'RE BOTH NINETEEN.

THEN YOU'RE CONSENTING ADULTS IN THIS STATE. NAMES?

TAP TAP TAP

I'M JERRY SPIEGAL.

AND I'M JOE SCHUMACHER.

SPIEGAL AND SCHUMACHER, EH? HAS A NICE RING TO IT-- I LIKE IT!

LET'S SEE THOSE JOHN HANCOCK'S ON THE BOTTOM LINE, BOYS!

AGREEMENT

UMM, WELL, COULDN'T WE TAKE IT HOME AND LOOK IT OVER? MAYBE SHOW IT TO A LAWYER?

WHO YOU GONNA' TRUST-- SOME LAWYER? OR ME?

OH, WE TRUST YOU, SID!

THEN DON'T WASTE YOUR TIME. IT'S JUST OUR STANDARD DEAL.

62

FROM *THE MAXIMORTAL.* © 1993 BY RICK VEITCH.

feeling this could be done, but I didn't have the skills at that point to do it—or even to see what had to be done. But reading Alan Moore's work on *Miracleman* brought it all into focus for me. I was definitely still developing my writing skills on *The One*. But I felt then and still feel today that there are many layers of depth to be explored. And possibly our own generation won't even understand the levels. It might take twenty or thirty years before people fully understand what we've been doing.

The One was the first step for me in that direction.

CBR: Why did you eventually leave *Epic* magazine?

VEITCH: Well, for various reasons *Epic* magazine died, and was replaced by the *Epic* comics line. Which was a slightly different animal—though I must say my experience with *Epic* comics was terrific as well.

But what really took me away from them was the work that John Totleben and Steve Bissette were doing on *Swamp Thing*. Up to that point, I wouldn't have *touched* the idea of doing a monthly comic book until I saw how that trio shook up the comic book world with *Swamp Thing*. Along with what Frank Miller was doing with *Daredevil* at the time, those guys really showed how a mainstream comic could be really good and creatively fulfilling. It could also be a real hotbed of ideas, and a very exciting thing to do. And once I saw that happening, I gravitated over in that direction.

CBR: Eventually you came on board to lend your talents, and after the above-named trio left the title, you were working full time as both artist and writer on *Swamp Thing*.

VEITCH: Yes, I started with a few fill-in issues, and then took over the penciling after Steve and John left the book. I worked with Alan for a couple of years, and when he left the book as writer, I took over the writing as well. This went on for a couple of more years. It was working out pretty well even though it was very hectic, and was probably more work than I cared to do all at once.

CBR: What we're leading to, of course, are the events dealing with the infamous issue #88 of *Swamp Thing*, which was killed by DC and to this day remains unpublished. What's your view of what happened?

VEITCH: I was working on a long-term storyline, over the course of a year, in which Swamp Thing went back in time. And each issue went progressively farther and farther back, with our hero meeting characters in the DC universe who were from the past, such as Tomahawk, as well as real people out of world history, such as Hitler. I then got the great idea of doing an issue in which Swamp Thing witnessed Christ's passion in the garden of Gethsemane. I knew it was a tricky subject to deal with in comics, so I discussed it with my editor, Karen Berger. And under her direction, I did a proposal, which we then showed to the powers that be at DC Comics, and they okayed it. I went ahead and wrote the complete script, which was then approved by my editor and, I assumed, by the powers that be above her.

It wasn't until a few months later, when the book was just being finished in pencils by Michael Zulli—who did a gorgeous job—that our problems began. Anyway, I think the first few pages were beginning to be inked, and somehow Jeanette Kahn saw it, and she stopped the whole project—dead. Refused to publish it. I got a call from Karen Berger, who was quite distraught, telling me that the book had been cancelled and that I had to write a new script within three days to replace it.

Which I wasn't going to do; as soon as I heard that they had stopped publication of the book, I resigned. Immediately.

CBR: The *Swamp Thing* #88 incident received a noticeable degree of media coverage, both inside and outside of the industry. Did it change anything for you in terms of effectively dealing with DC?

VEITCH: I first got a call from somebody at MTV News, and they ran a small news segment on it. Then I got a call from the *Wall Street Journal*. Then *Time* magazine. Then the AP wire service, and Scripps-Howard, and several other media organizations ran news items. The incident sailed around the country for a couple of weeks, which I must admit was kind of fun. But that was it for me, in terms of DC Comics, because I'd broken the Mafia-like "code of silence" that all freelancers are expected to abide by. Every once in a while I get a call from an editor at DC saying they want me to work with them again, and I always go, "Only if you publish *Swamp Thing* #88." And they never call back.

But I do have a feeling that someday, somehow, the book will get published. That DC will come to its senses, and realize they made a terrible mistake. I suspect if that ever happens, people will read the story and wonder, "Hey, what was the fuss all about?"

CBR: What's your personal assessment of why the issue was killed?

Veitch: On the surface, I think it had to do with Kahn's battle with Alan Moore and Frank Miller and a couple of other guys who had resigned—or threatened to—over her "standards of practice." About six or eight months earlier she had, just out of the blue, handed down a set of standards which the DC comic books were going to adhere to. And these standards drove just about everybody out. One of the points in the standards was that "There shall be no religious figures in DC Comics." She was later forced to publicly back down, even though Miller and Moore never went back to DC. So it was all part of that previous mess.

I think it also became tied up with the release of the Batman movie, and the corporate merger of Warner and Time, which was all going on at this time. I think there was this general feeling at DC Comics that everything had to be "safe"—they didn't want a bunch of right-wing Christians showing up at the Warner Building protesting Christ's appearance in *Swamp Thing*. Unfortunately I've never had the opportunity to sit down with Jeanette or any of the other powers that be and discuss why they did it. But in terms of my career at that point, when I left DC I was able to call Kevin Eastman and Peter Laird, and I was offered a job doing *Teenage Mutant Ninja Turtles* comics right off the bat. So, thinking back, it was really the best thing that could have happened to me, to get out of the clutches of DC Comics.

CBR: Was the DC experience what led to the formation of your own imprint, King Hell Press?

Veitch: Self-publishing was in my mind from the very beginning, but what clicked it for me was *Swamp Thing #88*. That just moved up my own timetable by about a year. Right now I still don't have the capital I need to make King Hell Press work entirely on its own, and I'm currently publishing my work in association with Tundra Publishing. I worked out a deal with them where I use their infrastructure and capital to get my projects off the ground and get them out into the marketplace. So far it's worked out really well for both of us.

I would like to see a lot more creators start up their own imprints. I think it would help our art form expand in new and exciting ways.

CBR: Would you ever consider working for a major mainstream publisher like Marvel or DC again? Or are they simply no longer necessary to make your career continue and succeed?

VEITCH: I don't want to say I'll never work for them again, yet I don't want to work for them under the terms that existed when I was working for them in the Seventies and Eighties. I don't want to sign work-for-hire contracts to barely make a living wage and work until I drop, which I've seen happen to a number of individuals. But things *are* changing. I think you're going to see a big change in how Marvel and DC do business over this next decade. Their primacy in the sales arena is going to start to erode, if it hasn't already. And even though they own the great characters, I think that to retain the best and most bankable creators they're going to have to change their ways because there're going to be too many attractive alternatives out there.

To take just one example from 1992: Image Comics, which changed the whole balance of power in the direct sales market. And if Image can continue to succeed, and continue to hold together without flying apart from centrifugal forces, it will change forever how publishers are seen. People won't approach publishers as if they are crime families any more. They'll be seen as service organizations. Or in the cases of Marvel and DC, service organizations which happen to own a lot of great characters. I think we're at a real turning point in our industry—and our art form—and that maybe the lid is going to blow off what's been bottled up by the monied interests.

CBR: So you're optimistic that, the more small publishers there are, the better off everyone working in the field will be? Assuming the industry giants are going to change their business practices if they're to thrive in the coming years as well.

VEITCH: It's my gut feeling that it's going to work, and that the people out there are ready for us. There's too much lingering resentment against the business policies of companies like Marvel and DC, and even they are beginning to realize you just can't go back to the way things were for the previous generations of creators.

But the major companies will always have the ability to attract young people who just haven't had the experience yet to understand how they screw themselves. *And I've been there.* I can see how certain decisions I made starting out are now causing problems for me, much later on. Or circumstances that happened in my career early on might somehow later lead me to stifle my creativity. Surely signing over ownership of a large body of work to a huge, amoral company was a major mistake.

But you can get hooked on the kind of money you make doing a successful mainstream title. You start out as a starving artist. All of a sudden you're making good, middle-class money, so it's really hard to just jump off and do something else on your own. Especially if by then you've got a family to support, and a mortgage to pay, and everything else. If there was a way of getting to the younger creators, and pointing all this out to them before they sign onto the slave ship, things would change in the industry a lot quicker.

CBR: Why your continued fascination with superheroes? Many creators who have been working in the industry as long as you have eventually burnt out on this subject.

VEITCH: I think one reason why other people get burnt out is because they don't get to do the type of superheroes that they might really want to do. When I established the King Hell imprint, it was to do *my* version of superheroes. Which are slightly more demented than anything anyone else is doing! [*Laughs*] But I tend to fly in the face of conventional wisdom because I see the superhero archetype as central to the twentieth-century American culture. To me, superheroes symbolize the American Dream itself. Certainly they're the foundation of comic books as a medium. Comic books didn't really happen as a mass phenomenon until *Superman.*

It's much more than comics . . . heroes in film are much closer to "superheroes" than they are to ordinary human beings. People in twentieth-century America live, eat, breathe, and defecate superheroes. All the time. Without even thinking about it. But the only problem with that is that nearly all the superheroes are owned—lock, stock, and work-for-hire—by a few major companies who have no reason to evolve their characters beyond a certain adolescent level. And if this archetype is as vital and important as I think it is to our culture, then it has to grow. To keep it stifled, is in a way to keep our whole *culture* stifled.

We have to break it out of the form it's been stuck in for so long. I think in the Eighties a great step was made in that direction, but we've got a long way to go. There's a depth to this genre that hasn't even been tapped yet. And it won't be tapped by companies who have a greater stake in licensing their characters—forever as is—than in allowing them to grow and develop in the way that they should.

CBR: Describe your master plan for developing your own vision of a superhero mythos. Clearly *Bratpack* and *The Maximortal* are parts of an even larger whole of still developing themes and concepts.

VEITCH: Right now I'm in the middle of the biggest part of the "master plan," which is the story of True-Man, being published in the series known as *The Maximortal*. That series will probably run about fifty issues, if not more. It's going to be broken up into four novels. This cycle of novels will detail, more than anything, where I'm going with this whole "King Hell Heroica" idea. A lot of it's still wide open, and forming even as we speak.

To begin with, I want to peel back the stratified layers that have grown over the real core of the genre. Some of that's nostalgia, some is adolescent addiction. Some of it is all the ridiculous marketing that goes with the pop culture territory. I want to get to the real human instincts that are at the heart and soul of this thing. I'll tell you, working on it—it's almost too easy. [*Chuckles*] Because so much of this stuff has been kept just under the surface, even used subliminally to sell the superhero comics for all these years.

CBR: *The Maximortal* also tells the story of the comic book industry through the fictionalized experiences of Maximortal's creators.

VEITCH: It goes back to the idea of art being an organic life-process that comes out of people. And the industry has always tended to crush that spirit, and to see creators as interchangeable cogs that can be taken in and out of any project. That it's the fictional characters themselves which make the "machine" go.

It's my feeling that you can't separate a creator from the characters that he or she creates. It's a *crime* to do so, unless it's done under the auspices and with the blessings of the original creator. The obvious parallel that I'm working with here is the Siegel & Schuster tragedy.

What happened to the creators of *Superman* kind of sets the tone for all creator-publisher relationships in comics in this century. I've fictionalized some real events that have been documented. I've also created some characters which aren't Siegel or Schuster, but definitely embody certain aspects of those pioneers.

It was done in the hope of enlightening current and future generations of comic book readers about what's been going on in "the backroom of the store."

CBR: Do you feel that you have total creative freedom at this point in your career? Apparently Tundra has never asked you to censor your work to meet their needs as a publisher?

VEITCH: Naah! They just egg me on! I'm sure there are areas I could touch upon that might cause Tundra problems, but I don't see any need to at this point. Nothing I've done with my current work is "X-rated," although an X-rated superhero comic might be interesting, and at some point I might pursue doing one. But I've been plying my art long enough to know how to get what I want, with the effect that I want, without having to resort to the type of material that would put the comic "behind the shelf," or in the "Adults Only" section. And by "X-rated" I mean showing actual sexual penetration which, when I started my career in the underground comix, was *de rigueur*.

CBR: Any negative response from fans with *Bratpack*, in terms of your blasting away the once rock-hard concept that superhero comics should just be "good, clean, harmless entertainment"?

VEITCH: Oh, I'm sure I gored some people's oxes! [*Laughs*] But I think I've discovered a niche, which the major companies don't dare to exploit. My audience is that reader who has been reading *X-Men* and all these other superhero comic books for a long time, and who might not be ready to pick up something like *Love & Rockets* or *Cages* or *Big Numbers* or *From Hell*. But *Bratpack* and *The Maximortal* are like a step between the tired mainstream superhero books and some of the most mature material being produced right now.

I believe that niche is created by the addictive quality of superhero comics. Kids get addicted on these comics, and they read thousands of them. And at some point they just burn out and it's usually for a good reason: because they picked up the latest issue of, say, *X-Men*, and they realize it's virtually the same story they first read from forty issues ago. They're still interested in superheroes—but they're kind of fried from reading too many comics with the same old ingredients. It's like eating too many hamburgers at McDonald's: You eventually never want to see another hamburger again! When they reach that point I believe they'll enjoy reading comics which conceptually deconstruct what superheroics supposedly are.

That's where I'm at, and that's where my niche audience exists.

19

Todd McFarlane
Breaking Rank

Among the most dramatic developments in the history of the industry has been the recent formation of Image Comics. Within only weeks of its gestation, Image Comics had turned the entire market on its ear, creating shock waves that all but literally reverberated onto Wall Street.

In February of 1992, Marvel's best-selling artists—Todd McFarlane, Rob Liefeld, and Jim Lee, as well as Erik Larsen, Whilce Portacio, Marc Silverstri, and Jim Valentino—announced the formation of their own publishing company. (Initially launching their titles through an existing independent publisher, Malibu Comics.) The news immediately spilled beyond the parameters of the miniscule comics-industry press, punctuating a controversial article in *Barron's* (February 17, 1992) that in turn prompted an immediate plunge in Marvel Comics stock.

The story was also reported in no less than the *Wall Street Journal* and the *New York Times*, where Marvel president Terry Stewart quickly belittled the import of the event. In effect, Stewart dismissed the movement of freelance creators within this industry as being simply business as usual: "Basically, they come, they go, and they come back again." ("Another Blow For Marvel," the New York *Times*, February 20, 1992).

Though Marvel stock did eventually recover, the first Image release—of Rob Liefeld's *Youngblood* #1 (1992)—became the best-selling creator-owned comic title to date. It was a record that was soon matched and bettered by subsequent Image titles, with the result being a significant cutting into the mainstream publishers' share of the market. The incredible early success of Image was interpreted by many as a telling blow against the empire, marking a major turning point in comic-book creators seizing control of their own creations, fates, and fortunes.

Not yet thirty years old, Todd McFarlane is among the oldest and most experienced creators in the Image area. His inauspicious debut in the pages of DC Comics' *Infinity, Inc.*, (1986–87) revealed a competent enough super-hero artist whose flair for unusual page design was compromised by the unwieldy plethora of costumed characters populating the title. A few years later, he made his mark (and fortune) with his highly inventive interpretation of *The Amazing Spiderman* (#298–328, 1989–90), rendering the web-slinging superhero with an energy and flair that was noticeably unusual for the plantation-production standards of Marvel.

Despite steady friction with the company's editors and management, the overwhelming commercial success of McFarlane's efforts made him an industry superstar: his *Spiderman* #1 sold a reported record 2.8 million copies. Then, having never written professionally before, he wrote and drew the first fourteen issues of the new Spiderman title. This effort earned him record sales, kudos from his legions of fans, and open derision from his critics and peers contemptutous of his awkward scripting efforts, affiliation with Marvel—and undeniable financial success.

Unfazed by either the adulation or contempt, Todd McFarlane has gone on to acquire an almost unprecedented harbor of stature and autonomy within the industry.

COMIC BOOK REBELS: What led to your leaving Marvel Comics after doing *Spiderman* #16, and then going on to form your own company, Image Comics?

TODD MCFARLANE: First off, I quit *Spiderman* when my daughter was born. That was ninety percent of the reason why I quit. It didn't really make any difference what else was going on, I was going to quit anyway. The other ten percent came to a head over a panel they wanted me to redraw in that issue. When they told me to redraw that panel, I pulled the book. I said, "Send it all back to me. I don't give you permission to use this issue." And they went, "But Todd, you'll lose tens of thousands of dollars in royalties." And I said, "Yes, but if I pull it back, you'll have to make every single one of your issues #16 returnable; you fuckers are going to lose a lot of money, too. And if you don't think that I just can't re-ink this and call it *Webberman* and take it over to DC as the unpublished *Spiderman #16*, and still make gobs of money, you guys are sadly mistaken. It's not like these are worthless pages I've got in my hands."

So my whole career became wrapped up in that one panel! I tried to tell these guys that they had finally worn me down to the nub, and that I had nothing left but bare skin now. So I was done. I'm tired of fighting to be successful, you know? "I'm putting money in your pockets—why are you always dickering with me all the time? There are guys who aren't doing half the job I'm doing—go fucking get them to fucking catch up to me instead of asking me to slow down!" You know?

This is one of those weird businesses where being successful is a hindrance. They go, "Wow! Your book is successful, so we'd better *not* promote it. We'd better promote the other books that need the help." Well, *fuck!* What other business does that? Remember the movie *Home Alone?* The studio didn't know it would be a sleeper, but it *was* a sleeper, and it made a bejillion dollars. So now that the video is ready to hit the stores, can you imagine them saying, "Oh, no, we'd better push *Pussycat and her Four Booties* instead." No, no, no! There were *Home Alone* videos in 7-Elevens, in pet stores—I was puking, I saw that video in so many places. But you know why? Because most businesses go, "We should make money off a successful product." But comic book companies are the opposite: "Ah, this book doesn't need any help. It's already selling."

So I quit and took a few months off. Around that same time, I was talking to Rob Liefeld. Rob and I were always the rebels in these companies. We always had a bad reputation.

CBR: With the editors?

McFARLANE: With everybody! [*Laughs*] You know what I mean. Hey, if I took orders, I wouldn't have drawn Spiderman the way I did. Marvel editor-in-chief Tom Falco once called me in the office and said, "Quit drawing your spaghetti webbing." I said, "Yes, sir." "Don't make the eyes so big. How come you put so much black in his costume?" I said, "Oh, yes, sir. I'll change it back, yes, sir." Then the next issue I'd make the eyes twice as big, I'd make the spaghetti webbing twice as long, and the sales would go up which would aggravate the editors even more.

NEXT ISSUE:
ALL HELL
BREAKS
LOOSE ON
EARTH!

At that point, Rob and I were looking to do something together. When Rob announced he was going to do *Youngblood*, as soon as he announced it, it was like, "Fine, I'm on board too." Now, Rob was just going to do it as a one-shot, and go back to Marvel or DC. But I was already gone from Marvel. So I said, "We've got to start a union." But nobody wanted to do it, so Image became our union. Here's the deal. I had been bugging Jim Lee for months, and Erik Larsen for months, and it became a matter of timing. I was already off the ship, so I told these guys that anytime they were ready to jump ship, I was ready. So I convinced as many people as I could, by giving them the biggest sales pitch that I could.

So I was ready, and Rob was ready. Now Marvel's golden boy at the time was Jim Lee. He was the company man. So it came down to him—if they lost me and Rob, and they kept Jim—it was a victory for them. But if we pulled away Jim Lee—the company man—then *anything* was possible! The editors already knew we were screwballs, and that we were gone, and that we were going to do something on our own. But we knew Jim would be like the last diamond in this crown of jewels. We knew it would be easy then to have other people follow us in the wind. So anyway, Jim goes, "Okay, yeah, fine." Nobody was as excited as I was.

So I set up a meeting with Terry Stewart, president of Marvel Comics, basically to tell him we're quitting. Not that we want to renegotiate, not that we want this or that. Just to tell him, "We're quitting. Here're our reasons why. Do with that information as you wish. If you want to ignore us, fine, we're gone anyway! If you want to change something, fine, we're gone anyway. It don't make no difference to us now." But God love Terry Stewart! He said the wrong things at the right time. Because for Jim Lee—who was wavering about leaving—that meeting was the one which solidified his jumping ship.

You see, Terry likes to count his pennies, and he was saying things like, "Well, you're not going to get this extra benefit, or we're not going to fly your wife to this or that meeting." They were things I didn't give a shit about, but Jim did! So it made Jim realize, "I'm your biggest artist, and I sell your most successful comic books, and you won't fly me and my wife in for a meeting?" And they went, "No." So he said, "Fuck it! If I was Mickey Mantle, you don't think they'd fly Mickey Mantle's wife around with him if he asked them to?"

Comics is an entertainment business. And in most entertainment businesses, the one who sells the most—not necessarily the best, but the one who's the most commercial—they usually get schmoozed the most, you know? But Jim Lee wasn't getting schmoozed. It was like, "You want to bring your wife, you're going to have to do this. You want to rent a car, you're going to pay for it." All the wrong things to say! At that point, it wasn't the money, it was the principle of the thing. So when the meeting ended and we walked out the door, they patted us on the back and said, "Oh, when you fail, please come back and work for us."

I remember when the elevator doors closed, and I turned to Jim Lee and said, "These guys are *dead*. And you know the reason they're dead? They forgot one fucking thing about us. Besides talent, they forget we got a fucking muscle up there called a brain."

They think we're dorks! They think we're the artists of thirty years ago, who just came off the streets. Unfortunately for them, since then most of us have university degrees or have started our own businesses, and know which end is up. Plus, my whole family has a background in the printing industry. These companies were always telling us that what they did was like magic. And you know what? *None* of what they did was magic in publishing comic books.

But they'd brainwash us! You know? They'd go, "We're doing five pushups here for you guys. And you wouldn't want to try it, because it's just a pain in the ass, and too hard for you guys to imitate." So we got down on our bellies and went, "Fuck! There's *ten* pushups. Ten? Hey, I didn't even break a sweat at five!"

What these publishers were doing for us was nothing, I'm sorry to say. One of two things has to be said: either the boys at Image are geniuses. Thank you, but I doubt if that's it. Or, the people at Marvel and DC don't know what the fuck they're doing. I'll argue the second point.

CBR: Tell us about your most popular character to date, *Spawn*. Some of our readers may be hearing about him here for the first time.

McFARLANE: *Spawn is the greatest character being published in comic books today, bar none!* [*Laughs*] Make that in big bold type, too! Spawn is a character I created in 1980 or 1981. It was a portfolio character, like we all have. I wanted to come up with a character from a creative point of view that I wouldn't get bored drawing. Sometimes you get bored with a character you're drawing at the time. So when you're doing

Spiderman, you say to yourself, "I'm tired of this fucking spaghetti-webbing! I just can't draw that webbing anymore. I'm going to *scream* if I draw that webbing!" That was why I would bring in Wolverine or Ghost Rider into the *Spiderman* books—anybody just to take my mind off Spiderman!

I wanted to come out with a character that is like Batman—who is essentially a human being in a costume—and Superman all mixed into one. I didn't want him to be too much like Superman, whose powers are basically unlimited. But I'm a bigger fan of Batman. He always has to dodge the bullet.

CBR: If you had created such an interesting character so early in your career, why didn't you introduce him to Marvel Comics or DC?

McFARLANE: "Why didn't a guy like Todd McFarlane, one of your more commercial talents out there, why did he never pull Spawn out of his portfolio? And as a matter of fact, why didn't he ever create a new character for these companies, period?" I mean, after a year and a half on *Spiderman*, I could have created *twenty* new characters. But you never saw one new character from me.

No—I made up my mind a long time ago not to. Being the psychotic shit that I was—and having read all the interviews—I knew that Jack Kirby got *fucked*. That was the biggest revelation for me: if "The King" can get fucked, *anybody* can get fucked! I always knew going in—from day one—that I wanted to start a union. Except nobody gave a shit, because back when I started on *Infinity, Inc.* I was a nobody. So I'm just saying today the same things I said five years ago. The voice is the same.

CBR: What do you think is going to give a small company like Image the staying power over the old-time giants?

McFARLANE: What's going to allow us to compete in the long run—and I'll believe this to my dying day—is the talent base that we have. Because we're *pro-creator*. Now, that doesn't mean we can't each try to create our own universal character like Mickey Mouse, but what's going to get Image in the same ballgame is not that we have huge corporate backing, or a firm of forty-five lawyers; we don't have any of that. But you know what I think we're going to have in the long run? The most *talent*.

And you know the only way we're going to keep attracting that top talent? On a basic level, there're only two things that really motivate most creative people: a) the bills getting paid or b) creative freedom. And we can offer them something sweeter than that: *both*. Usually you have to give up one to get the other. But we're saying: You can have all the freedom you want, *and* all the income you richly deserved over the past twenty years or whenever you started. That means we'll have the truly creative people. And if we get the creative people, Marvel or DC can put out 180 books a week, for all I care! If my mom draws them, it don't make no difference anymore.

CBR: Where do you see the future of the "Big Two" headed?

McFARLANE: They used to have the best comic books in the country. But I don't think that's going to be true in a few years. Because they're going to water down the product. They're pushing these gimmick covers over good stories and characters. They've got a bottom line now, they've got to keep bringing their profits up, and they're gonna forget the one factor that Image will not forget: *quality*. Quality and the good talents that produce it. Once you lose sight of that, you're dead. They may make a lot of money in the short run, but eventually it's going to blow up in their faces.

CBR: Do you think Image Comics represents the beginning of the end in terms of the way creators should now be treated by their respective employers?

McFARLANE: A little bit of yes and no. The guys who are going to benefit the most are those that have been brainwashed by this industry. I've called a hundred different creators, and most of them go, "Well, I'm not Jim Lee, and I'm not Todd McFarlane." And I've tried to pound it into their head that you don't *have* to be the hot artist of the month anymore. You can be somewhere between the best guy and the worst guy working out there, and realize—realize *this* if nothing, nothing else—that through your hard-earned work you're going to get paid what only one guy in the industry used to get paid: which was Todd McFarlane. It shouldn't matter how "famous" you are, it's a matter of what's a fair deal for all concerned. That fair deal is what I hope will bring more creative people running to our door.

Whether Image changes the way comics are done, I'm not really here to say it's time for us to change the way comics are published. I'm here to say there is *more than one way of doing the same fucking job*. You know? Whenever you show a big business a way of doing something different, they mistakenly assume their way must have been wrong for you not to have done it that way yourself. While my argument has always been, "I didn't draw Spiderman the way I did because John Romita was 'wrong.' I did it because John Romita did such a great job that I had to come up with something else that would set me apart." And their response was, "If you won't do it our way, then you must think we're idiots upstairs."

But no—I see the finish line as having twelve paths to it. I'm just taking one route. Marvel and DC are taking another route, and there are ten other ways to get to that finish line in this business. Once these big companies get out of that defensive mode, and they go, "Yes, we have to start to do business on more than just one level," then the situation will be a lot smoother. When they finally realize there is more than one way to do every single aspect of this business—from retailing to distributing to everything in between—then everybody will prosper.

The big guys call us weak, they call us unprofessional, and they call us disorganized. I say yes to all three charges. But you know what? We sell more comic books per title than any other comic book company in North America. So you know what my words of advice are to Marvel and DC?

CBR: We doubt you're going to hold back at this point.

McFarlane: I'd get a little more fucking unprofessional and disorganized—because it might sell a few more comic books.

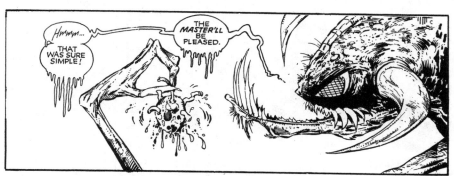

FROM *SPAWN*. © AND TRADEMARK 1993 BY TODD MCFARLANE PRODUCTIONS, INC.

20

WILL EISNER
The Old Man on the Mountain

Will Eisner is arguably the *first* comic book rebel.

Most of the artists who labored over the earliest original comic book stories aspired to having their own comic *strips*, or elevating themselves to the better-paying ranks of the well-heeled magazine illustrators of the day. Many more had resigned themselves to achieving little more than the meager living the comic page treadmill provided. But Eisner somehow knew the primitive comic books of  the Thirties were only the beginning for his legendary career.

In partnership with Jerry Iger, he managed one of the first studios designed to supply original stories and art to this newly formed industry. That partnership dissolved once Eisner was approached by a newspaper syndicate with an opportunity to create his own weekly series for a new audience. *The Spirit* was launched on February 6, 1940, as a "comic magazine" inserted into the Sunday papers (much like today's TV magazine sections). Furthermore, he had successfully negotiated control and rights to his own creation.

Will Eisner was the first American comic book artist to do so.

The Spirit immediately established Eisner as one of the medium's true innovators, crafting a new summit in comic book art. The synthesis of story and imagery to telling dramatic effect was orchestrated week after week by a new studio of artists working under his careful supervision, with Eisner writing, designing, and integrally involved with the completion of each and every page. The demise of *The Spirit* on October 10, 1952, marked the end of an era, and drove Eisner further beyond the established parameters of the comic book industry. His numerous one-shot industrial, educational, and government training comics sustained him throughout the next two decades.

In the Seventies, a new generation's interest prompted a revival of *The Spirit* and, more importantly, Eisner began work—alone this time—on an ambitious, self-contained volume of dramatic stories. The book was published in 1978 as *A Contract with God* (coincidentally appearing just weeks after the first independent "comic novel," *Sabre*), and Eisner coined the term "graphic novel" to distinguish the scope and ambitions of this new format from the standard periodical comic books.

Eisner has since forged a bond with European publishers and Denis Kitchen to create a remarkable body of graphic anthologies and novels. These include *Signal from Space* (1978–83), *New York, the Big City* (1981–86), *A Life Force* (1983–88), *The Building* (1987), and *City People*. A fictionalized chronicle of his early years in the comics industry is *The Dreamer* (1986), while a moving autobiographical portrait of intolerance and anti-Semitism in America during World War II exists in *To the Heart of the Storm* (1991).

Rather than distance himself from the creative community during this fertile period, Will Eisner remains a pervasive force within the industry, forever a passionate and eloquent advocate for positive self-awareness and growth.

COMIC BOOK REBELS: What did you think was possible in the comics medium when you started in the industry, back in 1936?

WILL EISNER: I have to give it to you from a personal perspective. I saw comics as a medium wherein I could realize my literary and art ambitions. Most people who came upon comics in 1936 simply saw it as an amorphic entertainment medium. Comics were divided into a few categories; there were daily strips, there were comic pages, and there were single panels. But comic "books" as we call them today were then the result of assembling six weeks of daily strips into magazines that sold for ten cents. Hardly promising as literature.

The thing that struck me, however, was that comics was the answer to what I was personally looking for: a medium which combined the elements which accommodated the talents I believed I had. I mean, I could draw. Also I wanted to be a writer. So I recognized very early that this form employed both elements, so it was possible to do things beyond slapstick in this form and devote a lifetime to it. Most of the other artists working alongside me in the field at the time regarded comics as merely a stepping stone on the way to the real, serious world of being an illustrator. The hope of landing a daily newspaper strip was remote.

So, no one saw comics as a lifelong pursuit. But I saw it as a great opportunity.

CBR: So you then decided to become one of the first packagers of turning comic stories into literal comic books by establishing your own cartoonists' studio?

EISNER: Yes, that was related to seeing the future of the field. In 1936, *Wow* magazine bought my first few pieces. It died after the fourth issue. But by then I recognized that there was a new market. The pulps were dying; the publishers were looking for a new market to replace them, it was easy to see that. It was also easy to see that the source material of comic magazines would soon dry up because they were using only daily newspaper strip material, like *Dick Tracy* and other adventure strips. Pretty soon those had to give out. Besides, there was a finite number of viable strips—clearly, new original material would have to be produced.

I had to argue with my partner Jerry Iger—who joined me when *Wow* collapsed—when I proposed the idea that we would manufacture the content material for these new comic magazines. He said, "I don't see much of a future here." And I argued, "There is a *tremendous* future here because there is no existing source of original material. There are also no complete stories in terms of material." The daily strips had merely continuing stories. So I told him I felt this was a great opportunity.

This may sound like great genius, but it was purely a reaction to being caught in a maze, and saying, "Hey, this is the only way out!" It was pretty obvious to me at the time. Well, Iger agreed after a little while that this *would* be a way to make money. Jerry was important to me because he could sell—he was eighteen years older than me, and "mature." [*Laughs*] I was still only nineteen or twenty years old, and still hesitant about selling. The product needed selling. Events eventually proved my point: complete, original stories came to be the backbone of the industry.

And, indeed, the unique thing about the early comic magazines or "comic books" was the fact that they presented *complete* stories. In fact, in the advertisements on the covers, we would always append the words "Complete Story!" That was a compelling idea for comics at that time. It was a concept that carried pulp magazines for many years.

CBR: So you took the theory that fans of short stories in prose would be fans of short stories in the comics medium?

EISNER: Not quite. There was no precedent. We really did not aim at the basic pulp readers—we just used the idea. There were no schools of comics. There was no theoretical comprehension. Sure, as a writer I borrowed from pulps—I was using my experience in the short story form. It was my early literary nutrition. I was also influenced by the work of O. Henry and Ring Lardner, and Saki, among others. The thirties, you must understand, was the halcyon days for the short story. It dominated American popular literature at the time. I based story concepts on them.

In fact, one of our big customers at Eisner & Iger was Fiction House, which was a pulp publishing company who were experiencing a downdraft in their sales and were looking for something else to invest in. We suggested they take on comic books, and they did! They distributed the comics the same way as they did their pulps. Part of my selling argument to them was that we were going to take a genre of literature which they knew and understood so well—namely the short story pulp—and simply transfer it to comics. It was a convincing argument.

CBR: You were one of the first—if not the very first—creators to retain ownership over your own comic book character. How did that come about?

EISNER: At that time it was standard practice for the publisher to own all the characters they published.

They felt, as their property, they could properly invest, develop, and exploit it. Besides, to the publisher, artists were really interchangable—and expendable. They bought the rights to these characters very easily. The rights to *Superman*, for example, were bought by a simple rubber stamp on the back of the paycheck that said, "For all rights and titles . . ." The creator would sign his check every week and ultimately had no claim to anything. But that was an accepted trade practice in the field.

My unique situation in owning *The Spirit* came about because I was in the catbird seat, if you will. I was approached by a syndicate to create a comic book supplement to newspapers. This was to enhance the newspapers' competitive position. They needed to compete with what they felt was a tremendously growing magazine force—the comic book—for the younger readers. So I was in a very strong position to retain the ownership of my character. They didn't give it up easily! The way we compromised it was that I permitted them to copyright the strip in the distributor's name because the argument was that daily newspapers would not buy strips that were copyrighted in the artist's name.

It was assumed the artist could get drunk, sick, die—whatever. There would be no guarantee of control or continuity. Whereas if the distributor owned the strip, then the newspaper would be assured of that continuity.

So in order to retain actual ownership, I had a reversion clause placed in my contract that in effect recognized my ownership of *The Spirit*. In effect it was a loan until there was a split-up between us; then the strip would return to me. The first few issues were copyrighted with the name Everett Arnold, but in effect I was the first comic book creator to own his strip. It was widely rumored that I threatened to set fire to the syndicate if I didn't retain ownership, but it didn't really work that way. [*Laughs*] It was just a good business deal.

CBR: Do you agree this has been the greatest injustice against creators—that it's always been assumed in this particular industry that it's the publisher who should own all rights to a character or comic book title?

EISNER: Injustice or ripoff is not a fair description. There are two sides to it. A publisher—just as the artist—works within the framework of what the market will bear. The publisher essentially felt he needed to have ownership because what he was doing was investing his money in a property, and he was not about to waive proprietorship. The publisher saw it in the long term and was prepared to promote, develop, and sustain the property. The creating artist neither had the resources or staying power. As a matter of fact—and this *is* a fact—there isn't a major superhero that has survived through today that is still being done by its originator.

Superman and *Batman* for example are the result of *years* of exploitation and creative refinement by many, many brilliant artists and writers. Thousands and thousands of dollars in investing in promotion and exploiting of ancillary product. Which the publisher claims he might *not* have done if he didn't own the property—or if his lease on that property was at the whim of some artist. On the other hand, the artist could not do it all himself. The real unfairness lay in the fact that creators did not share in the form of a royalty. It took many years for that to happen.

CBR: However, you stated the publishers believed writers and artists were interchangable and expendable. That attitude must have had some effect on the creative community toiling on the publishers' "plantations."

EISNER: Yes, there was a "slavery" syndrome in the fact that the artists were treated by the publishers as replaceable commodities. Saying, "If I own *Superhero*, I can hire anybody I want to do *Superhero*. I can easily find an artist somewhere to imitate the previous artist." Every artist knows that it isn't too hard to find an imitator of his or her style. For years, there was a big joke running around the comics community that if Milton Caniff died, four artists would go out of business; they were all imitating his style.

So, comic artists worked within a then commonly accepted attitude which the publishers had forced upon them by the sheer strength of their position. They could say, "You can be toughminded as you want, but we can replace you." As I recited earlier, the reason my negotiating position was so strong with the syndicate was that I was established, and in the position of owning a fine company, with a good income, and I didn't necessarily need what they were offering me.

Oh, yes, I needed what they were offering me in terms of a new arena, *that* I wanted badly. But I knew that unless I had the creative control—which came with owning the property—I couldn't achieve that new audience for *myself*. My strength with them lay in the fact that I was a proven producer and they could not take the risk of going with an unknown quantity. Not in the newspaper field.

CBR: What motivated you in "pushing the envelope" with the then radical approach you brought to *The Spirit*, right from the very start?

EISNER: From the outset I began to experiment. As far as I was concerned, I was taking on *The Spirit* because it would provide me with the opportunity to employ the medium as I felt it *could* be—innovatively! By 1940, '41, I believed earnestly that this medium was a true literary/art form, and that I was going to spend the rest of my life doing it. I *knew* it. As a matter of fact, somebody recently unearthed an old 1940 interview in the Baltimore *Sun* in which I said just that. I remember being embarrassed afterwards, because when I got back to New York, a number of the cartoonists accused me of being "uppity!" [*Laughs*]

But as I said, a "slave mentality" does inhibit creativity and innovation. If you tell a slave, "Look this is as far as you can go," a slave begins to accept this. He just says, "Yes, master," and does not make waves. The people who are constant experimenters by nature are the ones who resist creative enslavement, no matter what the cost.

I am one of these.

Even when I undertook *The Spirit*, I couldn't abide the rules and standards the syndicate wanted. Most were very simple but confining things: like they wanted me to draw the exact same logo every week! They'd plead, "We're just asking for a very simple request. We're not trying to interfere with your creative freedom—just please give us the same logo every week like they do for *Superman* so we can advertise *The Spirit* on our trucks! Is that too much to ask?" [*Laughs*] It *was* too much to ask! The logo was part of the story, you see! Integral to the ambience of the whole strip.

CBR: Was that your way of insuring your creativity wasn't running the risk of being "enslaved" by the practices of the industry at that time?

EISNER: Yes and no. I wasn't doing it because I felt enslaved. I did it because I felt *free*. I felt that here was my chance to exploit my career dream: I wanted to establish this medium as a literary/art form. That meant pushing on the perimeters (and parameters) of the medium as much as I could. What drove me then—and still drives me today—is the desire to always climb over the hill because I could see something new that could be done on the other side.

I'm an experimenter. Well, that's what *The Spirit* gave me: total freedom to experiment. It was far more free than working in any other comic book house—even my own publishing house! In newspapers I had found a place where *I* could be the master of my product rather than the newsstand marketplace! Because the newspapers at that time really had no accurate way of measuring the success or failure of a comic strip character. Not like a comic book publisher, who makes creative judgments by simply adding up the number of copies sold. So for me, it was total freedom. Not to run wild, but to try anything I felt needed to be tried. The precedent for me was *Krazy Kat, Polly*, and so forth.

CBR: In what other ways did you rebel against the status quo of your contemporaries of the Forties?

EISNER: Well, my tendency isn't toward sexual exploitation or mindless violence for the sake of violence. My discipline was my own creative integrity. I wanted what I was doing to be accepted, ultimately, as something serious. The fan mail that I was getting mostly dealt with *what* I was saying, rather than *how* I said it. I enjoyed that. My memories of that period of *The Spirit* was that I was a "Young Turk," if you will. I felt more revolutionary then; more *avant-garde* than I ever felt in my entire career. Except, perhaps, years later when I finished publishing and began *A Contract with God*.

I've always felt somewhat akin to the *avant-garde* comics. I don't know if I've ever been regarded as part of it, but I always felt a part of that movement.

CBR: You took a long career turn in the Fifties and Sixties by working outside of the mainstream comic book industry. Was that a conscious choice, or did you possibly feel that by then you were something of an "outcast" in terms of where you fit into the comic book scene?

EISNER: No, I wasn't an outcast—I never wanted to get into the comic book industry! Instructional comics was yet another adventure for me. It was more attractive to me.

Remember, a number of things happened to me along the way. During World War II, while I was in the Army, I made a pitch to the Department of Defense to sell them on the use of comics as training material. I had fallen into the training department somehow, and had sent up a memo saying that there is another medium which was not being used that could train soldiers faster than anything they presently had. When you're twenty or twenty-one you are cocky like that! I convinced the Ordnance Department to use comics as a training tool. I created a character called "Joe Dope" and I was then the first one to get a two-page comic in an official Army training manual.

This created quite a shock. It was an impertinence at the time. The military publishing commanders felt that what I was doing was a threat to them. My comics implied that their regular training material was not readable. Which was indeed true!

So during the war, I discovered a totally new application of comics which I carried in my mind when I got out of the military. When I got back to *The Spirit*, I occasionally received calls from former military types who were now involved in the publication departments of major corporations like General Motors and U.S. Steel. They asked if I could do any of their training material in comic form. Of course, being a New York City boy, I said, "Sure!"

So I started a new company because I saw this as an exciting opportunity. As far as I was concerned, the comic book world held no real interest for me anymore. I had no desire to be part of it. I suppose it sounds a little pretentious, but even though money was always important to me, it was not *that* important if it stood in the way of my doing something very, very valuable in itself. So I saw it as an opportunity to make money, as well as a way to open up a whole new field for the medium. Later, around 1952, I began to contract with the Defense Department to repeat the success of comics in World War II. I produced *PS Magazine* monthly.

CBR: The Fifties was also a time when the comic book industry was regularly under attack from parents groups and society in general as a negative influence in America, not a positive one.

EISNER: That never fazed me. The only way that attitude hurt me was when I tried to sell teaching material in comic form to schools. The teachers would have nothing to do with it! But from a career point of view, since I never saw the need to pursue doing pages for any of the major publishers of comics, it did not affect me. I also never really saw the need to publish my own comics, though I did do a couple on my own that were failures. But essentially I was interested in the industrial use and instructional application of comics as a very interesting educational tool.

CBR: Just what is it about comics that made you feel it could be such a potent educational tool? All of us were brought up with the general understanding from our educators that comics had virtually no intrinsic educational value.

EISNER: That concept confuses form and concept. Comics is a literary form that employs images. Imagery communicates ideas in milliseconds, whereas words have to be decoded. Images transcend language barriers. Comics is an arrangement of images in a sequence, if you will. This lies at the core of the idea that a comic, if well done and properly executed, can convey a complex thought. Those of us working in this medium had never realized, until others started writing about it, that the subject or the content tends to shape the way we *communicate* with this medium. That being said, let's carry it to what's happening today.

We're now living in an age where information is moving at such a startling rate that we must create communication that rapidly transmits ideas. What is needed is some kind of "visual machinery." So we invented electronic machines that can transmit pictures and ideas quickly, simply, widely and inexpensively.

Comics is a way of transmitting ideas through words and images via print. One does not eliminate the other; they are interactive. The culmination of the words and images that we string together is what makes it so easily understandable. There are limits to it, of course. Words also still convey a great deal of internal thought and abstract characterization. But the essential reason that comics work so well is because of the visual imagery. And imagery is the fastest means of written communication in existence.

CBR: When you came back to the comic book form in the Seventies, it was really as part of the underground comix scene rather than within the mainstream industry. What led you there?

EISNER: Several things happened. In 1972, I had the opportunity to sell my company. I had also reached a point in life where I wanted to continue to touch all the bases, do all the things I had wanted to do. The other thing that happened was that Phil Seuling had a convention, and invited me down there.

I was astonished to discover a lot of young men walking around carrying old copies of *The Spirit* that they were trading back and forth.

There was also a young fellow there with long hair named Denis Kitchen, and he was publishing underground comix. And he asked me if I would let him reprint some of *The Spirit* stories. I looked at all the underground comix and I suddenly realized what was happening: this was the new revolution in comics!

I attribute to that point in time as being the renaissance of comics as a literary/art form. With the artists like R. Crumb and Gilbert Shelton being the hard-core revolutionaries. They were using comics to attack the Establishment. They were not using comics purely as pandering entertainment. They were using it almost like graffiti. Sure they were writing for other "heads" who were dropping acid and such, but in the process they were still saying *something*. They had no other place to go to express themselves. It was *their* medium. They were being as "impertinent" as I was in the newspapers and the Army and the schools. Only more so!

"*My God,*" I said to myself, "*they are using this medium as a true literary/ art form.*" So I got caught up in that. This was a chance for me to do all the other things I always wanted to do. Again, I've always responded to opportunities in creativity, just as I've always responded to opportunities in business.

CBR: And that next opportunity for you was to basically create the first graphic novel, *A Contract with God* (1978). Creating an entire new market as well as a new format for the medium.

EISNER: I don't think in terms of market . . . I think in terms of audience. At the time there was no channel to the audience I sought except through the establishment bookstores. I hoped that I could break into the established mainstream market; I was in pursuit of the older reader. The format was intended to serve the content. I created the term "graphic novel" on the spur of the moment. I had written the book and rendered it in complete pencil form and started to look around for a publisher. I called Bantam Books because an editor there had known *The Spirit* and known of me. When I got the editor on the phone, I said, "I have something new for you here. Something very different." And he said, "Yeah, what's that?" I looked down and I suddenly realized: *I could not tell him this was a comic book!!* I wanted desperately to get a meeting, so I said, "Well, I have a graphic novel here." And he said, "Oh, that's interesting—I never heard of that. Bring that up."

So I came to his office a few days later and he looked at *A Contract with God*, and then he looked up at me and said, "You know, it's still a comic book." [*Laughs*] I was advised to find a smaller publisher. But that's how the form got started.

CBR: Do you think the general public in this country is at last changing their attitude towards the medium; that they're now seeing comics as a completely legitimate "literary/art form"?

EISNER: Yes, there *is* a substantial change. The fact that a comic book was recently given a Pulitzer Prize can't help but have a tremendous effect on the reading attitudes of the American public. All my professional life I've been fighting that stigma. I remember well that when I told a teacher, "I make comic books for a living," their eyes would go wide in horror, and you can see in the pupils of their eyes two superheroes battling one another. And I had to explain, "Wait a minute, wait a minute, this is something different. This is an entire *medium*."

Old reading habits die hard, but they are changing. The fact that *A Contract with God* is still in print after fifteen years is an enormous victory for me, because as a comic book by any other name, it has survived. The average shelf life of a "comic book" as you and I know it is quite brief. So people are paying attention to this form now, as they have been in Europe for years.

CBR: Of the graphic novels you've done since, which has been the most satisfying, overall?

EISNER: From a creative point of view, the book that gave me the most satisfaction when I finally completed it was *A Lifeforce*. The reason I say that is that I followed the conventions and the structure of a classic novel. *To the Heart of the Storm* was a kind of autobiography which took effort and angst and two years of my life.

But I haven't attempted yet to do something like Jack Jackson's historical comics. I regard what he's done as very important, and deserving of more attention than it's gotten.

CBR: Will, looking back on your career as a whole, what do you think has been your greatest influence on the medium?

EISNER: It would be hard for me to say; I think it should come from somebody who has a good overview of the field. Any answer now would be a carefully wrought guess! The influence I hope I will have left, above all, is that comics are a valid literary/art form, and that it will continue to enable us to ultimately achieve a serious, adult reading audience. Hopefully, the body of work I've produced proves it.

Appendix I

A BILL OF RIGHTS FOR COMICS CREATORS

Suggested Final Draft with Anotations by Scott McCloud

For the survival and health of comics, we recognize that no single system of commerce and no single type of agreement between creator and publisher can or should be instituted. However, the rights and dignity of creators everywhere are equally vital. Our rights, as we perceive them to be and intend to preserve them, are:

1. The right to full ownership of what we fully create.

2. The right to full control over the creative execution of that which we fully own.

3. The right of approval over the reproduction and format of our creative property.

4. The right of approval over the methods by which our creative property is distributed.

5. The right to free movement of ourselves and our creative property to and from publishers.

6. The right to employ legal counsel in any and all business transactions.

7. The right to offer a proposal to more than one publisher at a time.

8. The right to prompt payment of a fair and equitable share of profits derived from all of our creative work.

9. The right to full and accurate accounting of any and all income and disbursements relative to our work.

10. The right to prompt and complete return of our artwork in its original condition.

11. The right to full control over the licensing of our creative property.

12. The right to promote and the right of approval over any and all promotion of ourselves and our creative property.

Annotations

1. This means copyright and trademark. The term "fully create" is open to debate. Siegel and Schuster fully created Superman in my view, regardless of how much editorial input they may have received. It was their idea. Had they retained ownership of Superman from the start and later hired others to create stories for the character, such as DC Comics has, those others would be entitled to many rights, but ownership of Jerry and Joe's characters would *not* be one of them.

2. Without this right, the first one is meaningless. What difference would my full ownership of *Zot!* make if I could be forced, at a publisher's whim, to change my characters' appearance, bring villains back from the dead, to write long crossover scenes or even just to change a little piece of dialogue on page five, panel three, and in doing so undermine a message I may have been working to get across for over a hundred pages! No change is so important that it can't be discussed, but the final say over what goes into *Zot!* is still in the hands of its creator and owner. Companies that take on creator-owned properties do so at a certain risk, but when a creator trades in his or her control over their creation for a twelve-issue contract and some money in the bank, they do more than just *risk* that their message will be distorted in the long run. They virtually *guarantee* it.

3. This is my suggested wording change. I prefer "approval over" to "full control" in this instance because it's possible for both publisher and creator to agree on such basic matters as size, shape, printing

process and even pagination before the project is even begun. Unlike disputes over writing and art, these are matters that can be handled at the contract stage. If, while work is already proceeding, a creator or publisher wants to make a change in format, then agreement by both sides would be necessary. In the original draft of the Bill, a thirteenth right governing advisory labels was added. I've omitted it here, as I think this heading covers it well enough.

4. Again, a matter for the contract stage as I see it. This was also changed from "full control" and reworded slightly to avoid giving the impression that we all thought we had the right to walk into our local distributor's warehouse and start telling people how to pack boxes. This, and all the twelve rights, refer primarily to the creator/publisher relationship.

5. No, this doesn't mean we have the right to breach contracts and walk whenever we feel like it. (At least that's not *my* interpretation.) This simply means that, just as comic book writers and artists have traditionally competed for assignments from comic companies, the reverse should also be true. Creators wishing to produce work for more than one company at a time must be free from coercion of any kind.

6. I don't think this one needs any explanation.

7. What's good for the goose is good for the gander. This operates on the same principle as Number 5. I would add that such "multiple submissions" should be clearly labeled as such.

8. I think this is pretty self-evident.

9. These two articles apply to *all* comic writers and artists, not just creator-owners (also true of Numbers 5, 6, and 10). They aren't particularly controversial, but they are being violated—*constantly*.

10. Nowadays, this idea seems fairly tame, yet once this was the most radical, inflammatory thing an artist could possibly suggest to a publisher. It will be interesting to see how many of these other rights are taken for granted two or three decades from now, as this one has come to be.

11. Again, this one follows naturally from the first right. Ownership would be meaningless without this kind of control.

12. 'Nuff said.

Appendix II

BOOKS ABOUT COMICS

A. HISTORY AND CRITICISM

Bails, Jerry and Ware, Hames, editors: *The Who's Who of American Comic Books*
(four volumes), Jerry Bails, Saint Clair Shores, Michigan, 1973–76. A massive alphabetical reference work cataloguing every American comic book
creator who ever worked in the industry proper. A vital research aid, the
sorely-needed revised edition of this long out-of-print self-published labor-
of-love is currently in progress—watch for the upcoming multi-volume
edition; for comics scholars in particular, this is a vital work. *Recommended.*

Barker, Martin: *Action: The Story of a Violent Comic*, Titan Books, London, 1990.
Remarkable case-history of the short-lived but incredibly popular *Action
Weekly* of the mid-Seventies. Showcases full uncensored reprints of relevant
Action comic stories to document Barker's chronology and analysis of the
title and the rapid mobilization of authoritarian pressure that quickly led to
its demise. *Recommended.*

Barker, Martin: *A Haunt of Fears: The Strange History of the British Horror Comics
Campaign*, Pluto Press, London, 1984; reprinted by University Press of Mississippi, 1993. Martin Barker is one of the field's most intelligent and outspoken
analysts, particularly regarding censorship of the medium. By exhaustively
detailing the political realities of the British campaign against American
crime & horror comics in the Fifties, Barker perceptively dissects *how* the
genre and medium work, how they interact with the reader, and how political institutions distort and misrepresent that unique chemistry. Barker's
conclusions are chilling, and all-too-applicable to the American comic book
censorship crusade of the same era. A marvelous book. *Recommended.*

Barker, Martin: *Comics: Ideology, Power & the Critics*, Manchester University Press, Manchester, England / NY, dist. through St. Martin's Press, NY, 1989. Barker's densest study to date, a provocative reassessment of cultural interpretation and regulation of the comics medium via Barker's typically insightful analysis of representative case histories. A necessary companion to Barker's *A Haunt of Fears* and *Action: The Story of a Violent Comic*. *Recommended*.

Barrier, Mike and Williams, Martin, editors: *A Smithsonian Book of Comic-Book Comics*, Smithsonian Institute Press / Harry N. Abrams, NY, 1981. This companion volume to the earlier *Smithsonian Collection of Newspaper Comics* (1977) chooses to focus on humorous comics, with the exception of *Superman*, *Batman* (*Captain Marvel* and *Plastic Man* comfortably straddle the superhero and humor genres), *The Spirit*, and three excellent EC Comics stories. As such, the editors' prejudices subtly misrepresent the aesthetics and history of the industry, though one can hardly argue with the quality of the stories reprinted herein. *Recommended*, with reservations.

Bell, John, editor: *Canuck Comics: A Guide to Comic Books Published in Canada*, Matrix Books, Montreal, Quebec, dist. by University of Toronto Press, Downsview, Ontario / Buffalo, NY, 1986. Comprehensive short history of Canadian comic books includes "price guide" listing of titles, out-of-date for collectors but of lasting value to historians.

Benton, Mike: *The Comic Book in America: An Illustrated History*, Taylor Publishing Co., Dallas, Texas, 1989. Excellent, comprehensive introductory study of the comic book industry. Benton presents a great deal of information (accompanied by a most generous gallery of color comic book cover illustrations) in a briskly-written three-part historical overview: year-by-year "time capsule" summaries, concise analysis of the comic book publishing companies, and a well-crafted procession of genre studies. Highly *Recommended*.

Benton, Mike: *The Taylor History of Comics*, Taylor Pub. Co., Dallas, Texas, 1991-present. Ambitious multi-volume history of the American industry by genre: to date, they include *The Illustrated History of Horror Comics*, *The Illustrated History of Superhero Comics of the Silver Age*, *The Illustrated History of Science Fiction Comics*, and *The Illustrated History of Superhero Comics of the Golden Age*. Beautifully designed and illustrated, these are fine introductions to relevant genres for juvenile readers. Sadly, adult readers will find Benton's text too often inadequate. The superhero volumes are quite good, boosted by interviews and meticulous research, but the horror and science fiction "histories" are rendered inconsequential by the exclusion of underground comix (presumably receiving their own "genre" volume in the near future) and international contributions to the genres (of particular importance to the SF comics).

Craven, Thomas, editor: *Cartoon Cavalcade*, Simon and Schuster, NY, 1943.

Long out of print, but not too difficult to find in used book shops (particularly in its 1944 People's Book Club Edition), this provides a delightful overview of the growth of the medium in America from the 1880s to the War years. Ignores the proliferation of the comic book industry, as do three other worthy overviews of the medium we'll mention here: Coulton Waugh's *The Comics* (The Macmillan Company, New York, 1947) editors David Manning White and Robert H. Abel's compelling essay collection *The Funnies: An American Idiom* (Macmillan, 1963) and cartoonist Jerry Robinson's *The Comics: An Illustrated History of Comic Strip Art* (G.P. Putnam's Sons, 1974). As a rich visual history, though, Craven's book is particularly *Recommended*.

Daniels, Les: *Comix: A History of Comic Books in America*. Outerbridge & Dienstfrey, NY, 1971. Long out of print, but still invaluable, informative, and surprisingly comprehensive overview of the industry and medium up to 1971, accurately accessing key transitional publications ignored by more contemporary studies. *Recommended*.

Daniels, Les: *Marvel: Five Fabulous Decades of the World's Greatest Comics*, Abrams, NY, 1991. Definitive look at the history of the "Big One" of the "Big Two" in mainstream comic book publishing. Beautifully designed and almost overwhelmingly illustrated. Daniels' thorough history tells the reader more about "Mighty Marvel" than perhaps they even wish to know. Since this is an authorized company history produced *by* Marvel Comics, this is as much a work of propaganda as a laundered history, though Daniels' informative style remains impeccable—note that Daniels is currently at work on a companion history of DC Comics. *Recommended*, with reservations.

Davidson, Steef: *The Penguin Book of Political Comics*, Penguin Books, 1982. Translated by Hester and Marianne Velmans, this English-language edition of Dutch activist/author/editor Davidson's 1976 book is a lively compendium of international post-World War II propaganda comics, comix and comic-format posters. Though Davidson is clearly a child of sixties Europe, he wisely allows the diversity of ideologies and perspectives (from vicious rhetoric to rich satire) speak for themselves via comprehensive translations of the original texts. Despite often wretched art reproduction, this is an important tome bridging the gap between the relevant political comics covered in David Kunzle's histories (see author's listing) and the recent examples of the form, such as Joyce Brabner's *Brought to Light*. *Recommended*.

Dorfman, Ariel and Mattelart, Armand: *How to Read Donald Duck: Imperialist Ideology in the Disney Comic*, International General, NY; first published in Chile in 1971, translated U.S. edition 1975, revised and reprinted 1985. Seminal political analysis of Carl Barks' classic *Donald Duck* and *Uncle Scrooge* comics as a primary example of capitalist ideology spoonfed to the masses, in this case the people of South America under the thumb of U.S. political and corporate interests. A volatile and revolutionary work, translated and annotated by art and comics scholar David Kunzle (see author's listing). *Recommended.*

Eisner, Will: *Comics and Sequential Art*, Poorhouse Press / Eclipse Books, 1985; reprinted by Kitchen Sink Press. Eisner is one of the true masters of the medium, and his analysis of the art form and how it works is concise, intelligent, and definitely required reading for anyone interested in comics. *Recommended.*

Estren, Mark James: *A History of Underground Comics*, Straight Arrow Books, San Francisco, CA, 1974. Expansive, generously illustrated history and analysis of comix movement was source of much concern and controversy among comix creators at the time: many considered it an opportunistic and exploitative project, and denied permission to reprint their work. Often glib and stilted, but too valuable a document of its time and the movement to dismiss. *Recommended*, with reservations; see Kennedy, Jay: *The Official Underground and Newave Comix Price Guide* and Rosenkranz, Patrick and Van Baren, Hugo: *Artsy Fartsy Funnies*.

Feiffer, Jules: *The Great Comic Book Heroes*, Dial Press / Bonanza Books, NY, 1965. Seminal, affectionate showcase of thirteen Golden Age comic book heroes, reprinting their origin adventures in garish full color with an engaging introduction by the editor, who labored in the comics sweatshop studios long before earning celebrity as one of America's finest cartoonists and satirists.

Fuchs, Wolfgang and Reitberger, Reinhold: *Comics: Anatomy of a Mass Medium*, Little, Brown & Co., Boston, 1971. This European text (translated by Nadia Fowler) is of interest as one of the early studies of the medium, though it is dated and compromised by occasional misinformation (possibly due to translation confusion).

Fulce, John: *Seduction of the Innocent Revisited*, Huntington House, Lafayette, LA, 1990. Fundamentalist attack on the current comic book industry is poorly written and researched, presenting its case for an orchestrated corruption of young America with shrill accusations, paranoid rhetoric, and a sampling of comics covers and pages selectively censored to suggest more explicit content than actually is represented in the source material. Infuriating, tragically misunderstanding and misrepresenting the contemporary comic scene to alarmist extremes, and at best, a curiosity.

Garriock, P.R.: *Masters of Comic Book Art*, Aurum Press Ltd., London / Images Graphiques, NY, 1978. Handsome volume dedicated to brief but eye-filling overviews on ten international masters of the form, from Eisner, Kurtzman and Wally Wood to Crumb, Corben, and Moebius. Out of print.

Gerber, Ernst and Mary, editors: *The Photo Journal Guide to Comic Books* (2 volumes), Gerber Publishing Co., Inc., Minden, NV, 1989; and *The Photo*

Journal Guide to Marvel Comics (2 volumes), 1991. Invaluable reference guides and browsing delights, each set showcases full color comic book covers and relevant publishing statistics. Amazing labor of love aimed at the hardcore collectors' market, but a remarkable visual encyclopedia for anyone fascinated by the medium.

Gifford, Denis: *Happy Days: One Hundred Years of Comics*, Jupiter Books, London, 1975 / Bloomsbury Books, London, 1988. Gifford's text is characteristically slight, but this lavishly illustrated sampling of British comics from 1870 to 1974 offers an appealing showcase for much rarely-seen material.

Gifford, Denis: *The International Book of Comics*, Hamlyn Publishing Group, London / Crescent Books, NY, 1984. Expansive, entertaining, lushly illustrated volume is particularly valuable for its coverage of the British comics, proving—despite the persistent claims of many who claim comic books as being an *American* invention—the roots of the comic *book* lay in Europe (see David Kunzle's two-volume *The History of the Early Comic Strip* for further examples that pre-date Gifford's by centuries!). *Recommended.*

Goldwater, John L.: *Americana in Four Colors: A Decade of Self Regulation by the Comics Magazine Industry*, The Comics Magazine Association Inc., New York, NY, 1964. Rare and long-out-of-print, this remains an essential presentation of the Comics Code Authority's reign by its founding father, John L. Goldwater, who was also the publisher of Archie Comics. A slight but fascinating, infuriating, blood-curdling censorship (excuse us, we mean "self-regulation") document which tells the reader more about the Code than most comic book creators and editors who continue to work under CCA rules know!

Goulart, Ron: *The Great Comic Book Artists*, St. Martin's Press, NY, 1986 and *The Great Comic Book Artists, Volume 2*, St. Martin's Press, NY, 1987. Interesting but regrettably brief (one page of text, one illustration per artist) essays attempting to cover more than a hundred artists from the thirties to the eighties. Even at two volumes, Goulart does little more than cover the most basic turf. Most useful as an introduction to the subjects at hand, with both volumes including selected listings of the artists' published works.

Goulart, Ron: *Great History of Comic Books*, Contemporary Books, Chicago / NY, 1986. Exhaustive overview of the industry concentrates on the early years, where the author's affections clearly lay; the chapters on contemporary comics are, at best, an afterthought. Though hardly "the definitive illustrated history" proffered by the cover blurb, a creditable effort when covering the pre-Silver Age years.

Goulart, Ron: *Over 50 Years of American Comic Books*, Mallard Press, 1991. This handsome, lavishly illustrated history by science fiction author and comic book historian Goulart is considerably broader in scope than his previously published comic book studies, maintaining interest and focus right up through the contemporary chapters. *Recommended.*

Groth, Gary and Fiore, Robert, editors: *The New Comics*, Berkley Books, NY, 1988. Predecessor to the book you hold in your hand, attempting an overview of the contemporary comics scene through interviews with its key creative practitioners. A worthy effort seriously compromised by prejudices of editors and failure to introduce often complex material or issues to the layman reader, rendering much of its content unintelligable to the uninitiated.

Horn, Maurice: *Comics of the American West*, Winchester Press, NY / Stoeger Publishing, NJ, 1977. Well illustrated, comprehensive (to its date of publication) international history of the Western comics genre. Despite occasional factual errors, a worthy model for future genre histories.

Horn, Maurice, editor: *75 Years of the Comics*, Boston Book and Art, Boston, 1971. Sketchy overview of the medium, meshing comic strips and comic books. Though we are not particularly enamored with Horn's work—he is often glib, and his work is compromised by errors and unfortunate omissions—he remains an ambitious and tenacious historian of, and advocate for, the medium. Also see Horn's listing below.

Horn, Maurice: *Sex in the Comics*, Chelsea House, NY, 1985. This international overview of comic book sexuality, erotica and pornography is amply illustrated, offsetting Horn's shapeless and often labored text with a more engaging visual potpourri.

Horn, Maurice: *Women in the Comics*, Chelsea House, NY, 1977. Disappointing study of *fictional* female characters in comics, with nice visuals to offer and little else. Horn's shamefully brief chapter on women cartoonists is of note only because it provoked Trina Robbins and Cat Yronwode to write *Women and the Comics* (see listing).

Horn, Maurice, editor: *The World Encyclopedia of Comics*, Chelsea House/Avon, 1976; and *The World Encyclopedia of Comics*, Chelsea House, 1980. Ambitious tomes attempt to catalogue an international array of key creators, creations, and characters, embracing comic strips, comic books, and animation. Despite the domestic focus, we find Jerry Bails and Hames Ware's *The Who's Who of American Comic Books* a more expansive and reliable reference work, but Horn's encyclopedias are an important addition to any serious comic book library.

Inge, M. Thomas: *Comics As Culture*, University Press of Mississippi, Jackson, MS and London, 1990. Though the majority of essays collected here focus primarily on comic strips, Inge is an important authority on the medium, and he has played a vital role in the academic community's awakening to the importance of the art form (note how many of the texts cited in this bibliography are published under Inge's guidance by the University Press of Mississippi).

Jacobs, Will and Jones, Gerard: *The Comic Book Heroes from the Silver Age to the Present*, Crown Publishers, NY, 1985. Highly entertaining critical study of the

American superhero comics from the beginning of the Silver Age to the mid-Eighties, considerable "inside info" based on interviews with creators and editors behind the comics. *Recommended*.

Kennedy, Jay: *The Official Underground and Newave Comix Price Guide*, Boatner Norton Press, Cambridge, MA, 1982. Excellent reference volume on the comix scene up to its publication date, includes historical and autobiographical articles, artist indexes, and incorporates guide for "Ground-level" comix (*Cerebus, Elfquest*, etc.). Very worthwhile, sorely in need of a revised and updated edition.

Kunzle, David: *The History of the Early Comic Strip* (2 volumes to date), University of Southern California Press, Berkeley, California, 1973 (Vol. 1) and 1992 (Vol. 2). Kunzle is the most important and compelling archeologist of the medium to date, and these are simply incredible books. Exhaustive, expansive, and fully illustrated histories of the early *centuries* of the comics medium go far beyond anything previously attempted. Kunzle is to be applauded for and supported in his efforts; these books demand study by anyone seriously interested in the medium. The first volume is, sadly, long out-of-print and hard to find, and both are *very* expensive, but are most highly *Recommended*.

Kurtzman, Harvey and Barrier, Michael: *From AARGH! to ZAP!: Harvey Kurtzman's Visual History of the Comics*, Prentice Hall Press, 1991. Oversized, opinionated, and eye-drugging sprint through comic book history with one of the medium's key creators, the late, great Harvey Kurtzman, founder and original editor of *MAD*. A breathless introductory history, at its best when Kurtzman pauses for asides and evaluations drawn from his many experiences in the field. *Recommended*.

Lee, Stan and Buscema, John: *How to Draw Comics the Marvel Way*, Simon and Schuster, NY, 1978. A more than servicable introductory "how-to" book compromised, of course, by the questionable aesthetics and agenda of the Marvel "house style." More demanding and/or adventurous readers and aspiring practitioners should see Will Eisner's *Comics & Sequential Art*.

Lupoff, Dick and Don Thompson, editors: *All in Color for a Dime*, Arlington House, NY, 1970. Fine, early collection of essays and articles on comics characters, genres, and history by Harlan Ellison, Roy Thomas, and others. Long out of print, but worth the search.

McCloud, Scott: *Understanding Comics: The Invisible Art*, Tundra Publishing Ltd., Northampton, MA, 1993. Bravo! One of the most important studies of the medium ever published, a dissection of the art form artfully performed by one of its most insightful contemporary practitioners. *Recommended*.

Overstreet, Robert M.: *The Overstreet Comic Book Price Guide*, Avon Books, NY, annual new edition. *The* industry price guide for American comic books is an essential research tool for historians as well as collectors. An invaluable but problematic reference work updated annually, though its narrow focus on four-color mainstream comics (with selective inclusion of black-and-white titles like *Cerebus, Love and Rockets*, etc.) is unfortunate, excluding underground comix, many magazine, graphic novel, and book format titles. Also see Kennedy, Jay: *The Official Underground and Newave Comix Price Guide.*

Pearson, Roberta A. and Uricchio, William, editors: *The Many Lives of the Batman: Critical Approaches to a Superhero and His Media*, Routledge, NY / BFI Publishing, London, 1991. As stated on the book itself, "the first serious academic exploration of this intriguing cultural phenomenon" composed of essays and interviews, is often stimulating reading.

Perry, George and Aldridge, Alan: *The Penguin Book of Comics*, Penguin Books, UK/US, 1967. The authors rightfully dubbed this "a slight history," but for its time it did its job well. Sketchy but entertaining and informative. Out of print.

Reidelbach, Maria: *Completely MAD: A History of the Comic Book and Magazine*, Little, Brown and Co., Boston, 1991. Marvelous visual history of the celebrated satire comic, less a critical study than a self-congratulatory celebration with enough insight, information, and cleverly showcased reprint material to make the volume worthwhile.

Robbins, Trina: *A Century of Women Cartoonists*. Kitchen Sink Press, 1993. A companion to *Women and the Comics* offering a chronology of women cartoonists from the turn of the century to present. Published concurrently with *Comic Book Rebels*, we cannot offer any further information, though this is probably a worthy volume.

Robbins, Trina and Yronwode, Catherine: *Women and the Comics*, Eclipse Books, CA, 1985. Fine, comprehensive, and lovingly written chronicle of the many women who have worked in the medium, including the authors, both of whom are still vital members of the comics community (artist/writer and critic/publisher, respectively). Hopefully, a revised and updated edition will follow. See above entry. *Recommended.*

Rosenkranz, Patrick and Van Baren, Hugo: *Artsy Fartsy Funnies*, Paranoia, Holland, 1974. Published in English, this excellent history of the formative underground comix years has never been bettered. Comprehensive and informative, very rare but highly *Recommended.*

Sabin, Roger: *Adult Comics: An Introduction*. Routledge, London/New York, 1993. As of this writing, this is *the* most current and comprehensive book on contemporary adult comics (as noted in Sabin's introduction, this is a "somewhat arbitrary" term to define "any title orientated primarily towards an over-16 readership"). The author further acknowledges the book "is written from a British perspective," which accounts for its prejudices and occasional factual errors in the chapter on American comics, but it is an excellent book and highly *Recommended.*

Savage, Jr., William W.: *Comic Books and America: 1945–1954*, University of Oklahoma Press, Norman, OK, 1990. Interesting study of post–WWII and

Korean War American culture as reflected in comic books, and the culmination of those issues and tensions in the 1954 purge of the industry.

Schodt, Frederik L.: *Manga! Manga! The World of Japanese Comics*, Kodansha International / USA Ltd., dist. through HarperCollins, NY, 1983. Fascinating, richly detailed and documented history of the Japanese comic book *Manga*. An ideal introduction to some of the most compelling comics in the world. *Recommended*.

Steranko, Jim: *The Steranko History of Comics—Volume One*, Supergraphics, Pennsylvania, 1970; *The Steranko History of Comics—Volume 2*, Supergraphics, Pennsylvania, 1972. One of the first significant attempts at a comprehensive history, lovingly written, designed, and published by an artist who was, at the time, one of the most innovative in the business. Entertainingly written and impeccably crafted, these were intended to launch a six-volume series, exhaustively covering the entire history of the American industry and medium. Alas, for reasons unknown, only these two volumes saw print, bringing Steranko's history up through the World War II years. Well-researched, long out of print and hard to find, but highly *Recommended*.

Stevens, Carol and Fox, Martin, editors: *Print: America's Graphic Design Magazine*, Vol. XLII, No. VI, RC Publications, NY, November/December 1988. Yes, this is an issue of *Print* magazine, but it offers an extraordinary overview of the medium and industry. An essential volume, with insightful and abundantly illustrated essays by Art Spiegelman, Paul Gravett, Gary Groth, Leonard Rifas, and others. *Recommended*.

Thompson, Don and Lupoff, Dick, editors: *The Comic-Book Book*, Rainbow Books, Carlstadt, New Jersey, 1973. Scattershot but compelling collection of essays about early comics history, from psychosexual creation of *Wonder Woman* to Disney and EC comics. Out of print but worth seeking out; also see Lupoff and Thompson's *All in Color for a Dime*.

Twitchell, James B.: *Preposterous Violence: Fables of Aggression in Modern Culture*, Oxford University Press, Oxford/NY, 1989. Provocative study of the appeal of violence in mass media, with a compelling chapter on comics building on David Kunzle's seminal research. Though concerned with *all* media, Twitchell's expansive analysis of relevant comics and their kin is richer than that in many comic histories, embracing William Hogarth, EC Comics, *Batman*, and Roy Lichtenstein. *Recommended*.

Varnedoe, Kirk and Gopnik, Adam: *High and Low: Modern Art and Popular Culture*, The Museum of Modern Art / Harry N. Abrams, NY, 1990. Though compromised by some serious lapses in research and gross misinformation, this is an important study emerging from the controversial 1990–91 MOMA "High and Low" exhibition tracing the exchange between modern art and the pop culture, in which comics play a vital role. *Recommended*.

Wertham, Dr. Fredric: *Seduction of the Innocent*, Rinehart & Co., NY, 1954.

Notorious attack on the entire pre-Code comic book industry, citing comics as the primary cause of juvenile crime in post—war America. Though Wertham's book was only one in a small procession of alarmist, opportunistic titles, it remains the one to read, *the* fascinating, bloodcurdling catalyst of the decades-long castration of the medium and deep-rooted cultural prejudice that lingers to this day. Original editions are long out-of-print, though a reprint edition is being prepared by Kitchen Sink Press.

Wertham, Dr. Fredric: *The World of Fanzines: A Special Form of Communication*, Southern Illinois University Press, 1973. A remarkable document of the early comic book and science fiction fanzines, sympathetically analyzed as a subcultural phenomenon by none other than the author of *Seduction of the Innocent*! Rare, but fascinating on many levels, particularly coming from the good doctor.

Wooley, Charles: *Wooley's History of the Comic Book: 1899–1936*, Charles Wooley, Lake Buena Vista, Florida, 1986. Compelling attempt to chronicle the pre-history of the American comic book, though we urge you to also check out the British studies (see Denis Gifford listings) and particularly David Kunzle's remarkable archeologies of the medium.

B. BIOGRAPHIES, AUTOBIOGRAPHIES AND CAREER STUDIES

Bharucha, Fershid: *Richard Corben: Flights into Fantasy*, Thumb Tack Books, NY, 1981. Excellent retrospective of, and insight into, Corben's art, including complete stories, generous selection of his color covers, comics, and illustrations, and step-by-step example of the artist's unique hand-separated color process. Out of print, but *Recommended*.

Crompton, Alastair and Vince, Alan: *The Man Who Drew Tomorrow*, Who Dares Publishing, Dorset, U.K., 1985. Rich, detailed, ultimately devastating biography of British comics artist extraordinaire Frank Hampson, creator of the popular *Eagle* strip *Dan Dare*, and damning chronicle of how the industry typically dealt with its most vital practitioners. American readers unfamiliar with Hampson's seminal painted comics will appreciate the generous illustrations, many in color. *Recommended*.

Dean, M.: *The Studio: Jeffrey Jones, Michael Kaluta, Barry Windsor-Smith, Berni Wrightson*, Dragon's Dream / Big O Publishing, Charlottesville, VA, 1979. Stunning color showcase of "The Studio" composed of four of the finest artists to ever work in the comic book medium, who chose to complement (or in the case of Jones, abandon) their comics creations to pursue their interests in fine art. Fascinating portrait of these artistic rebels in prime, idealistic form at a time when they were pioneering a progressive but mismanaged and short-lived crossover market in art portfolios and prints. Alas, this book saw publication just as the Studio dissolved, and all but Jones returned to comics. Their respective post-Studio careers are worthy of study, though it would certainly be a sobering book. Out of print but *Recommended*. Also see Chris Zavisa's *Berni Wrightson: A Look Back*.

Dellinges, Al: *Joe Kubert: The War Years*, Al Dellinges, San Francisco, CA, 1991. Anecdotal labor-of-love, self-published career study of artist Kubert, a followup to an earlier volume by Dellinges published in 1977. This brisk collective of art, interviews, reminiscing by Kubert and many of his peers circa the late fifties to early seventies makes for interesting (if non-linear) reading, though with over forty years in the business Kubert deserves a full biographical study.

Fry, Philip and Poulos, Ted: *Steranko: Graphic Narrative–Storytelling in the Comics and the Visual Novel*, The Winnipeg Art Gallery, 1978. Ambitious, overly analytical study of the work of Jim Steranko, one of the prominent comic book stylists of the 1960s. Very scarce.

Harrison, Hank: *The Art of Jack Davis*, Stabur Press, Detroit, MI, 1987. Fine black-and-white overview of one of the most versatile cartoonists of all time. Very little on the man, but a treat to the eye.

Jacobs, Frank: *The MAD World of William M. Gaines*, Lyle Stewart, Inc. / Bantam Books, NY, 1973. Even given the context of Gaines' status as the publisher of *MAD* magazine, this biography is surprisingly irreverent and candid, and all the more valuable for that. Chapters on the early years of EC Comics and Gaines' role in the 1954 Kefauver hearings are of particular interest, before the self-promotional aspects of the book become more overbearing. *Recommended*.

Kane, Bob and Andrae, Tom: *Batman and Me*, Eclipse Books, Forestville, CA, 1989. Controversial (particularly regarding the contributions writer Bill Finger and cartoonist Jerry Robinson made to the Batman mythos, which Kane does confront herein—to his own satisfaction, at least) and self-aggrandizing autobiography is a compelling read, abundantly illustrated (much in color).

Kurtzman, Harvey and Zimmerman, Howard: *My Life As a Cartoonist*, Pocket Books / Minstrel, NY, 1988. Sketchy but engaging autobiography suffers from its brevity, especially given Kurtzman's stature and vital importance to the art form, and the wealth of material it could have explored. An interesting companion to Frank Jacobs' bio of William Gaines.

Lanes, Selma G.: *The Art of Maurice Sendak*, Abradale Press / Harry N. Abrams, NY, 1980. Opulent, delightful biography and career overview of the celebrated children's book author, illustrator, and comic book creator—though, of course, no one *calls* Sendak's relevant masterworks comic books. *Recommended*.

McClelland, Gordon: *Rick Griffin*, Perigee Books / G.P. Putnam's Sons, NY, 1980. The late Rick Griffin was one of the great stylists of West Coast rock poster, surf art, and comix scene, and this is a lush tribute to his work. Uncanny, even visionary artwork, ending with Griffin's lovely religious paintings. Rare (though occasionally remaindered) and *Recommended*.

Peeters, B.: *Tintin and the World of Hergé*, Little, Brown & Co., Boston, 1992. A fine study of European master Hergé and his internationally beloved creation; also see H. Thompson's *Hergé and His Creation*.

Simon, Joe and Jim: *The Comic Book Makers*, Crestwood/II Publications, NY, 1990. Fully illustrated memoirs of Joe Simon, co-creator of *Captain America* and long-time partner of dynamo comic book creator Jack Kirby. Thoroughly engaging, entertaining and bracing personal history of the early years of the industry, an individualistic tonic to the sort of company-spun propaganda that too often passes for history. *Recommended*.

Thompson, H.: *Hergé and His Creation*, Hodder & Stoughton, London, 1991. Another well-deserved overview of one of Europe's master cartoonists, creator of *Tintin*.

Topffer, Rodolphe, translated and edited by Wiese, E.: *Enter: The Comics— Rodolphe Topffer's Essay on Physiognomy and The True Story of Monsieur Crepin*, University of Nebraska Press, Lincoln, Nebraska, 1965. Long out of print, but important reprint of essay and complete comic story by the father of modern comics, Rodolphe Topffer (1799–1846), accompanied by a fine biographical introduction. Rare, but *Recommended*.

Van Hise, James: *The Art of Al Williamson*, Blue Dolphin Enterprises, San Diego, CA, 1983. Biographical essay, interviews, and fair collection of comic stories, strips, and art by one of America's greatest romantic adventure comic book artists.

Ward, Lynd: *Storyteller Without Words: The Wood Engravings of Lynd Ward*, Harry N. Abrams, Inc., NY, 1974. Magnificent oversize volume assembled, designed, and written by master artist Lynd Ward, whose six "novels in woodcuts" (1929–1937) are seminal masterpieces of narrative sequential art. They are *all* reprinted complete in this volume, an essential addition to any comic book library. Out of print, but most highly *Recommended*.

Witek, Joseph: *Comic Books as History: The Narrative Art of Jack Jackson, Art Spiegelman, and Harvey Pekar*, University Press of Mississippi, Jackson, MS, 1989. The first serious academic appreciation of contemporary comic book creators, hopefully the first of many. Comprehensive, compelling analysis and overview of the chosen subjects, particularly valuable if the reader familiarizes himself with the original works before plunging into Witek's text. *Recommended*.

Wyman, Jr., Ray: *The Art of Jack Kirby*, The Blue Rose Press, Orange, California, 1992. Lush, fully-illustrated historical career overview of the artist whose work practically invented the language of the comic book. The best of many books on Jack Kirby, including two volumes of *The Jack Kirby Treasury* by Greg Theakston (Pure Imagination, 1982, 1991); Wyman Jr.'s book is the best of the lot to date, featuring a good many color pages and rarely-seen Kirby pencil art. *Recommended.*

Zavisa, Christopher: *Berni Wrightson: A Look Back,* Land of Enchantment, 1979; reprinted by Underwood-Miller, Lancaster, PA, 1991. Massive biography and chronology, much of it in color, of premiere horror comic book artist and illustrator Berni Wrightson. Sadly, the 1991 reprint is not updated, though this volume still definitively showcases Wrightson's evolution and most mature work. *Recommended.*

C. VIDEO

Mann, Ron: *Comic Book Confidential,* Cineplex Odeon Films / Sphinx Productions, dist. by Pacific Arts Video, 1989. Uneven but nevertheless vital documentary about the evolution of the comics medium and industry, featuring interviews with over twenty contemporary creators. The often chilling archival film footage is, sadly, undated and uncredited, and erratic use of crude animation to "enliven" comics imagery is rarely effective, but there is much to recommend here, including Pekar's reading of one of his onscreen comic stories. *Recommended,* with reservations.

Viola, Ken: *The Masters of Comic Book Art,* Ken Viola Prod., 1987. Interviews with ten comic book masters (half of whom later appeared in *Comic Book Confidential*), hosted by Harlan Ellison. With the exception of Steve Ditko's dogmatic illustrated speech concerning his Randian philosophy, the personable subjects carry themselves well within the modest scope of the project. *Recommended.*

Appendix III

Source Material and Suggested Further Reading

The comic books and graphic novels referred to in this book are available in many comic book shops. Check your area telephone directory for name and location of your local store, and tell them we sent you.

Comic shops often carry back issues of out-of-print comics. If you are interested in out-of-print titles referred to in this book, ask your local comics dealer if he has (or can get) back issue titles for you. Before paying collector's prices, be sure to ask if the comics you want have been reprinted in book form—many of them are now included in long-lasting library editions that may be more affordable than the collectible comics themselves.

Comic book conventions are also a valuable source for many old, rare, or new comic books and graphic novels, and may provide opportunities to meet the creators themselves. Keep an eye on local newspapers advertising book conventions in your area. Conventions, mail order services and collectibles dealers are listed weekly in *The Comics Buyer's Guide*; write for subscription and sample issue information (see address listings below).

We have listed the names of publishers to help you identify and locate source and reading materials. Most of the publishers listed at the end of this appendix provide excellent mail order services.

If you are unable to find their publications in your local comic shops, we urge you to write for current availability of titles, ordering information, and for their catalogues, which offer many other worthwhile titles.

INTRODUCTION

The introductory anthology of underground comix *Best of Bijou / The Apex Treasury of Underground Comix* is still available directly from Kitchen Sink Press, Inc., and includes much early work by Robert Crumb and Art Spiegelman.

Robert Crumb's comix can be found in many shops. The multi-volume *The Complete Crumb Comics* (Fantagraphics Books) is an ambitious venture to reprint *all* of Crumb's work to date in book format. The initial volumes are currently available in stores or directly from the publisher, or from Kitchen Sink Press and Last Gasp. Kitchen Sink also offers Crumb's *Artistic Comix*, the classics *Zap* #0-12, *Homegrown* and *The People's Comics*, *Power Pak 1*, *Snoid Comix*, *Weirdo*, and his latest comix series *Hup*! (4 issues to date).

Issues of Art Spiegelman and Francois Mouly's annual anthology *Raw* (Penguin books), the collection *Read Yourself Raw* (Pantheon), and Spiegelman's 2-volume graphic novel *Maus*: *A Survivor's Tale* (Pantheon) are available at many book and comic book stores, or directly from Catalan communications, along with other *Raw*-related publications. Spiegelman's current work appears in *The New Yorker* magazine. (Note: Spiegelman's *Breakdowns*: *From Maus to Now*, Belier Press, 1977, is out-of-print and difficult to find, but we give it our highest recommendation.)

Wendy and Richard Pini's original *Elfquest* has been reprinted in a number of formats by WaRP Graphics, Marvel/Epic Comics, and the color Donning/ Starblaze editions (4 volumes). Check your local comic shop for these and current *Elfquest* series, or write to WaRP Graphics for information.

Gilbert and Jaime Hernandez's *Love & Rockets* and the many reprint collections of early issues from the series are available at most comic book shops, or directly from Fantagraphic Books, whose specialty imprint Eros comics also published Gilbert Hernandez's *Birdland*.

1. SCOTT MCCLOUD

Understanding Comics (Tundra Publishing) is currently available at most comic book shops or directly from Tundra Publishing.

McCloud's earlier series *Zot* (Eclipse Comics, 35 issues) is no longer in print, though the early issues were collected in *The Original ZOT*: *Book One*. *Destroy* was also published by Eclipse in two editions. Back issues can be found in shops, or write to Eclipse Comics for availability and ordering information. McCloud's "24-Hour Comic" was published in *Taboo Especial* (Tundra Publishing).

2. LARRY MARDER

The comic book series *Tales from the Beanworld* and first two collections of the early issues, *Beanworld*: *Book One* and *Book Two*, are available from most comic book shops, or by ordering directly from the The Beanworld Press, Inc.

3. JACK JACKSON

Jack Jackson's early out-of-print underground comix works (including a previously unpublished story from the early seventies) were recently collected as *Optimism of Youth*, with later works reprinted in a companion volume, *God's Bosom and Other Stories* (both from Fantagraphics Books).

Other collected works include *Comanche Moon* (co-published by Rip Off Press and the Last Gasp), *Los Tejanos* (Fantagraphics Books), and *Secret of San Saba* (Kitchen Sink Press). Jackson's work also appears in *Leather Nun* and various issues of *Death Rattle* (all available from Kitchen Sink Press), *Graphic Story Monthly* (#4-6, Fantagraphics Books), and his most recent work includes adaptations of *Last of the Mohicans* and *Columbus* (both from Dark Horse Comics).

(NOTE: Frank Stack/Foolbert Sturgeon's *The Adventures of Jesus* are available in Rip Off Press' *Underground Classics* series, #10, 11, 13, 14, from the publisher or from Kitchen Sink Press.)

4. RICHARD CORBEN

Richard Corben's self-published work, including the five-volume *Den* graphic novel series (*Neverwhere, Muvovum, Children of Fire, Dreams*, and *Elements*), the current series *Den Saga*, graphic novels *Jeremy Brood, Mutant World* and *Son of Mutant World* (script by Jan Strnad), *Rip in Time* (script by Bruce Jones), and *Richard Corben Art Book* can be ordered directly from the creator at Fantagor Press. Write for a current list of available titles.

Most of Corben's comix works have been collected in book form by Catalan Communications, and in many earlier editions from various publishers which may still be found in comic shops. Corben's early graphic novel, *Tales from the Plague*, is also available from Kitchen Sink Press. His collaboration with Harlan Ellison *Vic and Blood: The Chronicles of a Boy and His Dog* (NBM Publishers) is available from the publisher or from Heavy Metal.

5. LEE MARRS

Though much of Lee Marrs' early comicbook and comix work is scarce, they may still be found in comic book shops specializing in back issues. Besides those titles mentioned in her interview, look for *Unicorn Isle* and comics stories in *Plop!, Crazy Magazine, Epic Illustrated*, and *Heavy Metal*. More recent and readily available are her writing efforts, scripting *The Viking Prince* graphic novel *Viking Glory* (1991, DC Comics) and various issues of *Wonder Woman* and *Legends of the Dark Knight* (both DC).

Marrs is featured in many issues of *Wimmen's Comix*, which are still available from Kitchen Sink Press, and *Gay Comix* from Gay Comix; write for information.

Marrs is also a pioneer, consultant, and teacher in the blending of traditional animation and computer graphics, and is the co-author (with Leah Freiwald) of *Inside Autodesk Animator* (Macmillan, 1991).

6. HOWARD CRUSE

Wendel was published by Gay Press of New York, *Dancin' Nekkid with the Angels*, and *Wendel on the Rebound* were published by St. Martin's Press. *Wendel, Barefootz, Dancin' Nekkid with the Angels*, and issues of *Snarf* featuring Cruse's work are also available from Kitchen Sink Press, while some issues of *Gay Comix* are still available from the publisher (write Gay Comix for information). Most of Cruse's earlier comix work is long out-of-print, but shops carrying collectible comix may still carry them.

Stuck Rubber Baby is forthcoming from Piranha Press.

7. DENIS KITCHEN

Kitchen's own comix, including all three issues of *Mom's Homemade Comix*, are for the most part out-of-print, though they may be found in discriminating comic shops that carry back issues of underground comix. A compendium of Kitchen's comix stories and art entitled *The Oddly Compelling Art of Denis Kitchen* is forthcoming. Still in print are *Bizarre Sex #1*, *Twist #2*, *Grateful Dead Comix #6*, as well as a huge selection of work from other cartoonists published by Kitchen, available from Kitchen Sink Press.

8. DAVE SIM

Issues of *Cerebus* and the *Cerebus* graphic novels—*Cerebus, High Society, Church & State* (2 volumes), *Jake's Story, Melmoth*, and *Flight (Mother & Daughters Book One)*—are available in most comic book shops, or directly from Aardvark-Vanaheim, Inc.

9. KEVIN EASTMAN & PETER LAIRD

Eastman & Laird's comic book work, including collected volumes of the early issues of *Teenage Mutant Ninja Turtles*, can be found in most book stores and comic book shops. For a current listing of publications, write to Mirage Publishing Inc.

Kevin Eastman's recent work is available from Tundra Publishing. *No Guts No Glory* and *Zombie War* (scripted with Tom Skulan) are also available from Fantaco Publishing, and Eastman's collaborative novel (with Simon Bisley and Eric Talbot) *Melting Pot* is being serialized in *Heavy Metal* magazine (Heavy Metal Publications), sold on newsstands everywhere; back issues available from the publisher.

10. HARVEY PEKAR & JOYCE BRABNER

Current and back issues of *American Splendor* can be obtained at most comic shops, or directly from the creator at American Splendor. There have also been three collections, *American Splendor, More American Splendor* (both from Doubleday Books), and *The New American Splendor Anthology* (Four Doors Eight Windows Press). Pekar's work also appears in *The People's Comics* and various issues of *Snarf* (still available from Kitchen Sink Press). He can also be seen on "Late Night with David Letterman" upon occasion, and is featured in the video *Comic Book Confidential* (see Appendix II) giving a reading of one of his stories.

Joyce Brabner's *Brought to Light* and *Real War Stories* #1 and 2 were published by Eclipse Comics. Write to Eclipse, or to CCCO concerning *Real War Stories* #1 and Citizen Soldier for *Real War Stories* #2.

Pekar and Brabner's graphic novel *Our Cancer Year* (with artist Frank Stack) is scheduled for publication in Spring of 1994 from Four Walls Eight Windows.

11. JEAN "MOEBIUS" GIRAUD

Authorized translations of most of Giraud's work are available in the U.S. from Marvel Comics' Epic imprint and in special hardcover editions from Graffiti Designs. These include *Moebius* (8 volumes, plus *Moebius 0: The Horny Goof & Other Underground Stories* from Dark Horse), *The Incal* (script by Alejandro Jodorowsky, 3 volumes), *The Silver Surfer: Parable* (script by Stan Lee), *The Art of Moebius, Chaos,* and Giraud's classic western *Blueberry* (5 volumes), *Lt. Blueberry* (3 volumes), and *Marshal Blueberry* (all scripted by J.M. Charlier). *Young Blueberry* (3 volumes) were published by Catalan/Comcat, the publisher of the 3-volume *The Magic Crystal* (script only by Giraud). His early humor work was reprinted in *French Ticklers* (3 issues), available from Kitchen Sink Press, and *Moebius* ¹/₂ from Graffiti Designs.

The authorized translation of Giraud and Jodorowsky's *Eyes of the Cat* was published in *Taboo 4*, which is still available from SpiderBaby Grafix & Publications.

General inquiries about current availability of Giraud's work here in America can be addressed to Starwatcher Graphics, Inc.

12. ALAN MOORE

Most of Alan Moore's key works are still available in the direct sales market in paperback graphic novel editions, including *V For Vendetta* (DC Comics/ Warner Books), *Miracleman* (3 volumes, Eclipse Books), *The Complete BoJeffries Saga* (Tundra Publishing), *The Saga of the Swamp Thing* and *Swamp Thing: Love and Death* (DC/Warner Books), *The Ballad of Halo Jones* (3 volumes, Titan Books), *Watchmen* (DC/Warner Books/Graffiti Designs), and others. Recent works include *Brought to Light* (Eclipse Books), *A Small Killing* (U.K. only, Gollanz), the serialized novels *From Hell* and *Lost Girls* in *Taboo* (SpiderBaby/ Tundra; order from Tundra Publishing Ltd.), partially collected in *From Hell* (2 volumes to date, Tundra), *Big Numbers* (2 issues to date, Tundra), and *1963* (Image Comics).

13. EDDIE CAMPBELL

Though much of Campbell's early work is scarce in the U.S., his quintessential *Alec* strips are available in *The Complete Alec* (Eclipse Books). *The Deadface/ Bacchus* saga continues to appear in various issues of *Dark Horse Presents* and in collected series and editions from Dark Horse Comics, who also publish Campbell's collaborative title *The Eyeball Kid* in its own title and in various issues of *Cheval Noir*.

Campbell is also illustrating Alan Moore's serialized graphic novel *From Hell*, which appears in *Taboo* (SpiderBaby/Tundra; order from Tundra) and is being collected by Tundra Publishing (2 volumes to date). Also see *The Dead Muse, Little Italy, The Cheque, Mate, In the Days of the Ace Rock'n'Roll Club* (all from Fantagraphics Books), and Campbell's most recent graphic novel *Graffiti Kitchen* (Tundra).

14. NEIL GAIMAN

Neil Gaiman's collaborations with artist Dave McKean include *Violent Cases* (Escape/Titan Books; U.S. color edition from Tundra Publishing), *Black Orchid* (DC/Warner Books), *Signal to Noise* (U.K. Gollanz; U.S. edition Dark Horse), *Hellblazer* #27 (DC Comics), *Clive Barker's Hellraiser* #20 (Epic/Marvel), and the upcoming *Mr. Punch* (U.K., Gollanz).

Gaiman's ongoing *Sandman* series (DC Comics) has yielded the collected editions *Preludes and Nocturnes, The Doll's House, Dream Country, A Game of You,* and *Season of Mist,* which are also available in most comic shops as a boxed set. Gaiman's continuation of Alan Moore's *Miracleman* (Eclipse, #17-present) and the collected *Books of Magic* (DC/Warner Books) are also available in most comic stores.

His early books, *Ghastly Beyond Belief* (co-authored with Kim Newman; Arrow, 1984) and *Don't Panic* (Pocket Books, 1988), are difficult to find, as is the anthology *Now We Are Sick* (co-edited by Stephen Jones, DreamHaven Books), though the best-selling novel *Good Omens* (co-authored with Terry Pratchett, Berkley) is readily found in most book stores.

15. DAVE MCKEAN

McKean's series *Cages* (10 issues) and his first collaboration with writer Neil Gaiman *Violent Cases* are available from Tundra Publishing. *Signal to Noise* (U.K.

Gollanz, U.S. Dark Horse), *Black Orchid* and *Arkham Asylum* (both DC Comics/ Warner Books) remain generally available in comic shops.

McKean has also done many book and album covers for the U.K. markets, and all the covers for *Sandman* (DC Comics).

16. FRANK MILLER

Sin City (Dark Horse) is Miller's latest graphic novel, currently sold in most comic shops along with many of his earlier works. These include *Ronin, The Dark Knight Returns* (both from DC/Warner Books), collected editions of his early *Daredevil* and *Daredevil/Elektra* comics, *Wolverine, Elektra Lives Again* (all from Marvel or Marvel/Epic), and others.

Collaborative works Miller has scripted include *Elektra: Assassin, Daredevil: Love and War, Daredevil: Born Again* (all Marvel or Marvel/Epic), *Batman: Year One* (DC/Warner), *Give Me Liberty, Hard-Boiled, Robocop vs. Terminator* (Dark Horse), and others which are still available. *Robocop 2*, the feature film scripted by Miller, is available from Orion Home Video, for rental or purchase in most video rental shops.

17. COLLEEN DORAN

The original *A Distant Soil* series and Donning/Starblaze color graphic novel, and Doran's work for various other publishers (see interview) can be found in many comic shops. The current self-published *A Distant Soil* is available in many shops, or directly from the creator at Aria Press.

18. RICK VEITCH

Veitch's first graphic novels *1941: The Illustrated Story* (with Allan Asherman and Stephen Bissette, Heavy Metal; still available from Tundra) and *Heartburst* (Marvel) can still be found in many comic shops. Also available are *The One* (available from Tundra), *Teenage Mutant Ninja Turtles: The River* (Mirage Publishing), *Bratpack* (Tundra; note that the collected edition is considerably revised from the original series), and his current King Hell Heroica series *The Maximortal*. His collaborative series *1963* (script by Alan Moore, Image Comics) is currently available in most comic book shops, and those that carry back issues may still have back issues of Veitch's *Swamp Thing, Teenage Mutant Ninja Turtles*, etc.

19. TODD McFARLANE

McFarlane's current series *Spawn* (Image Comics) is available in most comic shops, as are his earlier works. Early issues of his work in *Amazing Spider-Man* were reprinted in graphic novel form as *Spider-Man vs. Venom* (Marvel) and the first five issues of *Spider-Man* are reprinted as *Spider-Man: Torment* (Marvel). McFarlane also drew various issues of *Infinity Inc.*, *Detective Comics* (both DC), *The Incredible Hulk*, *Spider-Man* (both Marvel) and others.

20. WILL EISNER

Will Eisner's *Comics & Sequential Art*, *The Spirit* comic magazine reprints, five volumes of *The Spirit: The Origin Years*, *The Spirit Casebook*, *The Spirit Paperback*, *The Will Eisner Reader*, his contemporary graphic novels *A Contract with God*, *A Life Force*, *The Dreamer*, *New York*, *To the Heart of the Storm*, *The Building*, *City People Notebook*, and his latest 3, *Invisible People* are all in print. These are available at most comic book shops or directly from Kitchen Sink Press.

ADDRESSES OF PUBLISHERS, SELF-PUBLISHERS AND MAIL ORDER OUTLETS

NOTE: At the time of this writing, we were notified of the merger of Kitchen Sink Press and Tundra Publishing. Denis Kitchen has instructed us to list the current mail order address for Kitchen Sink, which has moved its operations to Tundra's former editorial and mail order offices. The duplication of addresses is not a misprint: Kitchen Sink Press and Tundra Publishing share the same mailing address.

Aardvark-Vanaheim, Inc., P.O. Box 1674, Station C, Kitchener, Ontario, Canada N2G 4R2.
American Splendor, P.O. Box 18471, Cleveland Heights, OH 44118.
Aria Press, 12638-28 Jefferson Ave., Suite 173, Newport News, VA 23602-4316.
The Beanworld Press, Inc., 1926 D. Wilmette Ave., Wilmette, IL 60091.
Catalan Communications, 43 East 19th St., New York, NY 10003.
CCCO (The Central Committee for Conscientious Objectors), 2208 South Street, Philadelphia, PA 19146; CCCO Western Region office: P.O. Box 42249, San Francisco, CA 94142.
Citizen Soldier, 175 Fifth Ave., Suite 1010, New York, NY 10010.
The Comics Buyer's Guide, Krause Publications, Inc., 700 East State Street, Iola, WI 54990.
Dark Horse Comics, Inc., 10956 SE Main Street, Milwaukie, Oregon 97222.
Eclipse Comics, P.O. Box 1099, Forestville, CA 95436.
Fantaco Publications, 21 Central Ave., Albany, NY 12210.
Fantagor Press, P.O. Box 8632, Kansas City, MO 64114.
Fantagraphics Books, Inc., 7563 Lake City Way NE, Seattle, WA 98115.

Four Walls Eight Windows, P.O. Box 548, Village Station, New York, NY 10014.

Gay Comix, P.O. Box 3226, Portland, OR 97208.

[Victor] Gollanz Ltd., 14 Henrietta Street, London, WC2E 8QJ, Great Britain.

Graffiti Designs, Inc., 1140 N. Kraemer Blvd., Unit B, Anaheim, CA 92806-1919.

Heavy Metal, 584 Broadway, New York, NY 10012.

King Hell Press, RR1 Box 51, West Townshend, VT 05359.

Kitchen Sink Press, Inc., 320 Riverside Drive, Northampton, MA 01060.

Last Gasp, P.O. Box 410067, San Francisco, CA 94141-0067.

Mirage Publishing, Inc., 16 Market Street, Northampton, MA 01060.

NBM Publishing, 35-53 70th Street, Jackson Heights, NY 11372.

Rip-Off Press, Inc., Box 14158, San Francisco, CA 94114.

SpiderBaby Grafix & Publications, P.O. Box 2210, West Brattleboro, VT 05303.

Starwatcher Graphics, Inc., P.O. Box 17270, Encino, CA 91416-7270.

St. Martin's Press, 175 Fifth Avenue, New York, NY 10010.

Tundra Publishing, 320 Riverside Drive, Northampton, MA 01060.

WaRP Graphics, Inc., 5 Reno Road, Poughkeepsie, NY 12603.

ABOUT THE AUTHORS

STANLEY WIATER is a widely published journalist, cineteratologist, and observer of the popular culture scene. He is the author of two previous collections of interviews. *Dark Dreamers: Conversations with the Masters of Horror* (Avon, 1990)—which won the 1991 Bram Stoker Award for Superior Achievement from the Horror Writers of America—and *Dark Visions: Conversations with the Masters of the Horror Film* (Avon, 1992). He has edited two anthologies to date, *Night Visions 7* (Dark Harvest, 1989) and *After the Darkness* (Maclay & Associates, 1993).

In the comics field, Wiater is the author of *The Official Teenage Mutant Ninja Turtles Treasury* (Villard Books, 1991), an authorized overview of the Turtles phenomenon. Wiater has also written original scripts for the Turtles comics line, including numerous Turtles stories for the Archie comics line, as well as episodes of the syndicated daily Turtles comic strip. Several of his own short stories have been adapted for comic books. Wiater, who is currently developing his own comic book title, makes his home with his wife Iris and daughter Tanya in rural western Massachusetts.

STEPHEN R. BISSETTE is a prolific, award-winning comic book artist, writer, editor, critic, journalist, essayist, and publisher. With a group of fellow confederates in college, he self-published his first underground comix in 1975, *Abyss*. That work served as his portfolio to be accepted in the first year of the newly formed Joe Kubert School of Cartoon and Graphic Art.

Upon graduation, he then freelanced with the major comic book publishers, including Marvel Comics and DC Comics. In collaboration with fellow Kubert classmate John Totleben and British writer Alan Moore, Bissette began work on *The Saga of the Swamp Thing* for DC in 1983. His artwork on that publication helped it win six major American and British comic book awards, and made *Swamp Thing* the first "Mature Readers" title ever from the publisher.

In 1988 Bissette created (with John Totleben) the controversial adult horror anthology *Taboo*, which has been banned in some countries. In that year he also formed his own publishing company, SpiderBaby Grafix and Publications, with his wife, artist Marlene O'Conner. Beyond a wide range of acclaimed non-fiction and criticism in the horror genre, Bissette has returned to the medium to work with Alan Moore and Rick Veitch on the series *1963* for Image Comics.

Bissette currently resides in the wilds of his native Vermont with his wife and two children, Danny and Maia.